SAGE was founded in 1965 by Sara Miller McCune to support the dissemination of usable knowledge by publishing innovative and high-quality research and teaching content. Today, we publish over 900 journals, including those of more than 400 learned societies, more than 800 new books per year, and a growing range of library products including archives, data, case studies, reports, and video. SAGE remains majority-owned by our founder, and after Sara's lifetime will become owned by a charitable trust that secures our continued independence.

Los Angeles | London | New Delhi | Singapore | Washington DC | Melbourne

ADVANCE PRAISE

I am delighted to see a book being written about Dr Pritam Singh, a Midas touch leader and an institution builder par excellence. I have known him for many years and found that he was a person who made one feel enthused by his sheer presence. While the legend has moved on, the legacy continues. As a board member, he used to guide us in shaping our own JK Lakshmipat University, Jaipur, and as the chancellor of the university, I found his advice to be enormously sound, pragmatic and highly progressive. In many ways, Dr Singh was ahead of his time. I compliment Professor Asha Bhandarker and Dr Subrat Kumar for documenting the legacy of Dr Pritam Singh in this well-researched book. It is indeed a marvellous effort to describe Dr Pritam Singh—the great leader, an outstanding institution builder and an excellent human being—in such a lucid manner. I highly recommend this book to professionals, leaders, entrepreneurs and academicians and all those who want to make a positive difference wherever they work.

Bharat Hari Singhania, *President, J. K. Organisation; Chancellor, JK Lakshmipat University, Jaipur*

Dr Pritam Singh was among the select few personalities who traversed the multiverse of academia, policymaking and institution building with ease. His accomplishments across institutions are indeed a testimony to his distinctive management thinking and leadership qualities. It is great to see a book documenting his life, leadership and institution building. I am sure it will be a great resource for future leaders to become effective and outstanding in their chosen endeavours.

Shri Rajkiran Rai G.,
MD and CEO, Union Bank of India

The book, *Pritam Singh: The Alchemist Guru*, is a fitting tribute to the leadership and institution building of Dr Pritam Singh. The book comprehensively brings out the strategies and approaches used by him in transforming Indian management schools and provides a road map for budding leaders. I highly recommend this book to all those interested in leadership in organizations, especially in academia.

Professor Bharat Bhasker,
Director, IIM Raipur

Dr Pritam Singh is the unparalleled 'avtar purush' (the master incarnate) of management education and practice in India. In a slim and concise work of elegance and substance, Dr Asha Bhandarker and Dr Subrat Kumar have captured the philosophy and values of the guru. *Pritam Singh: The Alchemist Guru* will endure as the protagonist for a long time to come.

Manas Mohanty, *MD,*
Bharatiya Reserve Bank Note Mudran Pvt. Ltd

Dr Singh has been widely acknowledged as a guru, scholar and institution builder. This book has given insights into these aspects of Dr Pritam Singh's life. It is a wonderfully rare documentation of the life and contributions of an outstanding leader. I congratulate the authors for bringing out a fine book, well substantiated by the views of a large number of people who had the privilege of working with Dr Singh. It is a must-read for budding leaders, existing leaders and all those interested in the phenomenon of leadership.

Dr Santrupt Misra, *CEO, Birla Carbon; Director, Chemicals; Director, Group Human Resources, Aditya Birla Group*

Dr Pritam Singh was an institution for leadership and management skills. His work and life have inspired so many successful corporate leaders and transformed organizations. We are fortunate that his thoughts and legacy have been captured in this book, thereby institutionalizing his teachings for many generations to come. A must-read for current and future leaders.

Amit Malik, *CEO and MD, Aviva India*

Dr Pritam Singh had been a towering institutional builder. Rarely would you come across a personality who is as comfortable with policymaking as with teaching or researching. No surprise, he had left his indelible imprint on everyone he had met, on every place he dwelt. I am so thankful to Professor Asha Bhandarker and Dr Subrat Kumar, who have so painstakingly yet passionately penned this book.

There could never have been a better tribute to a person who was not only a teacher but also a change agent, a master crafter and a policy drafter, all rolled into one. The in-depth analysis of the persona behind Dr Pritam Singh has made it an interesting read. The authors have been able to weave in the anecdotes in a way that people like me, who could not have the opportunity to have a longer association with this great personality, could get a greater glimpse of Dr Pritam Singh. While I must thank the authors for chronicling a management

Guru, a rarity, I am sure the readers will not only thoroughly enjoy the book but will also be hugely inspired by this 'alchemist guru'.

Ranjan Kumar Mohapatra,
Director (HR), Indian Oil Corporation Ltd

The legendary Dr Pritam Singh has shown that there is no end to contributions if one aims high enough. He has been a constant mentor and guide to us for more than a decade. The book nicely brings out the path he has mapped to building top-class management schools. It also reveals many of the characteristics which have influenced his towering leadership over the last four decades. I unhesitatingly recommend this book to all budding leaders, especially in academia.

Sharad Jaipuria,
Chairman, Jaipuria Institute of Management

This book provides an in-depth understanding of what leads to building great academic institutions. I can also relate to practices in stakeholder management for the common greater good of the organization. A must-read for both academics and corporate leaders who are interested in understanding the Indian management education landscape.

K. S. Bakshi, *Group Head of Human Resources, InterGlobe Enterprises*

Dr Pritam Singh has not only led and built multiple excellent institutions but has gone on to mentor faculty and leaders who have built institutions themselves. He was that rarest of individuals, a true 'teacher of teachers'. I have personally benefited from being mentored by leaders who were, in turn, mentored by Dr Pritam Singh. The book, *Pritam Singh: The*

Alchemist Guru, by Bhandarker and Kumar, shows how and why Dr Singh was a guru and how he managed to build excellent institutions. I highly recommend this book to all leaders as well as budding leaders.

> **Dr Ranjan Banerjee,** *Dean and Professor of Marketing, BITS School of Management*

This book is a testament to the power of those individuals in our lives who touch us with their integrity and humility. The authors weave together the story of the late Pritam Singh as a thinker, leader and educationalist. Throughout, it is a study in values-based leadership, friendship and inspiration. Above all, it is a study of a man of quiet achievement, a gentle and thoughtful figure who shaped the practice and hearts of so many.

> **Professor Simon Mercado,** *Executive Vice President/ Directeur General-Adjoint for Business and External Relations, ESCP Business School Europe*

Pritam Singh

SAGE Response, our business books imprint, celebrates its silver jubilee this year. As we reflect on this transformational journey that began with a single title, we thank everyone who has helped us to produce content that is topical and relevant across a varied audience of aspiring managers, working professionals, practitioners and students. We feel privileged that eminent management and leadership experts, professionals and stalwarts from academia supported and trusted us with their work. Over the years, SAGE Response has built an enviable list of practice-based, reader-friendly books that provide creative strategies to keep pace with the rapidly changing global scenario. As we grow and evolve with the times, it is our endeavour to continue to publish books that offer innovative solutions, approaches and perspectives to the disciplines that we serve.

Pritam Singh
The Alchemist Guru

Asha Bhandarker
Subrat Kumar

Los Angeles | London | New Delhi
Singapore | Washington DC | Melbourne

Copyright © Asha Bhandarker and Subrat Kumar, 2022

All rights reserved. No part of this book may be reproduced or utilized in any form or by any means, electronic or mechanical, including photocopying, recording or by any information storage or retrieval system, without permission in writing from the publisher.

First published in 2022 by

SAGE Publications India Pvt Ltd
B1/I-1 Mohan Cooperative Industrial Area
Mathura Road, New Delhi 110 044, India
www.sagepub.in

SAGE Publications Inc
2455 Teller Road
Thousand Oaks, California 91320, USA

SAGE Publications Ltd
1 Oliver's Yard, 55 City Road
London EC1Y 1SP, United Kingdom

SAGE Publications Asia-Pacific Pte Ltd
18 Cross Street #10-10/11/12
China Square Central
Singapore 048423

Published by Vivek Mehra for SAGE Publications India Pvt Ltd. Typeset in 11/14pt Sabon by Fidus Design Pvt Ltd, Chandigarh.

Library of Congress Cataloging-in-Publication Data
Names: Bhandarker, Asha, author. | Kumar, Subrat, author.
Title: Pritam Singh: the alchemist guru / Asha Bhandarke and Subrat Kumar.
Description: New Delhi, India; Thousand Oaks, California: SAGE Response, an imprint of SAGE Publishing, 2021. | Includes bibliographical references.
Identifiers: LCCN 2021043928 | ISBN 9789354792045 (paperback) | ISBN 9789354792052 (epub) | ISBN 9789354792069 (ebook)
Subjects: LCSH: Singh, Pritam, 1941–2020. | Chief executive officers—India—Biography. | Leadership—India. | Creative ability in business—India.
Classification: LCC HC432.5.S519 B43 2021 | DDC 658.4/092 [B]—dc23
LC record available at https://lccn.loc.gov/2021043928

ISBN: 978-93-5479-204-5 (PB)

SAGE Team: Namarita Kathait, Shruti Gupta and Anupama Krishnan

To

Inspiring Leaders and Gurus

Thank you for choosing a SAGE product!
If you have any comment, observation or feedback,
I would like to personally hear from you.

Please write to me at **contactceo@sagepub.in**

Vivek Mehra, Managing Director and CEO, SAGE India.

Bulk Sales

SAGE India offers special discounts
for purchase of books in bulk.
We also make available special imprints
and excerpts from our books on demand.

For orders and enquiries, write to us at

Marketing Department
SAGE Publications India Pvt Ltd
B1/I-1, Mohan Cooperative Industrial Area
Mathura Road, Post Bag 7
New Delhi 110044, India

E-mail us at **marketing@sagepub.in**

Subscribe to our mailing list
Write to **marketing@sagepub.in**

This book is also available as an e-book.

CONTENTS

List of Illustrations ix
Foreword by Kumar Mangalam Birla xi
Preface xiii
Acknowledgements xix

Chapter 1 Leadership, Transformation and
          Institution Building in Higher Education   1

Chapter 2 The Quintessential Change Maestro   19

Chapter 3 A Commemoration and Remembrance   115

Chapter 4 A Holistic Portrait   227

Appendices 247
References 281
About the Authors 301

LIST OF ILLUSTRATIONS

FIGURES

2.1.	Strategies for Transforming and Building a Management School	106
2.2.	Work Culture Components	108
2.3.	Comprehensive Model of Organizational Transformation Process	109
2.4.	Mentoring Style of the Guru	110
2.5.	Influence and Organizational Transformation	113

TABLES

1.1.	Sample Details	17
2.1.	As a Leader—Festschrift Data	23
2.2.	As a Leader—Interview Data	24
2.3.	As a Person—Festschrift Data	26
2.4.	As a Person—Interview Data	27
4.1.	Comparison of FFM Descriptors with What People Said about Dr Singh	238

FOREWORD

Leadership is not just about actions and outcomes. It is, more importantly, about touching lives. A legacy that far transcends actions and outcomes.

Dr Pritam Singh epitomized such leadership. Over the arc of his career, he has donned several hats—educationist, author, institution builder, behavioural scientist, management guru and organizational transformer.

My first association with him harks back to the mid-1990s, when he curated a learning programme for the leadership team at the Aditya Birla Group. His deep personal involvement in the process was truly energizing. In the mid-1990s, an on-campus learning intervention for 150 top leaders of a business group was perhaps unheard of. But that's Dr Singh for you—transformative and unconventional.

His unconventional thinking was rooted in Indian values. He had this uncanny ability to blend traditional Indian wisdom with modern Western knowledge. In the process, he brought a refreshingly original lens to management thinking. Dr Singh's remarkable professional success is a consequence of not only his strategic thinking and leadership prowess but also a testament to his outstanding human traits—determination, resilience, clarity of thought and an agile mind.

This book, *Pritam Singh: The Alchemist Guru*, provides a powerful template for successful institution building and leadership. The book is interspersed with rich insights from a galaxy of business leaders who have shared their experience of working with Dr Singh. In each of these stories are pearls of wisdom. Participant observers, after all, can help capture moments of history and learning. They can help decode elements that contribute to success and leadership excellence.

The authors of this book have also been participant observers in the incredible journey of Dr Pritam Singh. Dr Asha Bhandarker, in particular, has worked with Dr Singh for almost three decades and has tapped into a rich reservoir of insights to build this narrative, which is a thoughtful guide to leadership.

There is inherent inspirational value in the biographies of pioneering leaders, and this book truly does justice to one such trailblazer. In conversation with Dr Asha Bhandarker, Dr Pritam Singh alludes to his role models, Swami Vivekananda—who profoundly impacted his life—and his high school teachers, whose sheer dedication to education inspired his own journey of pursuing excellence in academia.

Above all, this book will ensure that Dr Pritam Singh's rich body of work, wisdom and legacy will continue to power management thinking in India for generations to come.

Kumar Mangalam Birla

PREFACE

This book was long overdue. The right time to write this book was probably when the Government of India honoured Dr Pritam Singh with a Padma Shri—the 4th highest civilian award in India—in 2003 for his contributions to management education—a first in the history of the awards in management education. At that time, Dr Singh was going strong as a professional, busy creating the next curve of his contributions—Management Development Institute (MDI) V2, International Management Institute (IMI), role in the Institutions of Eminence (IOE; PM's committee for selecting IOE in Higher Education where he was the only expert from India), apart from memberships on various boards and committees. The thought of documentation just did not seem right at that time. He was an iconic personality who strode like a colossus across the landscape of management education in India for decades. As R. A. Yadav, former AICTE Chairman opined, 'he was a trendsetter in management education, and whatever trends he initiated continue to this day', His followers and fans are legion—numerous people in the academia and the corporate sector claim him as their mentor and guru and have taken inspiration from his words and shaped their own leadership talents.

> It is a sin to give recognition to those who don't deserve it and it is a greater sin to not recognize those who are deserving.

This statement was often made by Dr Singh. We hope that we have done the right thing by documenting the life and work of our guru, mentor, friend, philosopher and guide who deserves more than such an offering from us. His contributions to the country have been immense, and his legacy continues in the minds and hearts of those whose lives were touched by him in some way or the other. We believe that writing this book is one way of remembering and continuing the legacy and disseminating his vision.

The book has been titled *Pritam Singh: The Alchemist Guru*, in order to capture the spirit of transformation of the organizations he headed, almost magically, like alchemy.

The work on this book commenced in April 2020 when the team felt the urge to document for posterity, the unique and pioneering efforts at transforming and building great management institutions, as well as the unique brand of leadership demonstrated by Dr Singh. In the past five years, Dr Singh had declined our request to write a book, with a cryptic statement, 'I don't believe in self-promotion…my work should speak for itself.'

When one of his former students from MDI class of 1994—S. K. Bose, now Executive Director Human Resource (HR) Indian Oil Corporation Ltd (IOCL)—sent him a similar message in early April 2020, he took it seriously. Given his scientific approach to things, he sent the WhatsApp message from Bose to 25 different leaders from industry and academia asking them for their opinion. Only when he got an overwhelmingly positive response, did Dr Singh open his mind to this idea of the book being written. Once he accepted the request, he asked us to get more feedback from a larger group.

In turn we floated the names of three well-known names in management education, among 100 persons from academia and industry, and sought to identify whom they considered to be a transformational leader in management education in the last few decades. Around 95% of the respondents rated Dr Singh as the number 1 academic leader in the management domain. The researcher in Dr Singh was satisfied and he gave us the green signal to go ahead. Although the work started immediately (in April), he unfortunately passed away on 3 June 2020. However, he did get to read some of the Festschrift essays (discussed later) which he shared with his family and a few close friends.

This book seeks to highlight the contributions of Dr Singh, to institution building and leadership in higher education as well as the corporate sector, and to bring to light his complex, multifaceted talent and capabilities.

APPROACH TO THE RESEARCH

This book seeks to answer the following questions:

- What was Dr Singh's approach to transform the organizations which he headed?
- Who was he as a leader and as a person?
- What were his guiding values?

We sincerely hope that this book will provide a template for successful institution building and leadership in academia and bring out the key success factors in building institutions of higher education—especially in the field of management in India. The book seeks to throw light on leadership embedded in the typical Indian cultural context and as such would be of interest to academic leaders and also to future leaders in academia. It will also be an invaluable contribution to the scarce literature on academic leadership in higher education, in the Indian context.

This book is organized in the following four chapters.

Chapter 1: Leadership, Transformation and Institution Building in Higher Education

This chapter presents a literature review on the topics of institution building and leadership especially in the educational context. The literature review provides a background about the work done in these domains and offers the perspective in which the present research needs to be viewed. An exhaustive review has not been conducted since the Grounded Theory approach has been used, which focuses on developing the theory from the data, rather than viewing the data from the prism of a pre-established theory. Research methodology used in this work is also delineated in Chapter 1.

Chapter 2: The Quintessential Change Maestro

Chapter 2 analyses the views shared in the interviews and in the Festschrift write-ups. Other information available from participant observation is also utilized in developing various aspects of the case study. The chapter has been organized in the following five parts for ease of presentation and reading.

1. **Thematic analysis of the findings:** Findings from the NVivo data analysis about Dr Singh as a leader, institution builder and person are briefly presented in this part. The detailed narration has been done in parts 2–5.

2. **Architecting institutions—transformation code:** This part documents the case studies of institution building in MDI, IIM-L and IMI and seeks to identify commonalities in the approach taken to build transformation, along with bringing out the unique approach taken in each of the three institutions.

3. **Leaders go the way and show the way:** It identifies the leadership attributes and actions taken by Dr Singh in these institutions.

4. **Guru in a business suit:** It highlights the approach used by Dr Singh in advising, grooming and helping individuals, CEOs and organizations.
5. **Above all, be human:** It presents the attributes of Dr Singh as a human being from the viewpoint of the participants.

Chapter 3: A Commemoration and Remembrance

This chapter consists of the invited write-ups. They have been written by people associated with Dr Singh over his career span—from University of Rajasthan, Jaipur (late 1960s), Xavier School of Management (XLRI) Jamshedpur (1970s), ASCI Hyderabad (1980s), IIM Bangalore (early 1990s), MDI (mid 1990s), IIM Lucknow (late 1990s–2003), MDI (2003–2006) and IMI (2011–2014). There were others he was associated with over the decades who also contributed.

Chapter 4: A Holistic Portrait

This chapter pieces together the complete portrait emerging from the data gathered from multiple sources as well as from the authors' experiences.

ACKNOWLEDGEMENTS

This book is one of the many ways of honouring the memory of Dr Singh. In this connection, special mention must be made of Dr Anil Sahasrabudhe, Dr Poonia and the All India Council for Technical Education (AICTE) Team. They have made it possible to continue the leadership legacy of Dr Singh by instituting Annual Awards in the field of management in his name. Mention must be made next of the Dr Pritam Singh Foundation which is conducting various events to disseminate the teachings of Dr Singh.

Many people contribute to any good research work and this is more so for an unusual work like this one. Our friends, families, professional colleagues and most importantly those who participated in the research work deserve wholesome praise and deepest thanks for their contributions. It is impossible to mention each and every person who has contributed to the timely completion of this book. We have however made a modest attempt to do so.

The large number of academic and corporate leaders as well as policymakers who narrated their experiences with Dr Singh during the interviews deserve our deepest gratitude. They are not ordinary people; many of them are leading lights and luminaries in their fields. In fact, many of them are people of national and international eminence. The fact that they took the time to speak to us reflects their respect and regard for Dr Singh. Their names are presented here in alphabetical order: Anadi Pande, Anil Sahasrabudhe, Anurag Batra, Arun Maira, Arup Roy, Bhaskar Chatterjee, B. A. Metri, B. K. Chaturvedi, B. R. Singh, D. K. Bakshi,

Deepak Hota, Dhananjay Singh, Dilip Bandopadhyay, G. N. Pandey, Harivansh Chaturvedi, Jauhari Lal, K. K. Sinha, M. Damodaran, M. Jayadev, D. N. Khurana, Manoj Kohli, M. P. Jaiswal, M. P. Poonia, Nagananda Kumar, P. Dwarkanath, Prabhu Singh, Pradeep Dinodia, Puneet Dalmia, Pushp Joshi, Rajeev Dubey, Ravi Kumar, R. A. Yadav, R. B. Yadav, R. K. Dubey, R. V. Shahi, Sanjiv Bikhchandani, S. Acharya, S. C. Tripathi, Sunil Maheshwari, S. Y. Siddiqui, Udai Upendra, V. Chauhan, Vinod Rai, Vivek Mehra, Kedarnathan and Y. V. Verma. They provided rich insights into Dr Pritam Singh as a leader and as a person, by sharing their experiences with him.

We would like to warmly thank the Festschrift writers mentioned in alphabetical order: Alfredo Behrens, Anand Prakash, Anil Khandelwal, Anu Singh Lather, Ashok Banerjee, Atul Sobti, C. N. Narayana, D. P. Singh, Davide Sola, Debashis Chatterjee, G. N. Pandey, Jyoti Gupta, Jyotsna Bhatnagar, Kala Seetharam and V. Sridhar, M. P. Jaiswal, Mamata V. Singh, Nand Dhameja, Nupur Prakash, Premila Verma, A. K. Rath, Rajan George, Rajan Saxena, Rattan Sharma, Reeta Raina, R. L. Raina, Sanjay Srivastava, Sharad Sarin, S. K. Bose, Subir Verma, Sunil Mithas and Yogesh Singh. They took time out from their busy schedules and immediately responded to the invitation to contribute their write-ups.

We have derived a lot of support from Rajkiran Rai (Chairman Indian Banks Association [IBA]), Mallikarjuna Rao (MD Punjab Nation Bank [PNB]), L. Prabhakar (MD Canara Bank), Manimekhalai Arumugam (ED Canara Bank), Dr Raj Kumar (VC O. P. Jindal Global University [JGU]) and Prashant Bhalla (Chancellor Manav Rachna University).

Life throws up many challenges which can easily wreck all the plans made by mortals like us. Subir Verma, one of the original co-authors of this book had to withdraw from the project because his family was struck by Covid-19 and subsequently, he had to shift to Ahmedabad as Director Institute of Management, Nirma University. It is to his credit that he continued to help us by acting as a sounding board when it was most needed. Then Covid-19 attacked Subrat Kumar and his family and that in turn was a big blow to the planned timelines. My Research associate, Purva—a most dependable and capable young lady—had to withdraw from the project.... As they say when God closes one door, S/he opens another one. Magically people came in to fill the gaps, Shakila, Vira and Kshitija—my dear friends—thanks for all your help and support. Ashish Sharma and Mimamsa, what would I do without you two? You all absolutely took the load and helped with a significant amount of the background work.

A special warm thank you to the SAGE India team—Manisha, Namarita and others who were very patient with us at every step of the way in completing and bringing out a top-quality book. Above all, Vivek Mehra—the Chief of SAGE India—my warmest wishes and thanks go to you for your generous and kind-hearted support.

Finally and most importantly, Subrat Kumar would like to thank his parents, S. P. Singh and Vijoy Mala, his wife Neha, work colleagues as well as his newly born son Saurish, for bearing the long absences and providing their full support towards completing this book. Asha Bhandarker would like to thank her mother Vilasini, sisters, Sudha and Vidya, and brother, Vivek, and their respective families, for their enduring presence, faith and unconditional love. Above all, thank you Dr Singh for giving us the permission to write this book.

CHAPTER 1

LEADERSHIP, TRANSFORMATION AND INSTITUTION BUILDING IN HIGHER EDUCATION

The emergence of knowledge economies has fuelled a surge in the demand for a skilled and competent workforce (Gupta, 2008). Today high-quality talent has become a direct source of economic gains and has thus been rendered into a highly valued resource. As Blunkett (2000, p. 10) said 'The powerhouses of the new global economy are innovation and ideas, creativity, skills and knowledge. These are now the tools for success and prosperity as much as natural resources and physical labour power were in the past century.' There is no doubt that higher education has a key role to play in shaping talent, providing perspective, knowledge and skills. Thus, the shift to a knowledge society has made both talent and higher education a critical source of competitive advantage for nations and organizations.

Higher education acts as a centre for knowledge creation and human resource development required for a country's growth (Sukirno & Siengthai, 2011) and affects every area of national development (Chauhan, 2008). Higher Education drives the economy in a knowledge society and fuels innovation-led growth in a globalized world. Institutions of Higher Education contribute to national development through ideas and innovations (Rao, 2019) and by contributing to enhance international and intercultural experiences as well as the competencies and skills needed to work successfully across the globe (Tripathi & Bajpai, 2017).

Despite their importance, it is ironic that higher education institutions suffer from a financial crunch (Gansemer-Topf et al., 2018; Geiger, 2010) and their ability to become effective centres of knowledge creation and provide best in-class education is affected. The university system suffers from a lack of adequate resources (Geiger, 2010) as governments gradually reduce funding. The Indian government spends ₹54,873 crore on education, of which barely ₹38,350 crore is earmarked for higher education (see ET Bureau, February 2, 2021). It is no wonder that although India has top-quality institutions—IISc, IITs, IIMs—there are simply not enough of them equipped with top trained faculty (Hoque, 2018; Gupta & Gupta, 2012; Mishra, July 2019; Sharma & Sharma, 2015) who engage in knowledge creation, application and dissemination.

When higher education was opened up to the private sector in India, a large number of engineering (Reddy, 2018) and management (Unde & Bhor, 2013) institutions were set up by private players. Barring a few exceptions, however, the bulk of them suffer from low-quality of education (Aithal & Kumar, 2016; Ranjan, 2014). Many of them could not survive and had to close down. Data from the All India Council for Technical Education (AICTE) shows that the number of management colleges has dropped from 3,609 in 2014–2015 to 3,264 in 2017–2018 (Makkar & Waghmare, 2018). According to the AICTE, every year around 90–100 private colleges go into progressive closure. The AICTE website annually publishes the list of such institutions across various professional postgraduate programs, including management. Leadership is one of the key factors which contributes to the development of a top-class institution. It is an important factor impacting organizational performance, transformation and growth of higher educational institutions. Academic leaders directly contribute to building high-quality institutions with high-quality education. Thus, leaders can play a key role in shaping both the rise and fall of academic institutions. Leaders influence the well-being of employees and indeed all stakeholders.

The leader–follower relationship is an important element in the attitude and behaviour of a team. It has been found to influence job satisfaction, turnover, positive relationships and the well-being of followers and organizational productivity (Avolio et al., 2004a; Boyatzis et al., 2012). Not surprisingly, the behaviour of leaders triggers an emotional response in those they lead and affects their performance (Dasborough, 2006). According to Humphrey et al. (2016), there is a general agreement among researchers across a variety of theoretical approaches that leadership is inherently an emotional process. Leaders who can successfully trigger a positive emotional response can significantly influence their teams, thereby resulting in better performance of both the team and the organization. Furthermore, their ability to positively influence the emotional climate impacts work performance (Humphrey, 2002). Conger (1991) argues that arousing affect in others is an important mechanism by which inspirational leadership impacts performance. Chi et al. (2011) suggest that a leader's positive moods not only directly enhanced team performance, but also indirectly led to improved team performance through the mediating influence of transformational leadership and positive group affective tone.

Perusal of the literature shows that leadership studies have been conducted from two different perspectives: leadership as a person-centric phenomena and leadership as a process-centric phenomena. On the one hand, Leadership can be defined in terms of traits, characteristics and behaviours of the leader that focus on a clear vision, action, modelling the way, ethical relationships, congruence, trustworthiness and collaboration (Avolio et al., 2004a). On the other hand, leadership can be looked upon as 'a process whereby intentional influence is exerted by one person over other people to guide, structure, and facilitate activities and relationships in a group or organization' (Yukl & Becker, 2006, p. 3). Both approaches contribute to our understanding of the leadership phenomenon and both play a key role in institution building. While person-centric leadership is indispensable in motivating and inspiring people; process-centric approaches are important to ensure sustainability of organizational transformation and change. We now examine the research on the two approaches to leadership.

LEADERSHIP AS A PERSON-CENTRIC PHENOMENON

Some of the prominent theories which feature in this category are—servant (Greenleaf, 1970), authentic (Bernard, 1938; George, 2000), visionary (Nanus, 1992; Sashkin, 1992), shared (Pearce & Conger, 2003), ethical (Brown et al, 2005), moral (Beyer, 2012; Cheng et al., 2004), participative (Kahai et al., 1997; Koopman & Wierdsma, 1998; Spreitzer, 2007), collaborative (Chrislip & Larson, 1994), sustainable (Hargreaves & Fink, 2006), autocratic (Lewin et al., 1939), bureaucratic (Weber, 1947), paternalistic (Farh & Cheng, 2000), toxic (Whicker, 1996) and humanistic leadership (Fritz & Sorgel, 2017). Three of the most relevant theories from the perspective of this work—transformational leadership, responsible leadership and authentic leadership are discussed in the following sections.

Transformational Leadership

Transformational leadership models have dominated the understanding of leadership within the higher education sector (Astin & Astin, 2000) and tend to resonate positively with their apparent foundation upon human interactions and match the demands of faculty and campus-based leadership roles.

Transformational leadership was first identified by Downton (1973) and is often referred to as a 'new paradigm' or 'the new leadership' approach (Bryman, 1992). The term 'Transformational' is interchangeably used with terms like charismatic, visionary or value-based (Anderson, 2001). A transformational leader is also defined as one who 'articulates a realistic vision of the future that can be shared, stimulates subordinates intellectually and pays attention to the differences among the subordinates' (Yammarino & Bass, 1988, p. 2). Transformational leadership involves formulating and sharing a vision, encouraging followers and involving them in task performance, and promoting strong one-to-one bonds (in turn boosting their desire for self-development) (Jung et al., 2008; Winkler, 2009).

Transformational leaders involve employees in decision-making and value their ideas, in turn, making the employees feel important and motivated (Bass, 2000). Transformational leaders are passionate, energetic and have a long-term vision which they share with their teams (Torlak & Kuzey, 2019). This, then, makes change management and strategic decision-making relatively easier since people get co-opted into the change process. Transformational leaders are also appreciative of their employees' achievements and constantly motivate them (Burns, 1978) resulting in greater employee productivity (Ingram, 2018). Transformational leadership is the most prevalent style for change management (Indrawati, 2014; Kejriwal & Krishnan, 2004; Sarros & Santora, 2001). A transformational leader acts as guide, mentor and coach and enlarges the followers' vision (Pereira & Gomes, 2012).

People working with transformational leaders enjoy greater trust (Childers, 2009; Podsakoff et al., 1990) and opportunity for career advancement (Dubinsky et al., 1995). Besides, they experience greater self-efficacy (Walumbwa & Hartnell, 2011) and job satisfaction (Bushra et al, 2011; Mohammad et al., 2011; Yang et al., 2011). When a transformational leader is at the helm, there is reduced employee turnover (Erturk, 2014; Tse et al., 2013) and improved job performance (Dvir et al., 2002; Geyer & Steyrer, 1998; Koh et al., 1995). At the organizational level, transformational leadership leads to organizational commitment (Avolio et al., 2004b; Ramachandran & Krishnan, 2009), organizational citizenship behaviour (Humphrey, 2012; Lian & Tui, 2012) and organizational identification among the employees (Cavazotte, 2013; Humphrey, 2012; Walumbwa & Hartnell, 2011).

Responsible Leadership

'Responsible leadership is the global exercise of ethical, values-based leadership in the pursuit of economic and societal progress and sustainable development. It is based on a fundamental recognition of the interconnectedness of the world' (GRLI, 2005). Schraa-Liu and Trompenaars (2006) define 'responsible leaders as those who take responsibility towards the bottom-line and shareholders of the organization, while at the same time—through reconciliation—take responsibility to integrate all the stake-holders'. These leaders recognize and respect multiple demands, interests, needs and conflicts stemming from diverse responsibilities and reconcile them by mobilizing and successfully engaging the organization and varying stakeholders.

Doh and Stumpf (2005) emphasized the three important dimensions of responsible leadership: value-based leadership, ethical decision-making and quality stakeholder relationships. On the similar lines, Brown et al. (2005, p. 120) define ethical leadership as 'the demonstration of normatively appropriate conduct through personal action and interpersonal relationships, and the promotion of such conduct to followers through two-way communication, reinforcement, and decision-making'. Ethical leadership is crucial and vital in providing direction that enables the organization to fulfil its mission and vision and achieve declared goals (Kanungo & Mendonca, 1996). Ethical leadership is regarded as a key factor in the management of an organization's reputation in the external environment and in comparison, with competitors (Blanchard & Peale, 1996; Kanungo & Mendonca, 1996). An organization's moral health depends upon the standards and the example set by the chief executive (Kelly, 1990). According to Hitt (1990), senior leadership has two key responsibilities: (a) to ensure that ethical decisions are made and (b) to develop an organizational climate in which ethical follower conduct is fostered. This is where a responsible leader plays an important role.

Authentic Leadership

Walumbwa et al. (2008) define authentic leadership as

> a pattern of leader behaviour that draws upon and promotes both positive psychological capacities and a positive ethical climate, to foster greater self-awareness, an internalized moral perspective, balanced processing of information, and relational transparency on the part of leaders working with followers, there by fostering positive self-development. (p. 95)

Authentic leadership is the socialized leadership, which is concerned with the collective good. Such leaders transcend their own interests for the sake of others (Howell & Avolio, 1993). Authentic leadership results in building the credibility and reputation of the leader leading to acceptance of the leader and willingness to go along with them.

Authentic leadership has been found to have a positive effect on new venture performance (Hmieleski et al., 2012). It leads to employees'-level outcomes like better job performance among followers (Leroy et al., 2012; Wong & Cummings, 2009), greater job satisfaction and organizational commitment (Giallonardo et al., 2010; Avolio et al., 2004a; Jensen

& Luthans, 2006; Peus et al., 2012), higher work engagement (Hassan & Ahmed, 2011; Hsieh & Wang 2015), lower turnover intention (Azanza et al., 2015) and greater trust in leadership (Clapp-Smith et al., 2009; Wong & Cummings, 2009; Wong et al., 2010).

Authentic leaders foster positive emotional and cognitive development of their followers (Avolio & Gardner, 2005), and in turn, employees' self-worth perceptions and self-esteem will be enhanced as they acquire a more positive evaluation of self (Dutton et al., 1994). Authentic leaders may free followers from unnecessary psychological concerns, protecting their self-views from harm. Authentic leaders stress openness, honesty and respect by striving for these qualities in the interactions with their followers, and openly discussing their own vulnerabilities and transparently sharing their perceptions and feelings about their colleagues (Avolio et al., 2004a; Luthans & Avolio 2003; May et al., 2003).

LEADERSHIP AS A PROCESS-CENTRIC APPROACH

There are many process-based concepts of leadership like LMX (Leader-Member Exchange) theory (Graen & Uhl-Bien, 1995), motivation-based studies (e.g., Maslow, 1954; McClelland, 1985; Skinner, 1938), strength-based leadership concept (Rath & Conchie, 2008), Social Capital theory (Bourdieu, 1985; Coleman, 1990; Fukuyama, 1999; Portes, 1995; Putnam, 1996), Pygmalion effect (Rosenthal & Jacobson, 1968) and positive psychology (e.g., Spreitzer & Cameron, 2012) approaches. Social Capital theory and the Pygmalion theory are the two most relevant process-centric approaches to the current study and are now presented in the following sections.

Social Capital Theory

Bourdieu (1985, p. 248) defines social capital as 'the aggregate of the actual or potential resources which are linked to possession of a durable network of more or less institutionalized relationships of mutual acquaintance or recognition'. The whole notion of social capital is centred on social relationships and its major elements include social networks, civic engagement, norms of reciprocity and generalized trust.

Social capital plays a significant role in providing access to more information, increasing social cohesion, better engagement, reducing opportunistic behaviour, boosting participation, stakeholder responsiveness and efficiency, reducing transaction costs, providing buffer against risk and uncertainties, and solving collective actions problems (Coleman, 1990; Fukuyama, 1995; Lin, 2001; Paxton, 2002; Putnam, 1993; Welzel et al., 2005; Woolcock & Narayan, 2000). Therefore, the leaders with high social capital can leverage their networks for information to both protect and prepare the organizations, generate greater cooperation from various stakeholders and in the process generate goodwill for the organization and enhance its reputation.

Pygmalion Effect

Expectations of leaders play an important role in determining the performance of subordinates. Right from the 1960s (Likert, 1967; McGregor, 1960), it was assumed that the leaders who expect more get more. The same was reiterated by Rosenthal and Babad (1985), when they stated, 'When we expect certain behaviors of others, we are likely to act in ways that make the expected behavior more likely to occur.'

Harvard Business Review Classics (2003) summarized it the best when it highlighted that

> The way managers treat their subordinates is subtly influenced by what they expect of them. If a manager's expectations are high, productivity is likely to be

excellent. If their expectations are low, productivity is likely to be poor. It is as though there were a law that caused subordinates' performance to rise or fall to meet the managers' expectations.

It has been found that Pygmalion leaders set high expectations from the followers and at the same time make the followers feel more efficacious (Eden, 1992). Leaders set challenging goals, allow the followers to start on a clean slate and foster a high expectations culture (Eden, 1992).

IMPACT OF LEADERSHIP ON PERFORMANCE AND GROWTH OF ACADEMIC INSTITUTIONS

Leadership of academic institutions has grown in relevance in the present VUCA world. In fact, the volatility, uncertainty, change and ambiguity being faced by organizations in the corporate world, are equally applicable for academic institutions. There is a great need for the leaders who can cope with the challenges and find creative solutions to the problems; and the leaders who can steer their organizations in the right direction so that they can sustain for longer periods. Leadership has been found to contribute in many ways to the success of an educational institution (Fullwood et al., 2013; Leithwood et al., 1999).

It goes without saying that the type of leadership plays an important role in ensuring the growth and effectiveness of institutions. The role of academic leadership is important for leading research, setting teaching direction and encouraging industry–academia collaborations (Goel & Göktepe-Hulten, 2018). Academic leaders play a great role in fostering a culture which stimulates innovation, knowledge transfer, industrial engagement and entrepreneurship (Goel & Göktepe-Hulten, 2018). An academic leader must be a visionary and an agent of change (Dinu, 2017).

In addition to facing external challenges, academic leaders also face the internal challenge of managing and inspiring its faculty and administrators (Trivells & Dargenidou, 2009), encouraging them to discard old ways and embrace new values (Elwood & Leyden, 2000). An effective leader is thus needed to not only resolve these challenges, but also to carry all the stakeholders together. In this context, a transformational instructor-leadership has been found to be positively associated with 'students' motivation, satisfaction, perceptions of instructor credibility, academic performance, affective learning and cognitive learning' (Balwant, 2016).

Transformational leadership is one of the most appropriate leadership styles in higher educational institutions, as it facilitates development opportunities for the followers and where the culture demands higher level of involvement rather than just transactional work (Burke et al., 2006). Transformational leaders also lay great emphasis on learning and development, which is an important aspect of developing intellectual capital (Yildiz & Simsck, 2016).

Effective leadership in higher educational institutions enables a sharing, caring, innovative and growth-driven culture where the followers are involved and own up to their responsibilities. Higher education leaders try to establish a culture which reinforces knowledge sharing, retains faculty and builds loyalty to the university (Bollinger & Smith, 2001). As leaders facilitate the search for new opportunities, employees' responsibilities will be increased and their knowledge sharing will also inevitably flourish (Bass, 1999).

Effective leaders challenge their followers by setting ambitious expectations, making them aware about the future objectives and giving significance to the current job (Ndunge, 2014). This increases the performance capabilities of the followers, enhancing the entire team's results, which finally leads to organizational success (Gyanchandani, 2017).

LEADERSHIP AND ORGANIZATIONAL TRANSFORMATION

As organizations grapple with dynamic environments characterized by competition and other disruptions, managing change has become an important domain of inquiry. Effective change management has been found to be influenced by many factors and requires an effective management of people and resources, suitable to the context so as to maintain a competitive advantage (Teczke et al., 2017).

Hamel (2000) and Hamel and Prahalad (1996) view leaders as the driving force for change and suggest that innovation is a necessary force in creating change. At the same time, it requires a strategic intent and the active management process entailing motivating and communicating with people, leaving room for individual and team contributions, and allocating resources.

Different personal and interpersonal skills are necessary for effective change management (Aladwani, 2001; Kanter et al., 1992). A number of prominent models of change management have been developed, such as the Kotter's model of change management (1995), McKinsey 7s model (Peters & Waterman, 1982; Waterman et al., 1980), Lewin's 3 stage model (Lewin, 1951), Nadler's model (Nadler, 1997), Kanter's ten commandments (Kanter et al., 1992) and so on. These models have been used to effectively understand the functioning of different organizations and institutions (e.g., Alam, 2017; Malivan & Thanakunwutthirot, 2019; Mburu, 2013) and the scope for their improvement (Chappell et al., 2016; Hsu & Peng, 2012; Njeru & Kariuki, 2019; Paquibut & Naamany, 2019). These models have also been used in the context of higher educational institutions (Calegari et al., 2015; Kang et al., 2020; Wentworth et al., 2020).

METHODOLOGY

The approach used in the present work is broadly based on grounded theory (Strauss & Corbin, 1990; 1997) and as such the focus has been to capture the unique models emerging from the data itself. The above literature review has thus been presented more from the perspective of providing a background to the work rather than for hypothesis building. Glaser encouraged a broad reading of the literature to develop theoretical sensitivity; while Strauss felt that reading relevant material could enhance the researcher's theoretical sensitivity (Glaser & Strauss, 1967; Glaser, 1978; Strauss, 1987).

There is a normal human tendency to praise iconic leaders and this gets more pronounced when the person has passed on. The authors made conscious efforts to get past various biases in an attempt to develop a dispassionate account based not on eulogies but on factual 'on ground' experiences, events and information. Dr Singh's mantra, 'Leaders are known by their actions', helped us considerably. Whether it was the invitation to write a Festschrift for the book or conducting the interviews, we highlighted our request to the participants to mention events, experiences and facts, rather than praise.

The researchers used qualitative techniques (write-ups, interviews and participant observation) because they can provide in-depth insights into the nuances and dynamics of phenomena, which cannot be tapped adequately by quantitative research. For example, context and process are important to understand the leadership phenomenon (Kempster & Parry, 2011) and this needs in-depth understanding which only qualitative approaches can provide.

The present work used the case study method about one leader. According to Yin (1994), case studies can be helpful in providing complete details of a phenomenon. In the field of leadership studies, Kan and Parry (2004) and Rowland and Parry (2009) have applied and extended the approach of Glaser (1992) and Strauss and Corbin (1998), placing great importance on contextualized and processual elements of leadership for leadership theory. The observer ratings approach has been utilized in this work. For example, it has been found that observer ratings are reliable, if experienced professionals evaluate work activities based on observation and not only on job descriptions (Voskuijl & van Sliedregt, 2002).

Winston (2004) conducted a study on servant leadership on a single case—the leader. The study used multiple data sources followed by data triangulation. A similar approach has been used in the present work. Triangulation refers to the use of multiple methods or data sources in qualitative research to develop a comprehensive understanding of the phenomena (Patton, 1999). It was another way of obtaining complete and detailed data about Dr Singh as a leader, institution builder and person. We have used the inter-method triangulation (Denzin, 1978) approach—using interviews, write-ups and participant observation—to check whether different data sources lead to the same conclusions, thus adding to the validity of the findings (Cohen et al., 2000). Objective organizational performance data (ranking, revenue growth, accreditations, publications, reputation, placements and so on) have also been utilized in the study as supporting data.

Sample

A combination of purposive and convenience sampling has been utilized in this study. In line with Dr Singh's 'constituency' approach of connecting and involving all stakeholders, we interviewed not only those who directly worked with him at Management Development Institute (MDI), IIM Lucknow (IIM-L) and International Management Institute (IMI), but also people from the corporate sector, professional associations (AIMA, ISTD, NHRDN, EPSI), bureaucracy (MHRD at the Centre and Department of Industries/Finance UP), regulators like the AICTE, colleagues on some Boards where he was a member, as well as former students and leaders from the corporate sector. We also interviewed the Chairperson of the government appointed IOE committee—Shri N. Gopalswami.

Since we were interested to know about Dr Singh from his younger days, we tried to locate those who knew him from school and college. We managed to identify a few classmates and friends from Dr Singh's days in school and college and talked to them. We reached out to former students and colleagues from the Department of Commerce, University of Rajasthan, Jaipur, Xavier School of Management (XLRI), Jamshedpur, Administrative Staff College of India (ASCI), Hyderabad, IIM Bangalore as well. The authors contacted 100 different people from academia and industry requesting them to participate in this work. We found that some of the people we contacted were more comfortable to talk rather than write. We had to work through various such issues before the sample finalization.

The final sample size consisted of 31 write-ups, 46 interviews, observations by the authors and the interview with Dr Singh. The sample consisted of both internal (faculty and staff from that period whom we could contact from MDI, IIM-L and IMI) and external stakeholders (corporate sector and government sector). By standards of sample requirements for qualitative research this number is considered to be adequate. Our approach of using observation-based assessments has been supported by researchers (Schneider et al., 2019), who consider such data to be 'more objective' than self-ratings and results in greater validity of the findings.

Conducting the Interviews

The basic question we asked was framed thus—'What has been your experience of Dr Singh as a leader, institution builder and a person?' After the initial 5–6 interviews, we could identify key themes, which helped us to develop a set of probe questions. We could discern commonality in the perceptions about Dr Singh as a leader and as a person. In addition, there were two broad kinds of patterns visible: (a) those who worked closely with Dr Singh (at MDI, IIM-L and IMI) as a leader mentioned certain unique features; and (b) stakeholders from outside the system reported certain other unique features. This is in line with the context-specific nature of leadership phenomenon (Fiedler, 1967; Oc, 2018; Muna, 2011). Fiedler (1967) contingency model proposes that an effective group performance depends on the proper match between the leader's style and the degree to which the situation gives the leader control. Context plays a central role in leadership as leadership does not occur in a vacuum, but rather exists in a context where the leaders function (Oc, 2018).

The probe questions which we asked in the entire sample thus consisted of some common questions and some unique ones, depending on whether they were from the internal stakeholder sample category or the external stakeholder sample category. Each interview was for a duration of 45–60 minutes and were video recorded via zoom (except for 2 where this facility was not possible owing to Interviewee's lack of skills to use zoom). The external stakeholder category consisted of corporate, professional associations, international partners and government (including academic regulators and bureaucrats). The sample was thus heterogeneous enough across the relevant categories (Strauss & Corbin, 1990). Table 1.1 gives the sample details.

Festschrift Write-Ups

The same question used in the interviews was also sent out to the Festschrift writers—'What has been your experience of Dr Singh as a leader, institution builder and a person?' The writers were requested to write down citing events, episodes and examples.

The interview with Dr Singh was conducted in April 2020 (see Appendix A). Questions were asked to get an insight into the demographic factors, various key life experiences and value priorities to help gain deeper insights into the person.

Table 1.1. Sample Details

	Write-ups*	Interviews**	Total
MDI Gurgaon	06 (21.00)	05 (10.00)	11 (14.00)
IIM-L	05 (18.00)	05 (10.00)	10 (13.00)
IMI New Delhi (International Management Institute)	01 (4.00)	02 (4.00)	03 (4.00)
Other academicians	11 (39.00)	04 (8.00)	15 (19.00)
Corporate professionals	05 (18.00)	22 (43.00)	27 (34.00)
Government leaders	00	10 (20.00)	10 (13.00)
Childhood friends	00	03 (6.00)	03 (4.00)
Total	28 (100.00)	51 (100.00)	79 (100.00)

Note: *See Appendix B for details; **see Appendix C for details.

Self-perception data give valuable insights into a person's self-concept.

Data Analyses

Research assistants transcribed recordings of the interviews verbatim. The investigator who had conducted the interviews reviewed the transcripts for accuracy and conducted the primary analysis by coding them. This investigator and two others who had reviewed the transcripts extensively conducted the final analysis by reviewing and discussing the key themes. Several additional themes emerged and were included in the framework. Coding was an iterative process, which emerged from studying the data with a view to generate greater convergence. The NVivo qualitative data analysis software was used for the purpose of content analysis.

The data from the Festschrifts as well as the interviews were analysed separately. This has been done to separate out and check the effects of well thought-out sharing (write-up) vs. spontaneous sharing (interviews).

Thematic analysis focused on three broad domains—Dr Singh as an institution builder, leader and person. Post the thematic analysis we developed the narrative in Chapter 2 which has been constructed on the basis of the events shared by the sample group. Models emerging from the data were identified in three domains: Institution Building, Transformational Leadership and Person. Final triangulation was done across the different data sources to look for patterns of consistencies.

The present work was initiated with the following assumptions in mind—institution building is a function of the leadership style, which is in turn influenced by the leader's personality and values. The present work seeks to answer the following questions:

1. Who was Dr Singh as an institution builder and what did he do?
2. Who was Dr Singh as a leader and as a person?
3. What were Dr Singh's Guiding Values?

It must be mentioned here that it is extremely difficult to separate out the characteristics of the leader from the person. This is the reason why the literature review above did not deal with a separate section on the 'person' which is a broad and all-inclusive term. In fact, at the philosophical level it includes consciousness, rationality and a moral sense (Khuse & Singer, 2009; Varner, 2012); and at the psychological level it encapsulates personality, beliefs and values—individual differences in characteristic patterns of thinking, feeling and behaving (Holzman, 2020; Humphrey et al., 2016).

CHAPTER 2
THE QUINTESSENTIAL CHANGE MAESTRO

Dr Singh's contributions spanned institution building, policy making, mentoring and advisory. He was highly respected as a professor while at XLRI Jamshedpur, ASCI Hyderabad and at IIM Bangalore. He was well known in corporate circles, owing to the consulting and training work he carried out in Public Sector companies for many decades—especially in coal, steel, fertilizers and energy sectors. In the private sector he had by then worked for companies from the Tata Group like Tata Steel and others located around Jamshedpur; MNCs like Bayer India, Siemens India as well as Birla Group Companies in cement and fertilizers; and banks like Corporation Bank and Canara Bank. All this took place before he joined MDI Gurgaon. Subsequently he worked with numerous companies as well as banks through consulting, training, research and board memberships. He contributed in the government as well as in higher education through memberships on various committees (see Appendix D for details).

He won great acclaim for his successes in institution building (turning around/transforming) at MDI Gurgaon, IIM-L and IMI. His reputation as a Director with the Midas Touch got further burnished when he was awarded the Padma Shri in 2003, a first-ever Padma award for a professor in the field of management education. The award of the 19th Global Thought Leader by Moscow International Business School, University of Moscow, MIRBIS in 2005 (see Appendix E for various prominent awards received) further added to his stature, since he was the first in Asia to receive this award.

Dr Singh donned leadership roles from the early days of his career—he was Dean at ASCI and IIM Bangalore (late 1980s and early 1990s, respectively). He was Director MDI Gurgaon (1996–1998 and 2003–2006), IIM-L (1999–2003) and IMI New Delhi (2011–2014). In this part of the book, the dominant focus is on his contributions to building these three institutions.

The chapter is titled 'The Quintessential Change Maestro' and documents the organizational transformation scripted and delivered in the three leading Indian management schools, across three management institutions, each one belonging to a different sector—autonomous (MDI Gurgaon), private (IMI) and government (IIM-L). The term 'maestro' has been used because this feat has been achieved in institutions across sectors.

The chapter presents findings from the research conducted by the team to understand in-depth, the dimensions of organizational transformation and institution building, leadership as well as personal qualities displayed by Dr Singh. Qualitative analysis was conducted on the interview and Festschrift data. Tremendous unanimity of views was evident in the data regarding Dr Singh as a leader and as a person. Findings have been presented in five parts:

Part 1. Thematic Analysis of the Findings presents quantification and a brief analysis of the interview and Festschrift data regarding Dr Singh as an institution builder, as a leader and as a person.

Part 2. Architecting Institutions: Transformation Code presents how these institutions were transformed during Dr Singh's tenure. The sequence of initial events, the thrust areas and the type of work culture built have been described.

Part 3. Leaders Go the Way and Show the Way identifies what was done to bring about such transformations. What was the strategy, approach and style?

Part 4. Guru in a Business Suit puts together the views of the sample group regarding the mentoring, advice and guidance provided by Dr Singh, to individuals, institutions and professional bodies. Clearly, this has been an important route to Dr Singh's influence over the decades and has been presented separately. Strictly speaking, this part also covers an important aspect of Dr Singh as a leader; it has however, been presented separately so that it gets due importance.

Part 5. Above All, Be Human comes last. At the core of leadership is the person and their attitude and value systems, which have an important bearing on the leadership they provide. An attempt is made here to analyse what people said about Dr Singh as a person.

Needless to say, there are overlaps across the four parts. Our attempt, however, has been to tease out the conceptual strands for ease of analysis and presentation.

PART 1: THEMATIC ANALYSIS OF THE FINDINGS

Part 1 presents the data analysed from two sources: interview transcripts and Festschrift write-ups. There were 46 interviews and 31 Festschrift write-ups at this stage of the analysis.

Content analysis (Glaser & Strauss, 1967) was conducted on both the data sets and each one was treated separately using Nvivo (see Appendix F for details). Two layers of content analysis were conducted—a systematic analysis of the manifest content followed by a more interpretive analysis of the latent content. The two data sets were not combined for two key reasons: one, the data collection method in both the cases was different (interview vs write-up) and two, the profile of respondents was also largely different across the two sets (majority of the write-ups were by academicians, while the interviewees were largely industry experts and policymakers).

The transcripts were read carefully to come up with 'thought-units' and were organized into emergent categories. These emergent thought units were then categorized, and their frequencies were calculated.

Subsequently, latent analysis was carried out to club the units with similar thematic contours. These latent themes were then segregated into two broad categories of personal and leadership attributes. Further examination showed that an unwieldy number of sub-themes had emerged, in both the categories, making it difficult to bring convergence in the findings. In order to make the data more manageable and comprehensible, level 3 conceptual regrouping was done. Tables 2.1 and 2.2 present both level-2 and level-3 themes.

Table 2.1 presents the attributes of Dr Singh as a leader which emerged from an analysis of the Festschrift data. An examination of the themes in the table brings out that Institution Builder (25.80%) and Leader (24.90%) are the dominant themes here accounting for almost 50.00 per cent of the word count. Talent Shaper (12.10%), Stakeholder Focus (11.70%) and Team Builder (8.17%) follow and account for approximately one-third (32.00%) of the emergent themes. The balance themes—Result Focus, Indianness and Excellence Focus—together account for 17.33 per cent of the total. Dominant themes indicate the extent to which the Festschrift authors gave weightage to these attributes. Although the balance attributes are important but are, relatively speaking, less focused upon by the sample group.

Table 2.2 presents the attributes of Dr Singh as a leader according to the interviewed sample. Level 3 analysis of attributes in the table brings out the following dominant themes:

Table 2.1. As a Leader—Festschrift Data

Themes—Level 3	Themes—Level 2	Count	%
Institution builder	Institution builder	537	25.79
	Change maestro		
	Creating positive organizational culture		
Leader	Transformational leader	519	24.93
	Scholar leader		
	Visionary		
	Respected		
	Courageous		
Talent shaper	Holistic approach to development	251	12.06
	Talent spotter and nurturer		
Stakeholder focus	Ability to take all stakeholders together	244	11.72
	Connected to all		
Team builder	Egalitarian	170	8.17
	Excellent communicator		
Result focus	Action orientation	157	7.54
	Achiever		
	Creative		
	Innovative		
Indianness	Indian thoughts and wisdom	120	5.76
Excellence focus	Global connect and approach	84	4.03
	Keen observer		
Total		2082	100.00

Leader (25.25%), Stakeholder Focus (21.00%) and Talent Shaper (20.79%)—which account for almost 67.04 per cent (almost two-thirds of the word count). Institution Builder accounts for 12.39 per cent of the word count.

Table 2.2. As a Leader—Interview Data

Theme—Level 3	Theme—Level 2	Count	%
Leader	Leadership	1701	25.35
	Scholar leader		
	Thoughtful leader		
	Visionary leader		
	Transformational leader		
	Responsible leader		
	Strategic		
Stakeholder focus	Stakeholders' inclusion	1409	21.00
	Connected to all		
Talent shaper	Spotting talent	1395	20.79
	Developing talent		
	Holistic growth approach		
Institution builder	Change master	831	12.39
	Sustainable organizational architect		
Team builder	Motivating and inspiring teams	477	7.11
	Persuasive		
	Facilitator		
	Communicator		
	Transparent		
	Collaborative		

Theme—Level 3	Theme—Level 2	Count	%
Result focus	Action orientation	308	4.59
	Performance orientation		
Excellence focus	Global benchmark	307	4.58
	Nations		
	Professionalism		
Indianness	Indian thoughts and wisdom	281	4.19
	Total	6709	100.00

The balance themes—Team Builder (7.11), Result Focus (4.59), Excellence Focus (4.58) and Indianness (4.19)—together account for 20.47 per cent of the word count. Dominant themes indicate the extent to which the interviewees perceived these leadership attributes in Dr Singh. The balance attributes aren't unimportant but are, relatively speaking, less focused upon by the sample group. It must be mentioned that in both kinds of data sets, the same broad themes are evident. The orders of importance of the themes have varied probably owing to the sample composition, with the interview group consisting of a larger number of external stakeholders.

Mention must be made here that the themes which emerged based on the data analysis (see Tables 2.1 and 2.2) in response to the question on Dr Singh as a leader are important in the context of not only leadership but also institution builder and guru/mentor. As mentioned earlier, it is for the convenience of presentation that the content—though overlapping—has been discussed in separate parts.

Table 2.3 presents data from the Festschrift write-ups regarding Dr Singh as a person. This table consists of two meta-categories—interpersonal styles (59.50%) and impactful personality (40.50%). Strong personal connect, building

Table 2.3. As a Person—Festschrift Data

Themes—Level 3	Themes—Level 2	Count	%
Interpersonal style	Strong personal connect	182	59.50
	Informal relations		
	Encouraging attitude		
	Friendly		
Impactful personality	Strong character	124	40.50
	Passionate		
	Keen listener		
	Motivator		
	Impressive		
	Emotionally sensitive		
Total		306	100.00

informal relations, encouraging the team members and a friendly approach have been highlighted as the hallmark of Dr Singh's style of relating with people. The second category consists of attributes which indicate an impactful personality. A man of strong character, who is passionate about what he is doing; he is not only a keen listener but is emotionally sensitive and a motivator. Such attributes together make for an impactful personality especially when he is heading the organization.

The interview-based data (Table 2.4) have revealed similar findings about Dr Singh as a person. Interpersonal style becomes even more important here with more than 50.00 per cent weightage given to this attribute in the theme count.

In addition to the two categories evident in the Festschrift data (Table 2.3), the interview data revealed one more category—authentic human being. The reason for the same may be attributed to the interview format, which allowed people

Table 2.4. As a Person—Interview Data

Themes—Level 3	Theme—Level 2	Count	%
Interpersonal style	Strong personal connect	1101	56.06
	Informal relations		
	Understanding		
	Encouraging and supportive attitude		
	Recognition		
Authentic human being	Positive	621	31.62
	Spiritual		
	Genuine		
	Informal		
	Engaging		
	Humility		
	Humane		
	Acknowledging		
	Accommodating		
Impactful personality	Impressive	242	12.32
	Passionate		
	Reflective		
	Emotionally sensitive		
	Expressive		
	Good memory for names and events		
	Total	1964	100.00

to express themselves more. On the whole however, there is overlap between both categories of the sample (interview and Festschrift) and hence we can conclude that there is consistency in the way Dr Singh was perceived across both types of data sets.

PART 2: ARCHITECTING INSTITUTIONS— TRANSFORMATION CODE

He was not a change agent, he was a **Game Changer**, *a* **Change Master**. *That's the difference ... a change agent is one who facilitates organizational change, a* **Change Master** *makes it happen ....'*

Dwarakanath

Dr Pritam Singh was a widely acknowledged institution builder and transformational leader in the domain of management education, as indicated by the successfully executed transformations culminating in the awards and recognition which he was bestowed for his contributions in the field of management education.

According to Bhaskar Chatterjee, a veteran bureaucrat (then in the MHRD) who knew Dr Singh from his MDI days, 'It is only after a person leaves an institution, that what he leaves behind is really treasured. This was the case with Dr Singh. I saw his work at MDI (mid-1990s) when it was going through a bad patch. He came in, he pulled it up by the bootstraps, he made it into a vibrant institution. Many said, alright, he has done a good job, many others have done something similar; what's so great about Pritam Singh?

IIM Lucknow was a different kind of challenge; it was nothing when he joined. He literally had to create an institution, give it the kind of profile that people were expecting from established IIMs. So, how do you convert a new institution and take it up to the brand name of an IIM? That was his challenge, which he achieved very successfully; and again; only when he left IIM Lucknow, did we begin to realize just how much he had done!

And then he took over IMI. Here he was, each time, working in a different set of circumstances, Governmental ownership, private ownership, institutional ownership, and it's amazing how he was able to craft leadership, craft management, in a way that suited itself to different kinds of radically different circumstances. And yet, he acquitted himself so masterfully.'

This view perceptively highlights the challenges Dr Singh took on and the institutions he transformed.

Part 2 seeks to map out the ways and means used to build these institutions. The term 'transformation' has been used to indicate shifts in each organization on various dimensions, like strategy, structure, systems, shared values, styles, staff and shared values which, according to the McKinsey model (Peters & Waterman, 1982), is considered to be an effective way to bring about lasting organizational change. The term 'Maestro' hints at the ease with which the transformation skills were demonstrated in three management institutions. Thematic analysis presented in Table 2.1, Part 1 shows that institution building has emerged as a level-3 theme. At level 2 were descriptor themes like Institution Builder, Change Maestro, Creating Positive Organizational Culture and Sustainable Organizational Architect. This part has been presented in the following two sections:

1. Section 1: Context Mapping—brief sketch of each of the three institutions when Dr Singh took charge
2. Section 2: Creating a Suitable Work Culture

Section 1: Context Mapping

MDI Gurgaon: A Brief Sketch

MDI Gurgaon was established in 1973 by Industrial Finance Corporation of India (IFCI) based on conditions laid down by the German Agency, DLW (which was then funding IFCI) to spend a percentage of the funds on establishing an educational institution.

In the pre-1995 situation, MDI's activities were modest. They conducted a National Management Program (NMP) (1 section) from 1987 onwards; the Post Graduate Diploma in Management (PGDM) program had been started in 1994 by Professor Abad Ahmad who preceded Dr Singh as the Director. In 1994, there were 20 faculty and around 45 staff members and a budget of 3–4 crore. According to a staff member we interviewed, in those days, any visitor from IFCI—even a clerk was treated like God. Faculty were expected to mobilize management development programs (MDPs) as well as deliver them. According to R. B. Yadav (who was attached to the Director's office from 1993 until late 2000 and had a ringside view of MDI and its directors), before 1995, the financial position of MDI was not very good and IFCI used to pitch in now and then to bridge the budgetary gap.

MDI-V1 (1996–1998)

When Dr Singh took charge in 1995, he found to his dismay that there was little money to pay the salaries. Thus, in the first month itself it is said that he used his personal provident fund money (which he had received from IIM Bangalore) to pay the salaries. He found that the faculty and staff had not been promoted for many years and were clearly demoralized. The roads were full of pothole and the curtains in the offices had not been changed for many years (personal communication).

In fact, they went on a *dharna* (strike) demanding promotions shortly after he joined. According to an NMP participant (S. K. Bose) who had joined the program in 1995, a little after Dr Singh had taken charge, 'We were highly impressed by the speed with which the strike was resolved. Two days were spent in discussions on the issues, on the third day an interview committee was set up, people were promoted and on the fourth day we saw a group of smartly dressed staff. Suddenly, the strike was over. We saw a change in the dressing of the staff who began to wear ties; they had new designations—an officer in MDP was now called a Program Manager. All thirty-four erstwhile clerks were promoted, given new designations and increments. We came to know that Dr Singh had taken charge.

When the Director addressed the one-year NMP participants, one of them asked him: Why did you join MDI? What will you do differently? He answered, "I will take decisions with speed; I will grow the PGDM program; I will make MDI rank among the top 10 business schools in the country. I will create a hostel block for NMP."

People were quite sceptical at this bold vision. Bose said, "We could not believe what he said; in the government sector the tendering process (before construction) itself takes six months; to our utter surprise, the building was constructed right in front of our own eyes and was ready in less than a year..."'

Growing MDI Activities

Dr Singh quickly realized that new revenue streams were needed to make MDI self-sustaining. With this in view, many steps were taken—the part-time program (evening program) was started at MDI; and focus was shifted to increasing training and consulting activities.

One of the first persons Dr Singh contacted was Jauhari Lal, the then Director-Personnel of Oil and Natural Gas Corporation (ONGC), to explore the possibility of MDI conducting management programs for ONGC. He similarly went out and met Directors-HR and CMDs of companies wherever possible in the public sector. The number of training activities at MDI moved up to include policy-level programs; Advanced Management Programme (AMP) for top-level executives (with international component) commenced and many other short-term training programs were also started. The doctoral program was conceived and later launched in 1999. Faculty strength increased to around 30.

MDI became financially viable and it sprinted on a growth path. MDI was the first in India to be accredited by National Board of Accreditation (NBA)—establishing the credentials of MDI as a management school with high standards. In 1998, MDI was ranked in the top 10 management schools in the country. Within three years of his taking over, MDI emerged as a leading management school in India. It became financially viable; the PGDM program enjoyed top rankings (in the first ranking exercise by All India Management Association [AIMA]).

MDI-V2 (2003–2006)

After his stint as Director IIM-L (1998–2003), Dr Singh returned to MDI as a professor and was subsequently appointed as the Director for a second term in 2003. The period of 2003 to 2006 was one of the frenetic times for MDI.

As it grew in reputation, MDI expanded its activities. A host of international exchange programs were signed up, and dual-degree programs were developed with leading European schools like École Supérieure de Commerce de Paris (ESCP). Two new long-term PGDM programs were introduced—PGP Human Resources (HR) and PGP International Management.

The Executive Fellow Program in Management (EFPM) was also launched. The Post Graduate Program in Energy Management (PGPEM) was established in association with the Ministry of Power and USAID (R. V. Shahi). The Post Graduate Program in Public Policy and Management (PGP-PPM) and a program for army officers transitioning into civilian life were launched. A unique two-week integration program was initiated for senior officers of the RBI and senior commercial bankers. MDI became the first in India to be accredited by the International Agency Association of MBAs (AMBA) in 2005–2006. MDI became a trendsetter as subsequently, many other leading management institutions (including IIMs A, B and C) adopted this approach to highlight program quality. In fact, this was best summed up by Ravi Kumar who said that IIM Bangalore directors used to keep track of the latest developments in MDI. The faculty numbers grew from 35 in 2003 to 75 in 2006 (see Appendix G for details). The placement graph shot up and MDI was ranked among the top 5 management schools in India. During his second stint as Director, MDI was even ranked number 1 by one of the ranking agencies. In fact, for many years after 2006, MDI was consistently ranked among the top five management schools.

'MDI witnessed a total transformation under Dr Pritam Singh's leadership. He had the attitude of working selflessly, and he was a great institution builder, a skill which not many people possess. His focus was on institution building and development.' (Naga)

IIM-L

While MDI Gurgaon has been neither a fully public nor fully private sector entity, IIM-L was a government institution. Each type of institution had their own set of challenges and complexities which needed different treatment. While

MDI enjoyed autonomy once the Board reposed trust in the Director's capabilities, IIM-L was a different type of organization, being governed by the rules and regulations of the government sector.

Despite this, a significant transformation was brought even in IIM-L in terms of growing the institution and taking care of long-pending disputes which were a major irritant to its growth. The nature of some of the challenges at IIM-L was unique. It was a public institution funded and set up by the government, thus bringing the Ministry of Human Resource Development (MHRD) into the picture. Employees enjoyed job security unlike in the private sector management schools. Besides, in the 1990s, Lucknow was a backwater and the campus itself was located on the outskirts of the city. Attracting faculty was a tough task, since good schools (for faculty's children) were located at a distance. Besides, spouses of faculty did not have the scope to land jobs of any kind in the vicinity.

As the then Secretary, Industries of the UP Government, S. C. Tripathi, put it, 'He built IIM-L; I am telling you. Before him, when I would go there, it mainly had an agriculture resource centre funded by the World Bank; a good leader was lacking—many faculties worked part time, many positions were not filled yet. Towards the second half of the 90s, I learnt about how much it had changed. Dr Singh very remarkably filled the leadership vacuum and brought up the Institute during the period he was there, and it came on par with the IIM-A, B, and C. Today, many IIM-L graduates are leading industries in many countries.'

As a long-time faculty member from that period said, prior to 1998, when Dr Singh took charge as Director, there was nothing much to be appreciated at IIM-L. Good students were joining, studying, getting good placements and leaving. Hardly 15–20 MDPs were conducted; infrastructure—hostels, faculty housing and offices—was not that good. And that was the time when Professor Singh joined. He brought a tremendous amount of energy into the campus and he could totally revitalize the campus, according to Bandopadhyaya.

Dr Singh joined IIM-L as Director in November 1998, allegedly at the behest of the Government. He reluctantly shifted from MDI Gurgaon at a time when he was just beginning to enjoy the fruits of three years of hard work at MDI. His first experience at IIM-L was itself an uncomfortable one which perhaps gave him a flavour of the place and the impending challenges.

On 26 January, Republic Day, he was interacting with faculty and staff just before the flag hoisting ceremony on the campus lawns. In a friendly manner he politely spoke to the Staff Union representative, requesting for suggestions to make IIM-L a great place. The response, 'Everything is fine here. You can go back to MDI Gurgaon' was not only a public insult, but a challenge to the incoming head. Dr Singh knew that his reputation on the campus was linked to how he responded to this behaviour before staff, faculty and students.

The next day he called the registrar and said, 'We need to bring some discipline here—I want the Union representative to be suspended.' The letter came as a shock to the Union leader—who became so anxious, that she went to Mrs Singh, requesting her help and assuring good behaviour. Later, Dr Singh opined in one of the training programs when narrating this episode, 'My intent was not to trouble the lady but to give a signal to the whole campus that discipline and good behaviour were expected, and that bad behaviour would not be tolerated.'

Two key visionary decisions impacting the future of IIM-L were taken which served it well in the long run: (a) the long-pending land dispute with the farmers union (Tikait Group, operating in the surrounding villages of the campus) was resolved and this brought permanent peace in the region; (b) the then controversial decision to procure land in Noida to build a satellite campus, enabled IIM-L to get access to the corporate sector in the Noida area. During his stint from 1998–1999 to 2002–2003, the faculty strength increased from 35 to 66; MDPs shot up from 22 to 95; international linkages went up from Nil to six; revenues shot up from 5.14 crore to 16.77 crore and IIM-L was ranked number 1 among Indian business schools in 2002–2003 (see Appendix H for details).

IMI New Delhi

Dr Singh stepped down from MDI directorship in September 2006 and continued there as Professor of Eminence until 2011. In early 2011, he was invited for a meeting with Sanjiv Goenka, Chairman of the IMI Board and Chairman R. P.-Sanjiv Goenka Group. He was offered the post of Director General of IMI New Delhi, along with IMI Kolkata and IMI Bhubaneshwar. At the meeting, Dr Singh asked Mr Goenka about his expectation and he replied (Dr Singh—personal communication), 'Can you bring it up to the level of MDI?' Later Dr Singh said, 'this was like coming full circle—when I was interviewed on Doordarshan before taking charge as Director MDI V1 (1996), the interviewer had asked me, "Will you be able to bring MDI's ranking higher than that of IMI?" And indeed this was achieved in 2014, when NHRD ranked IMI 6th and MDI was ranked 7th.'

He took over as Director General of IMI in May 2011 and continued up to September 2014. According to C. N. Narayana, aka CNN (former Registrar IMI), prior to 2011,

IMI was ranked among the top 20 management schools. The ranking improved from 2011 onwards and in 2014, it was ranked among the top 11 management schools in India by credible ranking agencies. IMI was known for its PGDM program and Executive PGDM of 18 months duration. IMI conducted a PhD program affiliated to the Indraprastha University. The reputation of the school was more niche, faculty quality being one of its major strengths.

When Dr Singh took over, he came face to face with a unique set of challenges, which threatened to make his vision for IMI a non-starter. IMI had a small campus, not only located in the heart of South Delhi, but located at the edge of the city forest, Sanjay Van. Growing the institution by introducing new long-term programs and MDPs seemed next to impossible owing to the severe constraint on infrastructure, given that it was located on approximately two acres.

Vertical campuses are quite common especially in the west; IMI, however, could not grow vertically owing to it being located in a 'No Fly Zone', which prohibited its vertical growth as it lay in the aerial flight path. Clearances from multiple authorities were needed before the infrastructural expansion was possible, like Airport Authority of India, Forest and Fire Departments, Architecture committee, etc. (CNN).

Over the three-year tenure—April, 2011 to September, 2014—many initiatives were taken and the dream of building another high-quality management institution was largely achieved (see Appendix I for details).

It all started with taking on the challenge of growing the infrastructure by solving the 'No Fly Zone' issue and getting the multiple clearances. Since the Qutub Institutional Area was on the flight path located close to Palam Airport, the building height allowed in that area was only six floors.

As the then Registrar IMI, CNN, narrated, 'I initially went to many agencies and even visited the ministry. The officials said that it is not possible to shift the fly zone because of the location. Then Dr Singh suggested we go and meet the concerned people in the departments; he was not a person who would just delegate and watch from behind. We went to many meetings together- in fact we even went to the Ministry to get the clearances. He was not the type of person to be stuck on hierarchy. He had no problems, if needed, to even speak to the concerned clerk in a department. Only he could dream of shifting the fly zone and make the vision for IMI a reality.'

Parallelly, many actions were taken to grow IMI activities—new long-term programs were introduced, MDP activities with focus on senior levels were taken up, existing long-term programs were expanded, the Fellowship Programme in Management (FPM) was initiated, International accreditation (AMBA) was achieved and the process for getting the Association to Advance Collegiate Schools of Business (AACSB) was initiated. As all these activities were prioritized, construction activities were also in full swing and were completed by 2013. The number of faculty at IMI was around 30 in 2011 which almost doubled in 2014.

IMI witnessed some key achievements in this period: IMI was ranked number 3 on Intellectual Capital by Business World Magazine in 2012 and most of the leading ranking agencies placed IMI among the top 12 Business Schools of India. IMI New Delhi received the NBA approval and Association of Indian Management Schools (AIMS) approval for PGDM equivalent to MBA. IMI New Delhi was ranked among Top 10 Business Schools of India in credible surveys and National HRD Network (NHRDN) People Matters survey. The annual revenue, which stood at ₹25.82 crore, doubled to ₹50 crore in three years. In an unprecedented move, AMBA accreditation was given for a five-year period to an Indian management school (C. N. Narayana, former Registrar IMI).

Section 2: Creating a Suitable Work Culture

Findings indicated that strategic choices were made, and actions were taken on multiple fronts to support implementation of the strategy in each of the three institutions. Content analysis of the interview transcripts brought out some common patterns indicating the strategic choices made by Dr Singh while building these three institutions. Some unique choices were also evident, in response to the demands of each of the three institutions.

As Anadi Pande, who worked with him in IIM-L mentioned, the capacity for vision and strategy formulation along with executive implementation are critical for a leader which, according to him, Dr Singh combined amazingly well. As he put it, 'He created a vision that if at IIM-L we must really pursue growth, we need to build the Noida Campus. Back in 2000, even IIM-Ahmedabad did not have a satellite campus. That's when he conceived of the Noida campus—an apparently unattainable goal at that time. We are reaping the benefits today, because there was a Director with a vision and executive capability. I came to know very recently that he faced a lot of stiff resistance from the Ministry and had to go through a lot of personal pain - IIM-L had to seek a lot of approvals, but the fact that he could successfully do it, speaks volumes about Dr Singh as a Change Leader.'

Transformation was brought in through decisions and actions which created an empowered team and a vibrant work culture, conducive to performance and growth. Culture is one of the key pillars of sustainable organizational transformation. According to all the interviewees (who worked in MDI Gurgaon, IIM-L and IMI in that period), a highly conducive work culture was created. The authors have brought together the findings into the following work culture dimensions. Work culture is typically an outcome of the work values, leadership style and various processes and practices all operating in alignment with each other. Strong work culture brings clarity among people as to how the top management wants them to behave in a situation, and there is a connection between employees living the organizational values and rewards (tangible and intangible) they receive.

Exciting Work Culture

New faculty were brought in from diverse backgrounds from good schools like IIMs and Institute of Rural Management Anand (IRMA). Dr Singh would go out of the way to attract, motivate and retain faculty. In fact, according to Dhameja, it was not uncommon to find that Dr Singh would retain the faculty by offering them a raise or incentive in anticipation of the approval from the Board. These efforts contributed to generate excitement, and attract and retain talent. As M. P. Jaiswal said, 'I was working in Institute of Rural Management, Anand (IRMA) and had applied to MDI and other IIMs. To my surprise, I received a call from Dr Singh himself who said, "I am sending you a flight ticket, come over;" he was so warm and so welcoming. Although I received another offer from an IIM, I joined MDI because I wanted to work with this Director.'

There were others who saw his interview on national television (Maheshwari, R. L. Raina to name a few) and were inspired to work with such a leader.

Kala and Sridhar, both of whom had joined IIM-L from the USA said that in their endeavour to move back to India, they wrote to various IIMs and got no reply from any of them. They found it refreshing and heart-warming that the Director of IIM-L gave them a call and persuaded them to join, and they did so. Moreover, unlike typical management schools where appointment of spouses was generally frowned upon, here was a place which hired both husband and wife as faculties.

According to Ashok Banerjee, 'What struck me the most in our first encounter is, Dr Singh greeted me in a manner like we had known each other for a long time. While seeing me off after the meeting, he walked with me for a while and narrated his journey so far as an academic thought leader. He could have easily sent me off formally that evening and there was no compulsion to share his personal stories with an unknown person. He made every visitor feel important and at ease and in the process extracted a [psychological] commitment from them.'

According to Maheshwari who worked closely with him at IIM-L, he had the knack of picking up talent from various domains—corporate world, academia and various institutions. He would spot a promising person and say—'hey come and work with me.'

Many actions were taken to inspire people—faculty members at MDI were encouraged to interact with people from the industry, government and professional bodies and not just sit within the four walls of their offices. The director himself went to companies like ONGC, NTPC, BHEL and others and started MDPs for these companies. There was something new happening every day. The place was buzzing with activity. Dr Singh himself used to work until 10 pm at night—daytime was reserved for meetings and visits to companies, ministry and AICTE. Watching him work late also motivated many others to do the same.

A similar culture was built in IIM-L, to the extent possible. Owing to the relatively remote location of IIM-L, Dr Singh would travel to companies in Delhi, Bombay and other hubs to mobilize short-term programs, research opportunities, consulting assignments, attend meetings with the Ministry of HRD (MHRD) and so on. According to Jayadev, he utilized every opportunity to send faculty to meet senior-level corporate leaders outside Lucknow. The MDPs significantly helped to get senior executives to visit the campus and gave faculty the opportunity for interaction and for corporate executives to experience the IIM-L campus.

He tried to find unique ways to recognize people—for example, in the early days at MDI, to reward one of the hardworking faculty, he gave him one of his personal consulting assignments and said, 'Use the fees to buy a good car for yourself'—such actions kept up the excitement and developed positive expectations among all. Similar opportunities/rewards were given to those who could deliver.

Inspiring Workplace

Everyone who visited MDI and IIM-L appreciated the beauty of the campuses and the attention paid to maintaining them. According to his then personal secretary Yadav, MDI always had well-maintained gardens and lawns (35-acre campus). However, Dr Singh paid a lot of attention to improving the ambience. Statues of Mahatma Gandhi, Vivekananda, the main fountains—all this was done during his tenure. He was very particular about the beautification of the campus, as indicated by the following example: someone who used to accompany Dr Singh on morning walks on the MDI campus said, 'Even if there was a dried leaf on the trees, he would notice and get it removed.' The buildings were given specific names which were in themselves inspirational such as faculty offices were in the 'Scholars' building. The main entrance to the building had an imposing mural depicting great thinkers like Socrates and Aristotle and many others. The library building was named 'Gyangrih' (enlightenment place); buildings were given evocative names like 'Renaissance', 'Parthenon', 'Lakshya', 'Takshashila', 'Gurukul', 'Nalanda' and so on.

Likewise, in IIM-L, each building was given an inspiring name—the administrative block named 'Samadhan'; the library building 'Gyanoday'—enlightenment, with murals depicting Lord Buddha. Similarly, 'Chintan' was the name of the faculty block and so on, each name providing a specific meaning and focus, indicative of the role played by each one of them. Bhaskar Chatterjee, who visited the IIM-L campus in those days, expressed surprise that Dr Singh focused on the design elements of the campus when he had many more pressing issues to handle. As he elaborated, 'To me it appeared that he was trying to create a campus that would give it a geography, he would give it an ambience, would give it a presence that people who went from there would recall it so quickly. So, he was very conscious of how it should look. That struck me as very innovative at that time, because why would you get involved with architecture?! Why would you get involved with the way it looks?'

Even in the limited space of the campus at IMI, efforts were made to beautify the campus and plant trees to the extent possible.

Open and Informal with High Communication

Information-sharing and informality were an important part of the new work culture. Regular faculty meetings, as well as staff meetings, were normal in all the three institutions, where information was shared regarding the latest developments at the institution. Faculty across all the three institutions were introduced to a unique 'tea meeting' culture. Faculty could meet over morning tea and coffee between 11:00 to 11:30 am in a common area—they would drop in for a few minutes, catch up with colleagues and return to their offices. If the Director was in town, he made it a point to join the faculty for tea. This was a great way to provide a neutral space for internal networking, building camaraderie, as well meeting other colleagues for discussions. Dr Singh laid great emphasis on face-to-face meetings and discussions and did not care much for use of emails especially for conflict-laden matters. He discouraged faculty members sending mails especially copying the Director in their conversation, preferring that people resolve their own issues among themselves.

Since Dr Singh believed that the faculty were the major strength of an academic institution (in many interviews with the media, as well as when he addressed faculty, he would clearly state this) he realized that in order to attract faculty to join and stay; a suitable work culture needed to be established. According to Rattan Sharma of MDI, an academic culture, open and hierarchy-free, was created. Anyone could walk into the Director's office—whether faculty, staff or students—without an appointment. It was an open-door policy. According to all the faculty members (especially IIM-L and MDI) we spoke with, the Director rarely called faculty to his office. He would walk across to the office of the concerned faculty and discuss face-to-face.

This trend was evident in IIM-L as well. His morning calls to the deans and others are legendary. As the interviewed faculty members across the institutions put it, 'Dr Singh rarely asked his secretary to call a faculty to his office. He would either make a phone call himself or would walk over to the person's office. He would drop into my office and casually ask—"So how is your publication going? What are your research plans?" Another professor fondly recounted, he would visit my home; he knew my family members and what they were doing. Sometimes, we would have long discussions and together we made many plans.'

This was not unique to one person but to a team of people we interviewed. One of the former faculty members of IIM-L (Jayadev) said, 'I had just joined IIM-L as Assistant Professor and was looking for some data from banks for my research. I requested the Director for help. He immediately arranged a meeting and I got a chance to have interactions that enriched my understanding of the issue. I was not the only person he helped, anyone who reached out to him got help.'

Similar levels of information-sharing and accessibility were visible at IMI as well, and advance appointments were not required to meet the Director. In fact, anyone who wanted to meet would have the liberty to walk in. The only problem was the long wait for one's turn, in case other faculty had already dropped in to meet him.

Before the Director went on tour, a message would be sent out to all faculty members listing his visits and their purpose. More important—on his return, there would be a debrief session with faculty and staff to convey the successes and achievements made on behalf of the institution. The debrief sessions were given to staff as well so that both faculty and staff operated from the same information base.

This account by one of the Deans of IIM-L is especially revealing of Dr Singh's non-hierarchical approach (Bandyopadhyay), 'In the early days, for almost two weeks at a time, we travelled in a team of three, to major European management schools and universities across Europe. You won't believe it; he did not use the perks and privileges of the Director of an IIM. He said, "I am uncomfortable at the thought of wasting money when we are still trying to establish ourselves. I don't want people to point fingers." We used to travel by bus at night and by day we used to hire just one hotel room and take turns to use the facilities to freshen up and then set out for the day. That's when we got very close and we began to feel that he is one of us!'

Inspiring and Motivating the Team

He built strong teams at the three institutions. Various approaches were taken. Faculty members were encouraged to do what they were best at—be it teaching, training, research or consulting. Some faculty at MDI remembered what he spoke in the meetings—'I will not ask a rabbit to fly and a bird to run,' indicating that if a professor was asked to operate from his weak area, he was bound to fail and this approach would not be used. This was the beginning of the thought process of building a holistic approach to performance management in a holistic business school—focused on teaching, research, training and consulting, all of which fed into each other creating a virtuous cycle and generating growth momentum.

While at IIM-L, Dr Singh began to encourage some faculty to think of becoming future Directors in top schools. According to a former Dean, Dr Singh said, 'Many faculties join as directors without an iota of administrative acumen. So why not nurture those who have administrative ability and develop academic leaders,' and this was the beginning. Administrative portfolios were given to those who were inclined and had the potential. His wish from those days became a reality, according to a former Dean of IIM-L and of MDI Gurgaon. Today, there are as many as eight directors heading IIMs, who had, at one time, worked with Dr Singh at MDI, IIM-L and/or IMI.

At MDI, after initially supporting and helping staff members, Staff Union leaders were communicated to (according to a staff member we interviewed) in one of the meetings, in the local language—'My *maan* (reputation) is in your hands.' This gave the staff a sense of accountability and importance. As mentioned earlier, staff grievances at MDI were handled immediately, and promotions and increments were given. This created hope among the staff that 'If we work, this Director will take care of our requirements.' Those who never expected any promotion in their career, became officers in his tenure.

As in MDI, attention was paid to staff-level issues at IIM-L as well, and efforts were made to understand their problems and resolve them. According to the then Registrar at IIM-L, steps were taken to redress their grievances—80 per cent of the staff was promoted; work was done to bring about an attitude change to make them more positive—all 45 non-academic staff members were sent for sensitivity training conducted by an external expert. Besides this, a quick survey was conducted to assess their aspirations for IIM-L and their preferred department for job rotation.

Further, the Director held monthly communication meetings with the staff; these were open meetings for all staff from the peon to the officer. Such meetings were also held by the Registrar who regularly initiated and held department-level meetings. A staff welfare committee was formed to handle their grievances. A Director's medical fund was created and when staff needed more money for availing medical facilities, it was given from the Director's medical fund. An old shed was converted into assembly hall for the staff.

Tremendous emphasis was placed on faculty development, with faculty getting the opportunity to attend various national and international development programs. Many faculty benefitted from these opportunities and several went overseas for conferences or training. When a faculty introduced a client or contact to the institute, he was valued and recognized. For example, M. P. Jaiswal mentioned, 'When I brought the BAAN company to MDI, Dr Singh insisted that I be the person to sign the agreement with them. This was unique and made me feel special.'

The biggest inspirational factor was the role modelling by the Director, working hard for the well-being and growth of the institution. There were times when many people said, 'I was feeling lazy, disinclined to work more, yet, when Dr Singh requested, I would not dare say no—he was twice our age and he was working twice as much, how could I refuse!'

Performance and Reward

The PMS (performance management system) was introduced at MDI and IMI, and this had a motivational impact on faculty. At IIM-L, while the process of setting up a PMS was initiated by Dr Singh, implementation took place subsequently, according to Anadi Pande. At MDI, faculty members were given the chance to choose at least two activity areas in which they would like to contribute—be it teaching, training, research and consulting—to earn a minimum of 300 work points. Those working beyond 300 points were paid separately, in accordance with the number of sessions taken.

Some intangible rewards were instituted for publishing in well-known journals—faculty development and training abroad, for example. Faculty whose papers were accepted for a conference whether in India or abroad, could travel at the institute's expense to present their papers. This system came into place at MDI 17 years ago. Now it is common across top Indian management schools.

The PMS resulted in a high-performance culture, where people felt recognized, motivated and were eager to deliver more.

Research and publication were strongly encouraged by Dr Singh by providing research grants at MDI, IIM-L and IMI. A former professor of IIM-L shared in the interview, 'Dr Singh would say, "If somebody asks for one lakh rupees grant, I ask, why only one lakh? Take more money. When you give more money for research, it gives me an opportunity to ask after six months or a year: you took the money, what has happened, where is your paper/ book?"'

Empowering and Supportive

The administrative team (Deans and Chairpersons) was given complete empowerment to deliver. According to some of the faculty who worked in administrative positions with him, once a person was tasked with a responsibility, the Director would not interfere at all. An interesting example was shared by a then newly appointed faculty with an administrative role, who went up to him asking him for direction—Dr Singh's reply was revealing—he said, 'Professor XX, if I have to make the decision, then why have you in this position? He subsequently reassured and supported him saying go ahead and make the right decision, I am with you if something goes wrong.'

Deans/Chairpersons received full support to do their jobs, especially when they were in a crisis. Faculty had their own autonomy and independence to function. Every faculty was required to create a work plan for the year and once that was agreed upon, they were free to work without any interference. Timetables were decided and finalized in advance; classes could not be shifted easily after that.

According to G. N. Pandey, faculty were given the freedom to take company guests for lunch. The finance officer was advised by Dr Singh, 'If the faculty is taking a guest to lunch—don't question them. And if you require my approval, bring it to me and I will approve it.' That is how faculty also began to feel empowered that they could take financial decisions. On the other hand, when he would meet the faculty, he would advise them not to do anything without using their conscience. He would also assure them that he would take care of administrative matters.

At IIM-L, there was the instance of a student who was so inebriated that he ended up atop the water tank on the campus, threatening to jump down. The Director appointed an enquiry committee and the decision was taken to rusticate him from the program. The student had connections in high places and was confident that nothing would happen to him. There were some feelers from the Ministry, but the Director stood his ground saying, 'I have to maintain my integrity, I have to support my committee, sorry I cannot go against their decision.' In that sense the empowerment was of a very high order. According to Yadav of MDI Gurgaon, 'Although Dr Singh was high on empowerment, he was equally high on monitoring progress. He knew how to get people to work. For example, he didn't believe in sending out mails. He would directly walk into someone's office and ask them to get the work done; he would counsel them and give them a chance to improve. If they didn't improve then he would take it seriously. Such people would be treated differently.'

Certain norms were clearly put in place and strictly adhered to. Empowerment was combined with monitoring and follow-up to ensure that everything was on track—whether it was in academics or research, training, or consulting. A culture of discipline in maintaining class and program schedules and timings was adhered to.

Speedy and Result Focused

This was demonstrated right in the beginning of his tenure at MDI, in the way the staff strike was handled. It emerged later that the quick resolution of the strike was done by a committee appointed for the purpose. The committee identified the key problem bothering the staff—lack of promotions for long years—and solutions were then worked out.

Work was expected to go on, while the paperwork would take effect parallelly. According to M. P. Jaiswal, it was a refreshing culture where the paperwork did not delay the actions. Results were given greater importance and the earlier bureaucratic culture was changed into a result-focused culture. According to both faculty and staff at MDI, the Director worked not only with speed of decision-making, but he also worked with swiftness. As his then secretary put it, 'By day the Director was busy visiting companies, government departments, and the regulator, etc., office work began at 5 pm and went on until 10 pm. Meetings were held, files were cleared so that there was nothing pending at the Director's table.'

Another interesting example of how speed was achieved was given by Yadav, 'Many times, when things had to be moved fast, the Director would advise the concerned faculty or registrar to go ahead and start the work saying "I will take care of getting the Board permissions and we can sort out the paperwork parallelly."'

Similar was the case in IIM-L. As a senior professor put it, 'Dr Singh used to travel a lot on work and yet there were no delays in paperwork. He used to handle papers while he was travelling in the car to and from the airport.' One of the then faculty at IIM-L narrated how when he asked for a meeting appointment, Dr Singh agreed to a meeting right away—he invited the faculty member to drive with him in the car while en route to the airport to catch a flight.

According to the then Registrar IIM-L, he went to the staff offices, talked to people and made it clear to them that their job was to support faculty rather than ask questions on their spending decisions. This brought a change, which in turn led to faculty reaching out, talking to people from the government and corporate sector.

The greatest example of speedy and result focussed approach was the Noida campus plan. Dr Singh was so result-focused and concerned about providing industry reach that he initiated the acquisition of land for the Noida campus. In a government set up where MHRD controls expenditure, it is tough to take any initiative where big money is involved.

Even if old vehicles were to be disposed of, permission was required from the government. In such a situation, Dr Singh took a very bold decision. He went ahead and bought a plot for IIM-L in Noida and had to face some tough consequences for a while which were later amicably resolved. At IMI, he asked the administrative team to keep the construction work going on even as he visited different offices to get the clearances and permissions. One of the key administrative members said, 'Dr Singh was clear about the goal. He did not waste time. He had the ability to juggle multiple balls at the same time and handle things parallelly.'

Diverse, Inclusive and Boundaryless

All stakeholders—regulator, industry, media and local administration—were given the due importance and involved. Cordial relations were maintained with the Board members. The Director visited various companies and regulators and there was a plenty of scope for developing mutual understanding, information to flow within the organization and vice versa. No distinction was made across different cadres of employees—whether faculty or office staff, all were treated well (their needs were taken care of and information-sharing took place). Many women faculty were recruited and efforts were also made to recruit faculty across different regions in all the three institutions.

Dr Singh reached out to top managements of various companies and shared his thoughts and ideas on how MDI could contribute to their betterment. In this way the seeds were sown to acquire many training programs and consulting assignments. It was a win-win approach.

The move to bring 20 per cent teaching in every course by industry practitioners, was a great way to get corporate executives to interact with students and familiarize them with the corporate world.

Growth, mobilizing research funding, training and consulting, providing access to media as well as ranking agencies were prioritized and paid close attention to by the Director. One of the faculty members at MDI said, 'Earlier, we were expected to both mobilize and deliver programs but when Dr Singh joined, he assured us that he would-handle mobilization of the programs so that we could focus on high-quality delivery.' This was also a great change for the faculty and was appreciated by all. At both IIM-L and IMI, the foundations of high-quality training for the industry were put in place during his tenure.

His media handling was superb too. As an institution builder, he not only networked with professionals, his network and handling of the media was tremendous. He knew what and how to communicate with the outside world, about the institution. Media had access to information. In fact, in Lucknow anything which happened at IIM-L became news. Similar was the experience in MDI and IMI.

The following steps were evident in the transformation process across MDI, IIM-L and IMI:

1. *Communication to the internal community:* Addressing all students, staff and faculty, sharing the vision and inspiring people to join and support the cause.

2. *Sensemaking and building a common narrative and perception of issues*: Deriving specific meaning in the environment, observing opportunities was something Dr Singh did excellently well. This unique 'sensemaking' and interpretation, was then communicated to all, including plans for building the institution. People in the three institutions, especially staff and faculty, were addressed regularly in meetings. Updates regarding improvements and new assignments mobilized were a common feature of such meetings. There was a transparent process in place and information about the

financial position of MDI and IMI and the plans to improve the same were shared in these meetings.

3. *Creating hope and positivity by demonstrating quick results:* Keen efforts were made to soothe anxiety and train the collective energies in a positive direction for the growth of the institutions. This was dovetailed with the results on the ground as the institutions began to show growth and visibility.

4. *Attracting and retaining talent (Talent Shaper):* Faculty strength was increased in all the three institutions. Personal touch and recognition, creation of a conducive work culture and an incentive system contributed to attracting and retaining talent.

5. *Stakeholder relationships:* Efforts were made to reach out to public sector companies, as well as banks, with a view to establishing a win-win relationship by assisting the companies in developing their senior executives, doing consulting work. Thus, a two-way flow of information and ideas took place between industry and academia where both had a chance to learn from each other. Cordial relations were built with the regulator AICTE, with the media, and even with the local administration. Great relationships were cultivated with the Board members as well. In turn, all of them supported these institutions in their quest for greatness.

Part 2 reveals that there was a similarity of approach to institution building taken by Dr Singh across MDI, IIM-L and IMI. People were at the centre of all strategies for transformation and a suitable work culture was built which enhanced motivation and result orientation.

There is no doubt that at the core of institution building is the leader. Part 3 now delineates the leadership of Dr Singh.

PART 3: LEADERS GO THE WAY AND SHOW THE WAY

> *He was a creator; he was one who could manage things well and he was also somebody who could transform. The most important quality of a leader is to recognize who can be good at creating, who can be good at preserving, and who can do the transformation, and Dr Singh had that quality.*
>
> Poonia

This part attempts to answer the question regarding the How? What was the type of leadership which enabled Dr Singh to transform these organizations? The thematic analysis (see Part 1) revealed the presence of leadership attributes like transformational, intellectual, scholar leader, visionary, respected, thoughtful, responsible, strategic and courageous. Other important attributes of a leader which emerged from the analysis are—talent shaper, stakeholder focus, team builder, result focus and excellence focus. These are further elaborated in this part.

Part 3 is organized around the following subsections (see Part 1 for details of the content analysis):

1. Early days: The young turk
2. Leadership attributes
3. Behavioural and action attributes

Dr Singh has been widely viewed as a leader by the entire sample group of 77. Many called him a transformational leader while others called him a scholar leader. As a senior corporate leader put it, 'He was a very well accepted and highly respected leader both in the academic world as well as in the corporate world; besides, he enjoyed so much respect in government circles.'

Some others gave the following statements about Dr Singh as a leader:

- While I was in IIM-L, I heard so much from other faculty about how much he encouraged them.
- He was not only an excellent leader; he was an excellent administrator.
- His eyes were always on the goal.
- Highly result-focused.
- He gave plenty of empowerment but also conducted a good amount of follow up.
- A level 5 leader.
- A servant leader.
- Great facilitator leader.
- He was a balanced leader.
- A complete leader of a management school—balancing both academics and business.
- Purpose driven, vision-based leader—he accepted ideas and views from anyone that would fit in the vision.
- Result-focussed leader.
- Decisive leader.
- Great statesman, not at all the typical B-School professor.

Early Days: The Young Turk

Dr Singh's leadership drive and capability were evident right from his days as a young faculty in the Commerce College, University of Rajasthan, Jaipur. In those days he was excited and inspired by the thought of building a great department of management. As a young faculty in his late 20s, he worked very closely with the head of the Department to mobilize funding from a local businessman (according to Sharad Sarin, whose father was the Head of the Department there). The result of these efforts was the creation of R. A. Poddar Institute of Management, University of Rajasthan, Jaipur.

While at IIM Bangalore, although he was the Dean, he made a significant impact, according to Ravi Kumar (his colleague at IIM-B). He further added that Dr Singh was liked by faculty and in fact he was elected by the faculty body as the Dean of IIM-B (in accordance with their internal practice). The staff loved him and so did the students. In a surprising move, PGP students gave a farewell to Dr Singh when he was leaving IIM-B, something unprecedented at IIM-B (Ravi Kumar). Clearly, leadership was displayed much before occupying the position as the Director.

Leadership Attributes

The views of the interviewees regarding Dr Singh's leadership are presented below in five broad categories—transformational leader, scholar leader, a visionary dreamer, talent shaper, and inspirationally Pygmalion.

Transformational Leader

He first got the opportunity to lead an institution at MDI Gurgaon. That's where he demonstrated his leadership capability as an institution builder and transformed the institution on multiple fronts. The centrepiece of his leadership efforts were people. Our study showed that he influenced people by building interpersonal relationships, taking care of people, duly respecting them, developing teams, putting in place systems by which people were well incentivized and rewarded for performance—in the areas of research, teaching and training. The interviews and write-ups indicate that he was affectionate, he maintained a personal touch, and he developed one-on-one relations with many.

Before we conclude that he was a soft leader—in his terminology, a 'goody goody' leader—it is important to pay attention to other significant aspects which he stressed upon as a leader. People like Rattan Sharma, Anadi Pande, Subir Verma, B. A. Metri, said that they knew through their own experience that Dr Singh was highly result focused. This result-focus was within a given time boundary; he focussed on both high delegation and close monitoring.

Interviewees mentioned the following aspects of Dr Singh as a leader which illustrate his focus:

- His eye was on the ball—everything he did was linked to achieving the goals.
- He did not like the status quo. He questioned it.
- He was in a hurry to transform things, build things and make things happen.
- He practiced Tough-Love. He was tough on objectives but had tremendous love and affection for team members.

Although he was decisive, he never aggressively forced his decision. Instead, he would consider all the views expressed—negative and positive, and incorporate the constructive ones into the new decision. The interest of the organization was always in the forefront for him. Only when everybody agreed, would he take a decision (Bandopadhyay, Anadi Pande, G. N. Pandey, Maheshwari, Jaiswal, Rattan Sharma, Metri, CNN).

According to G. N. Pandey, he brought so much energy and enthusiasm and care for people that when they saw what he wanted to do, they were inspired by the cause of building an institution, and they were excited to work at a place where so much was happening.

As a true leader, he was with his team, and in case of mistakes, he would take the blame (D. N. Khurana); and when there was success, credit was given to the people concerned. That's how he groomed his administrative team to fearlessly make decisions (Metri, Jaiswal, Rattan Sharma, Subir Verma, CNN).

Scholar Leader

Dr Singh absorbed new ideas both by talking to myriad people in the corporate sector, as well as from regular reading of latest works in the fields of business, management and leadership. He used such information in his communication with his faculty colleagues, and in the numerous workshops that he conducted in the industry. His reading habit was cultivated right from his college days—one of his good friends from college days (B. R. Singh), said that he would read from domains ranging from management, philosophy, mythology, and poetry. Udai Upendra who studied at XLRI, mentioned in the interview—I used to see Dr Singh very often in the library. According to Anil Khandelwal, while he was faculty at Department of Commerce, University of Rajasthan Jaipur, Dr Singh had written a paper on Meaning of Work. Khandelwal indicated his surprise at the fact that a commerce faculty would write on such a topic core to human values.

Almost all the interviewed persons (90%) were quite amazed that he continued to personally conduct research/be involved in research projects, even while heading institutions. All the colleagues whom we interviewed at MDI, IIM-L and IMI mentioned that he emphasized research and publications and had the style of encouraging faculty members to publish. In fact, he used to discuss with young faculty across disciplines, by suggesting topics on which they could conduct research and also guide them on how to go about it.

He was unabashedly focused on original thinking and research, rather than blindly replicating work done in Western universities. He believed that management schools should develop a research-based body of local knowledge to serve Indian organizations. Most of his own research work focused on writing for Indian audiences and documenting institution building efforts and leadership in Indian organizations (see Appendix J for details of publications).

He was also of the view that in the management domain, practice precedes theory (unlike other disciplines like physics for example), since a lot of experimentation to solve current problems happens in the corporate sector. In fact, many times, given the pace of experimentation in the corporate world to solve emerging problems, research has to race to keep up with what is happening in the industry. Thus, the key requirement in the management domain is to capture this knowledge, research and theorize about it and then link it to global best practices.

Visionary Dreamer

This refers to the capacity to dream lofty dreams and visualize audacious futures. He was a visionary who nurtured high aspirations and dreams from his younger days. He not only spoke about 'Himalayan Vision' in his lectures, he also had tall visions for the organizations which he headed. Whether at MDI, or IIM-L or IMI, people were taken aback by the scale of the vision.

According to Maheshwari, who had joined IIM-L in the late 1990s, the first introduction to Dr Singh was his interview on Doordarshan, even before taking over as director of MDI: 'I heard him talk about his vision for MDI—it was absolutely wonderful! When the anchor asked what his message was, he said, "IIM Bangalore, watch out! I am going to compete with you!" That interview made me believe that here is a man who will make a big difference to MDI; and we know what a difference he made to the institute. Wherever he was, his motto was making the institution one of the best in its own field of activities.'

This clearly reflected his high aspirations since in those days, MDI was nowhere in the reckoning at the national level. According to Nangia, former Registrar MDI, 'during his second stint at MDI, Dr Singh and team had worked on a ten-year vision, such was his passion and commitment to build the institution.'

Metri cited a discussion with Dr Singh, a week before his retirement from MDI Directorship in 2006. To his utter amazement he found Dr Singh mapping out how he visualized the institute grow over the next decade. Metri said, 'It was unbelievable that Dr Singh's focus was on his vision for MDI, at a time when most people would focus on their retirement planning. That is the big difference between visionary leaders and those who work as position holders.'

Another example of his visionary approach was conveyed by Pushp Joshi while Dr Singh was Director IIM-L. On one occasion, the Board approved only 20% of the budget that the Director proposed, saying it was enough to run the institute. To this, Dr Singh replied, 'This is the institute in which we are investing—I need to make something which is world class, something which will survive for 50 years.' According to Pushp Joshi, who heard about this episode while at IIM-L for training—this indicated the power of his vision, and indeed, his total commitment to the institution he was heading. It also shows the level of responsibility he took to build the institution. His visionary approach was combined with passion to make things happen; this was evident in the manner in which he transformed the institutions he was heading.

Talent Spotter and Talent Shaper

People said that he had the knack of recognizing potential in a person, and he knew how to accelerate potential. Talent was not only spotted—in this case, potential faculty with capacity and fervour to grow professionally—it was also shaped. Most people said that he was a great talent spotter; he kept track of good faculty from premier institutions, sometimes invited them over, sometimes persuaded them. As an institution builder, Dr Singh would go out of his way to attract, motivate and retain faculty.

Many of the interviewees said they joined because of Dr Singh and the way he treated them. The Director of an institution giving faculty special attention and inviting them over, was unusual. People may have had other offers that they left, to join MDI/IIM-L because they wanted to work with such a Director. Dr Singh treated incoming faculty with respect; made the effort to understand their concerns regarding their children's education as well as the job of the spouse. Whenever he saw a faculty with their family, he would reach out, call them by name, inquire about their studies, etc. When new faculty joined, he would help the person settle by facilitating school admission of the children and other requirements. The belief was that if the faculty was comfortable on the family front, they would give their best to work commitments and responsibilities, and work to build the institution. Similar was the case at IIM-L. As many faculty members said, 'Dr Singh made us feel very comfortable—the whole team, he made them feel confident, he elevated the people.' His fundamental belief was that the institute is the faculty and students, not the physical structure (Jayadev). Unlike MDI and IIM-L of those days, IMI was well-located in the heart of Delhi, and as such, faculty did not need such support.

An important aspect of Dr Singh's style was to groom and develop people. One part of this was to build the confidence of the incumbents in the administrative role. As Metri put it, 'After I was asked to Head the PGP program at MDI, he asked me how things were going—I responded that people were unhappy because a newcomer like me has been given this position. He replied, "Don't bother Metri, just do your job," In this way, he ensured a smooth transition for me. He not only appointed people to positions, but also ensured they could function. He would encourage through positive feedback and ensure improvement. He would say "well done…. I am sure that you will do even better next time."

Another perspective was given by Maheshwari who worked with him at IIM-L, 'Dr Singh wanted to develop leaders—for the corporate sector and academia, promote them quickly and then give them important administrative roles. The more you promote people, the more administrative freedom you give them for administrative tasks, the more they will be ready to become Directors in other academic institutions in the country—this was his view. He wanted professors at IIM Lucknow to become Directors across the country and he went on to realise that dream. He was grooming academic leaders. "Let them go and lead institutions"—that was his thinking.'

He was concerned that professors became Directors without any administrative exposure, and this was detrimental to the growth and performance of many IIMs and others. This motivated him to groom many faculties to become administrators.

Dr Singh was an exceptional leader because, above all, he developed and groomed many leaders—the hallmark of a great leader. Anil Sahasrabudhe opines, 'Great leaders are great mentors; Dr Singh has been a father figure grooming and guiding many faculty who later became Directors.'

Jauhari Lal observed, 'Dr Singh encouraged others to reach higher levels, dream and achieve their goals, rather than just be content with what they had. Talk to most of them (many current directors of IIMs), and you will find that they have very good things to say about Dr Singh, which itself, is a great manifestation of his contribution and significance of his achievements.'

Inspirationally Pygmalion

Dr Singh was himself an inspired individual, captivated by ideas, excited about creating something new, taking on challenges and risks. He had the knack of conveying his ideas through anecdotes and stories which ensured that the ideas easily reached the minds and hearts of people. He had a simple and earthy way with words, and created tremendous positivity and hope in the minds and hearts of his team. He could achieve this by focusing on their strengths and painting for them the likely direction in which they could grow, and in turn contribute to the growth of the organization. Growth and shaping of faculty were linked to organizational growth and opportunity. By providing appreciation and recognition and giving them a peek at the possibilities of what they could become in the future, Dr Singh gave faculty the highest form of motivation.

All the faculty we spoke to highlighted instances where he would introduce them to visiting dignitaries by speaking highly about their skills and capabilities in public meetings. D. N. Khurana who once observed this during a visit to MDI, asked Dr Singh, '*Pritam bhai, aap thoda zyada nahi kar rahe ho?*' (Pritam, don't you think you are going a bit overboard?); Dr Singh replied, 'No, I see potential in this man. What is lacking is a mentor, somebody who will hold his hand and lift him up.' D. N. Khurana said, 'I never heard him talking in a way that affected a person's esteem or self-respect. On the face of it he will build them up. Even in their absence he would never tear them apart.'

An example given by another faculty at MDI offered insights into his Pygmalion approach. Dr Singh appreciated a faculty member in a public forum, boasting he has 25 publications in International journals. The conscientious person went up to remind the Director that he had only 18 papers. Pat came the reply, 'I have announced that you have 25 papers, but that does not mean that you have them as of now. It means that within no time you have to publish 25 papers. I said 25 only because I want to set the bar for tomorrow.' The interviewee further added, 'Dr Singh would come on his rounds sometimes and he would drop into my office and enquire about what I was doing, the status of my publications, and how many were in the pipeline.' He attributes his prolific publishing of papers to the push Dr Singh provided him as a mentor.

The former Registrar of IMI noted that when he was deeply conflicted, he would go to Dr Singh and the latter would try to inspire him by saying, 'Sometimes we need to go through the grind of stress for the selfless cause of institutional interest. We need to sacrifice our personal comforts, sometimes listen to people who you know are not right, but it will build resilience in you to become a great leader in the long run. People may make mountains out of your mistakes but in the end, truth will survive.'

'He had the enviable style of urging faculty to embrace changes and would urge his colleagues to venture out of the comfort zone to experiment with new ideas.' (Ashok Banerjee)

Behavioural and Action Attributes

Six behavioural and action attributes—bringing people together; accessible, open and patient; a creative thinker and persuasive communicator; outward looking and networked; connecting horizon with ground; and performance focused—are now discussed in the following subsections.

Bringing People Together

Dr Singh was keenly aware of the need to build teams and create bonds among team members, and he worked at it diligently in all the three organizations. Tea meetings ensured that many people met each other every day in all the three institutions. Bringing people together to celebrate small wins and achievements was practiced. Faculty meetings and staff meetings were regularly conducted, and this again brought people together. Faculty members were treated more like colleagues than as subordinates. In fact, he was known to say, 'People already know you are the boss, where is the need to rub it in?'

Other faculty we interviewed mentioned how they could walk into the Director's office and talk to him, seek his help, and get ideas. As Maheshwari said about his experience at IIM-L, 'He always led the team by example—Dr Singh, in my view, established trust with candour and transparency.'

Anadi Pande elaborated in the interview regarding Dr Singh's style by using an analogy from the Mahabharata, 'A leader must work through people—like Lord Krishna worked through Arjun—and accomplished many things without himself lifting a finger,' Dr Singh brought that capability to delegate, but would still take the responsibility. This point was further reinforced by D. N. Khurana who visited MDI when he was Director General AIMA (All India Management Association). He observed, 'You could see that Dr Singh's thoughts were flowing through the team, his thoughts were actionized through the team. I also observed that in some of the meetings when things went wrong, he would take the blame saying, I am the leader and ultimately, it's my responsibility.

Celebration was an important pillar for building bonds, which came about through informal dinners on important occasions like institute achievements, milestones, and faculty achievements. One of his favourite Sanskrit prayers from the Rig Veda, which he never tired of repeating was, *Sangachadwam samvadadwam*—let's live together, let's work together, let's enjoy together.'

Accessible, Open and Patient

Anyone could reach out to Dr Singh—faculty, students and staff. In this respect, Dr Singh was different from most other directors. He had a great reputation, whether within the institutions he headed, or outside in the corporate world, as a great listener—he listened with rapt attention and tried to help to the extent possible. As Banerjee opined, a busy man always finds time, and that adage perfectly describes him. He was super busy flying between Lucknow and Delhi almost every week and yet one could easily reach him whenever there was any urgency.

Sometimes he would go to meet faculty and staff in their offices, instead of calling them into his. This informality appealed to everyone. The ease of access to meeting him for any issue that arose was widely appreciated. This atypical, non-hierarchical style inspired and motivated people, making them feel that he is one of them. As Bandopadhyay explained, 'Everyone felt more connected and more productive. His collegial behaviour actually melted the ice, and everyone started to think that "He is one of us and he thinks about our welfare." That's how he influenced and inspired people. Everybody became productive, that is a very interesting thing. I used to say to him that you have a Midas' Touch.'

He was open to suggestions from anyone and everyone. Be it from a class 4 employee or an officer, he would take suggestions and implement them. He always took criticism positively. 'We considered him a family member as he gave us that sort of liberty. I sometimes criticized him', said Yadav, his former personal secretary. He added that Dr Singh gave him this liberty to speak even in MDI V2 when he came as Director in 2003. Sometimes he implemented and sometimes he did not, but he always listened.

Nagananda Kumar recalled an incident in 2006, when a staff union leader came to his office and shouted at him. Dr Singh was calm, he told Naga, 'As the Director it is my job to get both bouquets and brickbats.' When Naga asked, 'Don't you think she should be thrown out', he replied, 'I will give her another chance—after all, she has a family and I don't want to jeopardize their future.'

Creative Thinker and Persuasive Communicator

Many people lauded Dr Singh's creative ideas evident when he was trying to solve problems, 'He thought differently, he often broke the mould in terms of how things should be, what to think, what one should say, and how one should act. And he was always open to new ideas and fresh thinking.' (Sanjiv Bikhchandani)

A striking example comes from IIM-L where the sight of half-built buildings inherited by him from the previous regime bothered Dr Singh. On the one hand, built up space was required for new activities. The contractor was not doing his job, in fact, he was probably waiting for IIM-L to go to court so that he could get some advantage. Going to court was the worst option for IIM-L, as problem resolution would have taken too long. Dr Singh concluded that in order to crunch the timelines, they should in some way get the same contractor to do the work and pay him as the work progressed. This creative solution was implemented, adhering to the processes of decision making of the IIM-L system, and the work was completed as planned.

A similar observation was made by Rajiv Dubey, 'He was always questioning the status quo, looking to improve, to completely change the paradigm. He added, Dr Singh was not looking for incremental changes, he was looking for paradigm shifts. In fact, he did not accept any ideas until he applied his mind and linked it to the larger purpose for the organization.'

The manner in which he handled the problem of attracting good faculty to IIM-L indicates his creative and solution-centric mind. He did not follow the typical norm of not hiring couples and did not shy away from hiring qualified spouses. According to Anadi Pande, he believed that the institution should facilitate spouses to work in the same organization as it would help people to relocate and stay longer with the institution. Dr Singh saw it as a way to attract and retain people. During his time, five couples were hired at IIM-L.

As Mr Jauhari Lal, former director HR of ONGC put it, 'I knew Dr Singh from the training programs I attended in ASCI. When he came to MDI, he visited me and discussed and advised how future leaders for ONGC could be developed. He was so clear and persuasive that we signed the annual agreement to conduct management development programs for our senior level managers. What was more surprising was that he could also convince us to pay advance to MDI. In PSUs, it is extremely difficult to get advance payments made but then that is what Dr Singh was all about. 100s of ONGC executives were trained at MDI. Many of them reached top positions—all seniors for a long time were those who had attended those programs at MDI. What I liked was that the programs were customized for ONGC after doing a diagnosis and identifying the needs of the company and the training needs of the people.'

Another facet of his creative thinking was his capacity to explain his out of box ideas. According to D. N. Khurana, 'He could communicate difficult and out-of-the-box ideas in an acceptable manner without rocking the boat, and they were well-received. This is where he was different from the conventional distinguished teachers and leaders—in his capacity to convey ideas.'

Similar views were shared by Jauhari Lal who admired how Dr Singh could turn a situation positive through the power of personal connect and communication. B. K. Chaturvedi went a step ahead when he said, 'Other Directors of IIMs may have good ideas but the way he could put his (idea) across in a persuasive fashion is to be appreciated. He had the knack.'

The idea of inviting HR leaders from the industry to co-design the PGDM HR program at MDI in 2004, was a highly creative idea to get the industry involved in teaching, get their buy-in of the fledgling program and bring in fresh thoughts to enhance program content, and build program visibility. Siddiqui wonders, 'Why is it that nobody thought of this before Dr Singh?' Many of his ideas in developing this program have now been adopted by other institutions. The MDI-HR program became one of the leading programs in HR in India. It was the type of idea which kept giving back to MDI. It was a part of Dr Singh's vision to have HR leaders of MDI occupying important positions in the corporate sector and this is now happening, and the strategy continues to benefit MDI when it comes to placements.

Outward Looking and Networked

He was a highly outward looking leader—he strongly believed in reaching out to all stakeholders, internal (faculty and their families, students) as well as external—companies, regulators, ministry, alumni, local administration, and management associations. Dr Singh always worked to build a successful institution. To this end, he was willing to do whatever was required; he would visit and meet persons relevant to the institution and solve pending problems. As his former driver would say, 'Dr Singh would get into the car, and make myriad calls and talk. He would, for example, call up the AICTE Chairman and say, I am coming over to have a cup of coffee with you. It all looked so easy when Dr Singh handled things. It was only later when he left that we realized that it was not so easy. If it was, why did other Directors after him not do the same?'

High-ranking officials of various institutions would be invited to MDI to address students during numerous events. Dr Singh would give the visitors full respect; he would climb down to the ground floor lobby entrance to welcome the guest; sometimes there was a formal welcome, offering a shawl and memento. Yadav adds, 'These were small gestures which brought a lot of goodwill to MDI; I have seen many directors during my tenure in the Director's secretariat at MDI. None of them treated visiting dignitaries with this level of respect and welcome and this greatly benefitted MDI.'

A similar example was given by Dr G. N. Pandey (when he was working with ONGC) of the negotiations on training programs for ONGC. There was a deadlock in the negotiations and instead of holding the meeting in the ONGC office, the team was invited to the MDI campus. Dr Singh walked down to the entrance of the main building to welcome the team. The ONGC team (including Dr Pandey) was so impressed and touched by his humility that a win-win solution was reached and ONGC awarded a long-term training contract to MDI.

Corporate sector executives felt happy to be invited to visit the campus—whether MDI, IIM-L or IMI. They knew that they were welcome. MDI suddenly became a happening place—it had visitors from the corporate world, entrepreneurs, visiting researchers and scholars and it became a hub of activity and came into focus.

Taking the board into confidence and delivering by establishing the clarity of expectations was something Dr Singh did with elan. According to Yadav, initially (V1 at MDI) he did have some difficulty with the Board, in terms of their speed—the speed at which the Board decided and the speed at which he wanted to take MDI ahead, although they never refused his suggestions. Once the Board had the confidence that he was a Director who could deliver, they didn't hesitate in cooperating with him.

According to Anurag Batra, 'Dr Singh knew what needed to be done with the faculty, what needed to be done with media, and what needed to be done for placement—he would work with all the stakeholders, 360 degrees. Dr Singh's internal and external stakeholders' management skill and engagement was 11 on 10, not 10 on 10 and that's what built the institutions he worked for.'

Connecting Horizon with Ground—Integrating Ideas with Execution

This refers to the capacity to not only come up with strategy but also have the skills to ensure implementation. There is a myth in the minds of many that bright ideas are rare and that it is implementation which is easy. In the current knowledge era, ideas are available on tap. The real challenge is implementation because that is not a solo game and has to be done through people. As A. M. Naik, Chairman of L&T, once opined (see the case study on L&T in the book, *In Search of Change Maestros*, 2012), 'There are hundreds of micro-steps to be taken before any idea is implemented, indicating that implementation is itself an art and needs to be meticulously planned.'

Dr Singh was known as a hands-on leader who not only had ideas but also the skills to implement them. As Nagananda Kumar put it, 'This is unlike most academic leaders who have great thoughts which are never acted upon. Ideas don't get converted into actions because leaders are insecure, scared, and have a fear of failure. Therefore, there is status quo and mediocrity from the top leadership. Most academic leaders live in the world of generalities and focus on concepts and ideas. They are not really interested in execution because they shy away from commitments, and because they hesitate to back, support, and provide resources.'

According to Maheshwari, he brought together both thought and action. You can have great conceptions of a very worthy institution but how do you bring it to reality, right? That was his competence. He was the master at bringing together both thought and action; he could identify the right person for the right job and constituted teams accordingly.

Dr Singh effortlessly integrated both strategy and execution, according to Y. V. Verma. Anadi Pande analysed his leadership thus, 'He had intellectual capabilities and the perseverance to go with it. I called him a Master of Executive Action—he could somehow create a way. No doubt he was a thought leader; his effectiveness in implementation came from his being able to connect with every constituency, at their level. For instance, even today, if you look at his relationship with the administrative staff of IIM Lucknow, they have only reverence, love, and anecdotes to share when they talk about him. On the other hand, if he connected with, say, the Deans of global schools, he would never be second to them in any way. The span of his ability to relate, empathize, and connect with everybody on issues close to their hearts is the effectiveness of a leader.

He carried a vision in his mind, but ultimately, he had to execute the vision through people. These people were not necessarily faculty with doctorates from various institutions, they could also be those at the administrative level. How many leaders do we come across who can empathize, connect, and elicit reverence from such a diverse group? That's what I marvel about.'

Performance Focused

There are two kinds of leaders—those who focus on growth (numerator management) and those who focus on the bottom line through cost cutting (denominator management). The former is more difficult while the latter results in easy wins.

Most leaders tend to focus on the latter which is a low risk/quick return option. Everyone said Dr Singh focussed on growth. Some people called him a numerator manager; others said he focused on growth; some others said that he was always thinking of expanding the activities; and that he was not penny-wise and pound-foolish. According to Maheshwari, even in the most difficult of situations, Dr Singh looked for opportunities for the institutions he led.

According to Sanjiv Bikhchandani, Dr Singh used to say 'There are people who manage the numerator and there are those who manage the denominator. To grow, you have to manage the numerator, to survive in the long run maybe, you must manage the denominator. So, if you don't do both, you won't move forward.' Anadi Pande explained that Dr Singh's focus on growth, efficiency and effectiveness made him an excellent numerator manager. He always believed that there is enough for everybody in this world. According to Rattan Sharma, Dr Singh said, 'If we want to improve return on investment (ROI), let us increase the numerator and under normal working conditions, the denominator will take care of itself.'

This part of the chapter vividly brought out the examples of the leadership displayed by Dr Singh. It has revealed a range of leadership styles as well as behaviours which people have observed and provides rich insights on how he went about making things happen. An important facet of Dr Singh's influence has been his scholarship and wisdom which is presented below in Part 4.

PART 4: GURU IN A BUSINESS SUIT

I have seen him wearing multiple hats, and whichever role he took, he did a splendid job. You can call him a Guru, a Thought leader, a Mentor, a Coach.

Siddiqui

This part has been titled as 'Guru in a Business Suit' to convey the spirit with which Dr Singh exercised influence and gave advice—like a typical corporate leader in a suit, at the same time carrying the guru-like spirit of detachment from self-gain, concern for the well-being of all and working for the greater good. The business suit represents the typical corporate values of business growth, wealth creation, excellence, and result focused, all of which Dr Singh espoused. It would be interesting for the reader to know that for many years Dr Singh was informally considered the corporate priest in Maruti Suzuki India Limited (MSIL). This is indicative of the stature he enjoyed with the top team of this company from 2005–2006 onwards for almost a decade. The several 'mentoring top management' workshops which he conducted for companies, are indicative of the value which Dr Singh was able to provide to the corporate world, both in the public and the private sector.

This part is divided into two sections:

Section 1: Guru style and advice and transformative impact

Section 2: Contributions made to leaders in government departments, organizations and professional associations

The following sections convey how Dr Singh appeared to people through his words and deeds (see Part 1, Tables 2.1 and 2.2)—a thought leader, a scholar leader, a guru, a wise man; absolutely selfless, a person interested in the well-being of others, who never sought anything for himself, who believed in working for the larger cause; who advised others keeping in view the best interests of the person, the organization, and the nation. Talent shaper—emerged as an important theme, reflecting the spirit of spotting, grooming and developing people, with a holistic growth approach, which characterized Dr Singh. Scholar leader and Indianness (Indian thoughts and wisdom) are two important themes which have a bearing on Dr Singh being viewed as a guru and are discussed here.

He was viewed as a mentor and guru not only by many of the students and faculty of the institutions that he helmed; there were others heading organizations, professional associations, and bureaucrats who also viewed him with great respect and admiration, his wisdom and how he generously shared it with others. The advice ranged from one-to-one mentoring advice, for example, mentoring CEOs and HR leaders, influencing boards as a board member, mentoring at the institution level, mentoring professional associations (without being a member of any association) and so on.

All the interviewees expressed their opinions on this facet in different ways:

- He was undoubtedly a guru.
- He was my friend, philosopher and guide.
- A man of Indian values, grounded, hardworking, humble, truly simple.
- An Indian guru, deep-rooted in Indian philosophy.
- Always a teacher.
- Always concerned about others.
- Concerned about the country.
- Wanted to do more for the country.
- Inspired us to do more; he was a Vishwa Guru.

Detailed findings have been presented in the following two sections: section 1—guru style and advice and transformative impact, and section 2—contributions made to management education, government departments, organizations and professional associations.

Section 1: Guru Style and Advice and Transformative Impact

This theme presents details about (a) the quality and type of advice given by Dr Singh as a mentor and guru and (b) the style used as well as its transformative impact.

Quality and Type of Advice

Following are some quotes which provide insights about the quality of advice given by Dr Singh:

'He was a Guru at heart, always guiding others whether a Manager or a Board member.' (Y. V. Verma)

'A teacher should be able to show the way...he had that sort of competence and that authority to convince you.' (Jauhari Lal)

'He used to inquire and guide me.' (Hota)

'He was always there, like a friend, philosopher and guide.' (Acharya)

'When he gave advice, it went far beyond knowledge. He would bring in practicality and speak with an approach which combined idealism with ground realities. He was a very wise person.' (Bakshi)

'He used to always show me the right direction, he always left me with a good idea, or something which was a solution to my problems either personal or professional. He was always inspiring me to do something positive....' (Rajan)

The above quotes indicate that the advice was valued because it went way beyond knowledge and logic, it consisted of guidance, showed the way, helped both professionally and as a friend, as well as helped find solutions to problems.

Below are some examples of the type of advice and guidance which Dr Singh gave. Addressing PGDM students at IIM-Bangalore, Dr Singh said, 'All of you are going to be leaders in organizations, make sure that you treat people as people. Remember to address people by name. It is not one more number on the payroll, it is not just one more person on your team.' (Puneet Dalmia)

'He said, your mind is most important, your thinking is most important. It can either lift you up, to make you a great man or it can take you down. This means that your mind is the most powerful thing. It is not about the outside; it is all about the inside.' (Rajan)

According to Manoj Kohli, who knew him over many decades, 'I always discussed every career move I made with him, every challenge that I faced. He would personally nudge me to make good decisions. When I first met him at ASCI Hyderabad, I think it struck a chord in me—we shared similar values of honesty, humility, hard work, and resilience. Dr Singh used to radiate such positive energy; right then I adopted him as my mentor, teacher, and guide.... As a leader, his lessons to me were very valuable. Leaders are meant for large things, meant to think big, meant to do big, meant to inspire; it's ok for leaders to neglect a few small things so that they can focus and reinforce the big things. This was a very big learning experience. It helps to prioritize your mind, your time, your attention, and your entire journey, because then you don't waste time on things which are secondary. I don't think any other Director or Dean, had deep insights into leadership the way Dr Singh did.'

'Dr Singh would say that a company needs high ethical standards—that is something I absorbed from him, from his words and actions. For me he was a great teacher though I never learned from him in a formal class but being with him was enough to learn.' (Dinodia)

'When I was the CEO of a large company, he really helped me with the issues of building a large organization–he encouraged me to follow an innovative idea on the business model and secondly, he advised me to build a large company with a professional culture. He gave me two tips—build high communication and a personal touch with informality. In that way, the dangers of becoming bureaucratic and rigid can be minimized. I follow this advice to this day.' (Manoj Kohli)

'By using his wealth of experiences and knowledge to contribute to any industry Dr Singh could advise any sector. For example, when I was heading BSES as Chairman and Managing Director he gave ideas which helped us to give a fresh look to the business.' (R. V. Shahi)

The above advice ranges from guidance for future leaders, managing the mind, leadership guidance with focus on being large-hearted; maintaining high ethical standards, focus on bigger issues rather than getting stuck in the small stuff; focus on the institution which is bigger than the individual; advice on how to build a professional culture in a large organization and redefining the business of a company. The advice appears to be geared to enable people to be more self-managed and more effective as leaders. No wonder that they respected Dr Singh so highly as a mentor.

Style Used and Transformative Impact

The following observations bring out the way he conveyed his advice and provided guidance: 'He conveyed gently, not rudely. This was his *tehzeeb* and *adaa* (style and grace). I would like to compare Dr Singh with a brilliant professor who taught me in IIM Ahmedabad. He could not make an impact as a teacher because he was two different people in his head—the professional (westernized) and the personal (Indian). In contrast, Dr Singh was impactful because both the selves were integrated; he was very genuine, speaking from his core self, without any false sense of ego and could easily reach any audience.' (Naga)

As Vinod Rai explained, 'Whenever he spoke in a professional capacity or a lecture, his approach was not theoretical, not distanced, but had an air of informality as if we were sitting together and chatting. He would convey any advice informally; it was never a bureaucratic top-down exchange. It was always like—ok why don't you consider this? This was a winning approach and made people feel comfortable with him.'

Sometimes, he asked profound questions, designed to make a person reflect. For example, according to Maheshwari, in response to his query about making a career decision, Dr Singh once asked him, 'See, Sunil, you have the choice of being a *Guru* (wise man) or a *Rajguru* (royal advisor)! You decide.' He went about making his colleagues reflect and feel inspired by showing them different perspectives on a situation, to help them make better choices.

'Dr Singh questioned the core of the person. He made people ask themselves questions: Who am I? What am I doing? In this way, he could touch your identity and nudge you to reflect and transform yourself. Human beings are being atomized by the West. It's all pulled together by the soul, values, vision, and purpose. That is what Dr Singh strove to do—he asked these questions, about Purpose, Vision, and Values. He had a profound impact on my identity.' (Naga)

'Dr Singh made me believe in myself. He would always talk about the contribution of the team rather than individual achievements. I learnt from him how to take the team along to become successful.' (CNN)

'He would blend the personal with the official, showing concern for your growth. Without explicitly saying so, he'd asked searching questions. His incisive observations would make you feel like he was there for your development; there was a coaching and mentoring approach, constantly asking what one has done.' (Hota)

'He would give so many instances from his own life to illustrate his message on leadership—this made it very believable.' (Bose).

'I was very much impacted by his style of asking questions—I once sought Dr Singh's advice regarding a dilemma I was facing about recruiting a very bright person as my next in command. I asked him, "Don't you think if I take him, he will soon prove to the organization that he is much better than I am?" In response, he asked me, "Do you want to lead, or do you want to follow?" I said I wanted to lead. He said, "If you want to lead, you need to have a team that is better than you and that is the only way to lead. You can't be insecure; you need to be fully secure with them," and let me tell you, that changed my life.' (Manoj)

Another distinguished person [Former Secretary, Industries, UP Government (Tripathi)] who saw Dr Singh while he was at IIM-L noted that what impressed him about Dr Singh was that he could go down to any level to explain the situation to somebody who was unwilling/unable to understand. 'A very highly qualified person like him reaching a person of any level (of job profile, education) to explain ideas was quite unexpected and highly impactful.'

'If somebody asks me what Dr Singh taught me, I will say Dr Singh didn't teach me anything. But if somebody were to ask me "what did you learn from him?", I would definitely say that I learnt how small things make a big difference in life.' (Ravi Kumar)

The above quotes indicate that Dr Singh's style of giving advice created a deep impact because it was given in the spirit of a guru with concern for one's overall well-being and because it was gentle and never directive. The impact seems to have been deep and life altering, touching upon one's identity and making one look at one's own life in perspective. In other words, the approach was transformative.

An important aspect of the style was the way Dr Singh integrated Indian wisdom with management knowledge.

According to many corporate executives who knew him right from his tenure at ASCI Hyderabad, Dr Singh taught, using insightful quotes and episodes from the Mahabharata and Upanishads, and applied them very aptly to issues and challenges of the contemporary management world.

'What I liked best was that while he was rooted in Indian knowledge, systems and traditions, he equally respected western knowledge without getting swayed to either extreme.' (Sahasrabudhe)

According to Gopalaswami, 'He could recite Sanskrit shlokas and apply them while discussing issues (during the IOE meetings) with such consummate ease. That is something amazing. I loved it.'

'He used Sanskrit shlokas at a time when it was not at all fashionable to do so. He was the pioneer; he did not bother about what others thought about it. The best thing about his approach to teaching, using stories from mythology, was that he was able to connect these stories most appropriately to the issue at hand so ingeniously and so simply.' (Joshi)

The former CMD of NLC Ltd (Acharya) said, 'His command of the Vedas and Upanishads, Bhagavad Gita, and Ramayana was rare in the management world. He had the knack of relating our mythological teachings and cases, to management, business, and to industry. Quotes were shared and made relevant to the current challenges and dilemmas and gave a pointer for the future course of action.'

'It was for the first time that I found a very distinguished management teacher and educator, who had experienced the world and returned to India. I had read many quotes from American industry, British colonial times and things like that; but for somebody to quote from Mahabharata and Ramayana and make it very topical, it did really bowl me over. This made me a great admirer of Dr Singh apart from his other fine qualities as a person.' (Tripathi)

'His ability to distil wisdom from our ancient culture and ethos, quoting from the Mahabharata or the Bhagavad Gita and, at the same time, bring in knowledge from Peter Drucker, Jim Collins, Gary Hamel and C. K. Prahalad. That distilled wisdom came from very deep thought, connecting the two knowledge systems.' (Joshi)

'His thought leadership and insights were like none other. He would connect Indian philosophy with modern management so effortlessly.' (Rajan)

'I very much valued that he shared the best of Indian knowledge and wisdom along with western knowledge. For someone like me, returning to India after spending many years in the US, this was very refreshing.' (Mehra)

The above cited views highlight how and why Dr Singh's style was characterized by that of an Indian Guru. The approach of using quotes in Sanskrit, stories from mythology and from one's own life, made the learning far more powerful because of its authenticity and its alignment to the Indian philosophical and cultural context and feeding into one's own cultural identity.

Section 2: Contributions Made to Management Education, Government Departments, Organizations and Professional Associations

The following section presents the contributions made to (a) management education and departments of the Government of India; (b) company boards as independent director; and (c) professional associations like AIMA and National HRD Network (NHRD) and the Indian Society for Training and Development (ISTD).

Management Education and Departments of Government of India

Dr Singh influenced the thinking in the government through involvement in many committees (see Appendix C for details) the latest being the IOE, where he was the only management professor from India. He was involved on many government committees over the years, sometimes as a member and sometimes as a Chairman of the committees in education as well as in other domains. He left his mark on management education in India. Some of the contributions are as follows:

'He could persuade the MHRD to protect autonomy of the IIMs' (B. K. Chaturvedi). This was at a time when the MHRD was planning to bring greater centralization.

'As a member of the All India Management Board of AICTE, he impacted management education in India. Besides, he was responsible to design and implement learning outcome-based assessments as a member of the NBA (National Board of Accreditation).' (R. A. Yadav)

'He supported the Department of Finance, UP Government to develop and implement wide ranging changes through workshops and management programs.' (Tripathi)

'He helped the banking selection board to conceptualize, architect and structure the policy of deep selection and in fixing the tenure of CMDs.' (Vinod Rai)

'Advised ONGC Academy to broaden their offerings and bring an international component to top level training to develop the global mindset of the top team.' (Jauhari Lal)

Contributions at the Board Level

Dr Singh made significant contributions at the Board level of companies as an independent director and as a mentor to boards. Following are some of the examples.

As an Independent Director

Dr Singh was on the board of many organizations, both public and private, over the last few decades. The following experiences and observations narrated provide us an insight about how he influenced at the Board level.

According to a veteran director of one India's large companies, where Dr Singh served as an independent director for many years, 'The difference between Pritam Singh and others was that all board members knew what was happening on the Board (which we were on), yet it was only he who had the commitment to voice his concerns. He would be thoroughly prepared and ask questions. He would not give up, he would speak out. I think he was an example for how a Board member should be.'

His reputation as a board member among the top team of the company can be gauged from this observation made by another board director: 'He was always accessible for advice to internal Board members—I have observed that somehow the people who needed some comfort, some validation, would reach out to him, ask him a couple of clarifications, they would not just let him go, or they would just walk with him down the length of the corridor till he reached the elevator.'

Another Board member opined that Dr Singh, with his extraordinary ability to communicate and persuade using his deep intellectual competence, asking questions relentlessly, provided guidance to the owners of the business.

According to Damodaran, 'He was very insightful, but as an Independent Director he never said, "do this" or "do that." He would converse, ask questions seemingly casually, and prompt the other person to come up with solutions. Whenever somebody spoke, he would listen with rapt attention.'

According to Poonia, 'Dr Singh was very concerned about governance issues on academic boards, the ethics and values of heads of academic institutions. He felt that those who govern the organization should themselves exemplify such values. This is one criterion which has been adopted in the IOE selections.'

Mentoring Boards and Influencing Top Management Groups

Dr Singh's capacity to bring together board members and members of the top teams of organizations has been legendary. Many people said that he had the knack of bringing people, parties, and partners (whether Indian or foreign) on boards of companies as well as top teams to work together. This has happened in companies like Siemens, Bayer, New Holland Tractors, MSIL, SAIL, NTPC, Corporation Bank, Bank of Baroda, among others. Some of the views are shared as follows:

Arup Roy, former CMD of NTPC said, 'On large boards like in NTPC, he could talk to people of high stature at their level and therefore he could successfully address and resolve conflicts at that level.'

'He was responsible for helping the newly created Power Grid Corporation of India (PGCIL) in its efforts at integration of the hived off transmission divisions of many power companies when Narayan was the Chairman and Managing Director. Through his unique and persuasive style, he was able to bring Board level executives from different companies and cultures to work together as one team. He set the foundation for this.' (S. K. Chawla, former Director Personnel PGCIL)

Director HR of a company in the manufacturing sector shared: 'Dr Singh could relate so well with our international Board members—British, Italian. They were at ease with him and he could create a situation where all would cooperate not only in the class but in the day-to-day working for the company. That was his great contribution.'

Siddiqui shares, 'In the workshop for the MSIL Board in Bangalore, even though his session was being translated for the Japanese board members, his impact was so strong that they wanted the workshop every year. Mr Khattar became a great fan of Dr Singh although both were diametrically opposite in nature.'

The capacity to convert a top management group into a top management team was his forte. Over the years he had done such work with innumerable organizations including Siemens, Bayer, New Holland tractors, SAIL, Indo-Rama, PowerGrid, NTPC, BHEL, NLC and many others. The example of the Maruti Board mentioned by Siddiqui is illustrative, 'There existed some difference of views at the senior level in Maruti at one point of time. It all concluded at the Bangalore workshop, because of Dr Singh who could bring people around to the common perspective of building this company for the future. The communication gap between the Suzuki Japanese colleagues and Indian management was solved and all members worked together with mutual respect for each other.'

'He worked well with top management groups…he had the knack of putting people at ease. His track record (achievements) was too good…and yet he was so humble. The way he spoke, he made it so credible…' (Arup Roy)

Advising Professional Bodies and Committees

This aspect of Dr Singh's work was completely focussed on supporting and developing the management profession by helping professional bodies, such as AIMA, NHRDN, ISTD, and the Education Promotion Society of India (EPSI). According to Dwarkanath, 'Dr Singh has been the key architect for the last two decades in the NHRD, where he contributed guidance, support and added immense value; he contributed similarly to AIMA, ISTD, and NIPM. Dr Singh was sought after as the academic leader for large conferences put together by professional bodies. He helped in every way possible to make these grand successes, purely out of a spirit of respect and service to the profession.'

According to Dhananjay Singh, the guidance given by Dr Singh to AIMA and NHRD helped them become national-level bodies, expand their product offerings to better serve the professional community. Emphasis was placed on creating platforms to get industry and academia together which was a win-win situation for all. Dr Singh also encouraged NHRD to launch a quarterly journal to publish thought leadership papers.

According Sanjiv Bikhchandani who was associated with NHRD in the early 2000s, 'He challenged us a lot, pointing out directions where NHRD could move. He was not a person who was content with the status quo, and he always wanted organizations to move to the next level.'

'Becoming a member of the Defence Acquisition Committee, and later becoming Chairman of the committee, speaks volumes about his capabilities; he played an important role in keeping the committee members together.' (Hota)

According to Gopalswami, Chairman of the IOE, 'Dr Singh was highly respected—presenters (who were heads of management schools) would have one look at him and go silent. He knew their background in-depth, and they knew him. He shared a lot of ground level knowledge about what was happening in the institutions that had applied for the IOE status and that played a big role in the IOE making good quality decisions.'

Sahasrabudhe, AICTE Chairman, concurred, 'Dr Singh had an amazing depth of knowledge about Indian higher education, and I am yet to meet a person who has a higher level of understanding of Business Education in India than him.'

According to H. Chaturvedi (Chairman of EPSI—Education Promotion Society of India), 'Dr Singh supported and guided us whenever we approached him. He was with us when we visited the then Minister of HRD to present the concerns of the private sector management schools; he advised us at the right time on steps to be taken so that the image of EPSI did not suffer.'

This Part brings out that Dr Singh played an important role in influencing the thinking of the corporate sector and policymakers as well as professional bodies in the field of management and education. The approach combined the core thought leadership and style of a guru, with the mindset of a business leader. This appealed to all because of the unique amalgam of wisdom and practicality conveyed more as guidance than as expert sharing.

PART 5: ABOVE ALL, BE HUMAN

Be kind, for everyone you meet is fighting a hard battle.

Socrates

The inner kernel of a leader is the person, their beliefs, values and attitudes and the way they conduct themselves. There is no doubt that the unique leadership quality of an individual is deeply influenced by the person and their qualities. Since leadership is a type of relationship, the person becomes equally important in either enhancing or reducing one's leadership capability and influencing how one's leadership unfolds. Since there is no leadership without followership it is important to understand the person at the core of the leader. In fact, the basic assumption of this research is that personal and interpersonal qualities play an important role in the leader's ability to influence followers. It is the person who carries the values, temperament and attitudes which are manifested in the leadership role which one plays. At many levels, the leader and the person meld into one and beyond a point, it's impossible to tease out the threads and differentiate the two.

In Parts 1–3, we have examined Dr Singh as an institution builder, leader and a guru. This part has been titled as 'Above All, Be Human' to capture the essence of what Dr Singh stood for as a human being and as a person as elucidated in the following text. We now examine the characteristics of Dr Singh as a person viewed by the sample group.

Analysis indicated that the following categories emerged from the basic coding of the interviews and Festschrift write-ups—personal touch, relationship, understanding, supportive, encouraging, recognition, humane, acknowledging, accommodating, positive, spiritual, genuine, informal, engaging, humility, impressive, passionate, reflective, emotionally sensitive, expressive, recollects names and people (for details see Part 1). These were further regrouped (level 3 analysis) into three broad themes—interpersonal behaviours and connect, authentic human being and impactful. The detailed thematic presentations are given in the following three sections.

Interpersonal Behaviour and Connect

This section presents the views shared by the sample group regarding Dr Singh's personal and interpersonal qualities such as relationship building; listening; voice; sense of humour; and being respectful, polite and calm.

Personal Qualities

People have a tendency to conclude about others from their behaviours and leaders are no exception. The most visible characteristics are behaviours and body language from which we piece together our views about a person. People expressed in the following ways when asked about Dr Singh:

'His eyes used to speak a lot. When he spoke, each one in the audience felt like he was speaking to them.' (R. K. Dubey)

'He would always remember people's names and details of their families and ask about them.' (Jaiswal)

'Highly appreciative, he focused on the good qualities of others.' (Hota)

'He always had a smile on his face, it communicated so much.' (Jauhari Lal)

'Dr Singh was my O.B. faculty at IIM-B—he had a great ability to connect with people, he was very sensitive and observant. He was so affectionate and loving, he made us most comfortable. He touched me very deeply. He was firm, never angry, never irritable. He touched people's hearts.' (Puneet Dalmia)

'A very loving person. He appealed to many people because of the love he gave others.' (R. K. Dubey)

'He could relate to anyone. He could go to the level of his son, or the level of someone senior, whether a bureaucrat, an academician, a PSU chief, a managing director of a company or a promoter. There were no barriers to his reach.' (Dwarkanath)

'We were deeply moved by his gentleness and his compassion, that he was not confined or concerned about only his own interest, but he was taking care of other's interests also. If needed, he would go to any extent to do what he promised to someone. This was not just for me but for so many people. He did not expect any kind of special attention, despite the age difference between us.' (H. Chaturvedi)

'Dr Singh would appreciate people, even in a large crowd. Once, while addressing a large group where I was also sitting, he said—"I didn't do much work, the gentleman sitting there, he did most of it and I am getting the credit; please give him a round of applause." That made me feel that every time I should deliver more than what he has asked for.' (CNN)

'He was a man with tremendous foresight and an incredible capacity to carry people together —he never gave me the feeling that he was my boss—and that is his greatness. Even if we were implementing his ideas, he used to give us the credit. He would say, it's all because of you.' (Bandyopadhyay)

'He was a friend of friends, there was honesty of purpose in his relationships; a magnanimous person—made people feel important.' (Siddiqui)

'Long long ago, while Dr Singh was in Jamshedpur, a close friend needed a large sum of money for his daughter's wedding. Dr Singh gave him the needed money. The gentleman was overwhelmed and later said—what a man! Neither did he ask for the money back, nor did he brag about it to anyone.' (Y. V. Varma)

'Highly empathetic—he felt my pain and stood by me when my mother died. He lived empathy; he was so caring, like a fatherly figure.' (Acharya)

'He was so nice and so helpful to all, he was so well liked because of this.' (Maheshwari)

Relationship Building

Dr Singh had the knack of building relationships right from his college days as the following statements indicate:

'He kept in touch with everyone while in college. Even then, he would take others along, organize picnics and take us to the movies spending from his pocket.' (B. R. Singh)

'He was a great human being, never talked about his own self-interest. He would think about the interest of the person who was sitting with him. I vividly remember the way he warmly received us during our first visit to MDI, interacted for some time, offered lunch, and treated us as if we are very close with him.' (H. Chaturvedi)

According to Sharad Sarin, while at XLRI, he knew everyone including the *Daroga* (local Police Inspector). All the interviewed people told us that they were in touch with Dr Singh over the years. When asked who would take the initiative, in 90% of the cases they said, 'He would call me regularly.' Santrupt Misra made a very apt statement about Dr Singh, 'He was the original networker before the idea of networking gained currency.'

Excellent Listener

People lauded his listening ability in the following ways:

Everyone expressed that he was respectful, polite, and calm.

'He listened with rapt attention.' (Metri)

'Even when people criticized him, he would listen patiently, and only then speak.' (Naga)

'We loved to meet him whenever we felt low on motivation and self-belief. Even when he did not have any concrete suggestions to offer to address our problems, he would listen to us and leave us with a sense of positivity.' (Banerjee)

According to his fellow colleagues on some boards, 'in Board meetings, he was invariably the last one to speak—he would patiently listen to all and then speak.' (Damodaran)

'In faculty meetings, he would listen to faculty views first, and then speak.' (G. N. Pandey, R. B. Yadav, CNN)

'In the IOE meetings, his was always the moderating voice.' (Gopalswami)

'He was always so polite and respectful of everyone.' (Rajan George)

'He gave a lot of respect to everyone, whether visitors, staff, or students.' (Yadav)

'He did not belittle anyone in the way he spoke to them.' (Jaiswal)

'Never talked at a person; never talked down at a person even though he was so knowledgeable.' (Damodaran)

'Very calm personality, most of the time. He would get very angry only if people were dishonest at the Board level.' (Dinodia)

'He was always calm, except when others did not maintain discipline—he would tick off anyone, no matter at what level—an MD, a Director—they could not afford to come late to his class.' (K. K. Sinha, D. N. Khurana)

The listening skills, coupled with his friendship, positivity, affection, gentleness, effervescence, charm and calmness endeared Dr Singh to many people. They found comfort in talking to him and discussing their problems with him. This was one of the reasons why his relationships were deeper and sustained over a long period, much after the formal association had come to an end.

Voice Modulation

Observations made by people about his voice are given as follows:

Everyone we spoke to mentioned that he was soft-spoken even in meetings, whether with faculty or in Board meetings.

'In the IOE meetings, he was soft spoken, never used any harsh words.' (Gopalswami)

'He never raised his voice or shouted at anyone.' (Naga)

'He was such a role model, that within a short time he could captivate and make people his own. His quality of being soft spoken, his smile, energetic face, beautiful personality, he would make people his own and you would want to meet him again and again.' (Poonia)

'I knew him for 30 plus years, having first met him at ASCI Hyderabad—he spoke with the same grace then and now.' (Jauhari Lal)

'Although he was generally soft spoken, when it came to class, however, his voice was bold like a lion, the way he would thunder away when making a point with conviction.' (Bakshi)

'In class he spoke with great energy. I saw the same energy recently which I had seen 25 years ago.' (Jauhari Lal)

Sense of Humour

Many people mentioned that Dr Singh had a sense of humour. Some of the quotes are given as follows:

'I enjoyed meeting him as he was a man with a great sense of humour and didn't mind laughing. He had twinkling and mischievous eyes, he was a positive and a loving person.' (Rajeev Dubey)

'He conveyed his message in good humour, without tearing anyone down. He would crack jokes one-on-one. In classroom sessions, he used both humour and satire to make his point.' (Acharya)

'He had a sense of humour and would sometimes laugh at himself.' (Maira)

'As a college student, he would regale his friends by sharing jokes with a straight face.' (Kedarnathan)

'His laughter and chuckling—I miss it a lot.' (Dinodia)

'He would laugh a lot.' (Khandelwal)

'A well-known story illustrating Dr Singh's sense of humour, was in connection with his visit to the Raymond's clothing store on Lucknow's crowded main street while he was Director at IIM-L. Having completed his purchases, Dr Singh asked the security guard at the entrance whether anyone in a Safari suit had come asking for him. The security guy gave him one look and began to berate him, "Don't you know, *Sahib (Sir)* has come thrice looking for you, wait here!" Dr Singh would narrate this in class and break into peals of laughter. He would then explain that while at IIM-L he preferred to mostly dress in a *Kurta-Pyjama-Jacket*, the typical local mode of dressing and his driver used to wear the Safari suits which he had discarded; and the security guard mistook one for the other.'

The above cited findings clearly indicate that Dr Singh displayed characteristics which made him attractive in the interpersonal sense and easily drew people to him. He won people over, through his personal qualities and self-presentation and the way he related with others through his excellent listening skills, gentle voice, sense of humour and laughter.

Authentic Person

This section highlights the many attributes which make people look up to and respect a leader. Two themes emerged and these are presented as follows.

Humility, Genuineness, Fairness, Positivity and Pragmatism

These qualities are a part of being an authentic and decent person, without misusing and unnecessarily displaying the trappings of power and privilege. Examples of some of the typical statements which highlight these qualities in Dr Singh are as follows:

'He was so distinguished, yet so humble; he never threw his weight around.' (Hota)

'He was so humble, he would listen first and only then give his views.' (R. V. Shahi)

'What impressed me was that Dr Singh was very humble and easily approachable.' (Tripathi)

'I loved him because he was realistic, no throwing of attitude, no snobbery, no speaking of his international degree, or prestigious awards.' (Naga)

'He never spoke from a higher pedestal despite all his achievements.' (Verma)

'I came to know that he was a Fulbright scholar only from the newspapers, he never talked about it personally with me.' (Ravi Kumar)

'Not seen a person so balanced in his views; he had no ill-will towards anyone, nor did he have any favourites—everything was on merit, absolutely balanced.' (Gopalswami)

'He was remarkably pragmatic, and his views were grounded and practical.' (Dinodia)

'I have never seen somebody get so popular in more than one constituency. Students were fond of him; he was liked by faculty; he was loved by the staff, whether a gardener or a canteen boy or someone in the dining hall. He became very popular with clerical staff in administration. It's because he would meet people, he would remember their names, he would talk to them, he would listen to them and try to help them. He showed a lot of compassion.' (Ravi Kumar)

'He did not feel the need to throw his weight around despite being so distinguished. I tell you he was the same person wherever you met him; he could deal with all the (trappings of power) so easily because he was so grounded. I think that quality is the rarest of the rare today, and there are not many leaders like that.' (Manoj)

Everyone we talked to said that he was very positive, warm hearted, and highly approachable —those personal qualities which are bound to attract others to relate to a person, and more so a leader. Some of the statements are as follows:

'He was a man of clear heart and transparency.' (Sahasrabudhe)

'His perspective about people was that everyone has strengths and weaknesses, let's work with the strengths.' (Damodaran)

'Dr Singh was a very positive, very optimistic and a highly inspirational person.' (Hota)

'He was so positive, enthusiastic, and hopeful, it was contagious.' (Rajan)

'He praised people and in fact he did not speak against anyone.' (Jaiswal)

'While teaching in class, Dr Singh was always so positive, gave positive energy to the class.' (Udai)

'I remember the first class I attended at ASCI—there was another distinguished faculty there who was highly analytical, and there was Dr Singh, who brought so much positivity in the class.' (Manoj Kohli)

'It was difficult to dislike anything about him. The reasons to like him were many, as he always helped people. I think he was one who could never do any harm to anybody.' (Maheshwari)

'I concluded he was a good man, from the way he talked about the staff, about the way he wanted to run the Institute.' (B. K. Chaturvedi)

'Whatever he did was born out of the spirit of Satya, Prem, and Seva—Truth, Love, and Service.' (Rajeev Dubey)

'Never talked down to anyone, nor snubbed.' (Acharya)

'Meant very well, very thoughtful.' (Maira)

Vinod Rai narrated an episode where Dr Singh was expressing concern about a junior colleague and wondering how to help him. He said, 'This touched me—here is a Director who is running a large institution and is bothered about one junior faculty. Another aspect of his behavior which touched me was how he made the effort to ensure that candidates coming for ED and MD selection (Banking Selection Board) were comfortable. He didn't show off his knowledge as a Professor, he was making each candidate comfortable; then he would ask questions, which would help us gauge the candidate's suitability for the position. I thought this was really kind of him. The concern didn't stop there. In case of a candidate who didn't do well, he urged me to counsel him and build his confidence.'

Honesty and Integrity

Integrity is an extremely important quality for leaders to be accepted and followed. Perceived leader integrity includes the perceived consistency of a leader's words and deeds, as well as the perceived consistency of these deeds with the values shared by the leader and the follower (Moorman & Grover, 2009). Integrity is being honest and firm and adhering to a code of morals and principles.

People talked about Dr Singh's integrity as follows:

'Dr Singh had no vested interests, he was focussed on the national interest.' (Sahasrabudhe)

'I don't want to belittle his character by saying that he was an honest person, of course he was an honest person; that's why we got along so well.' (Chauhan)

'He did so much at IIM-L and IMI, without being corrupt or politicking; he achieved by using fair means.' (Acharya)

'He was a man of high integrity, yet he never talked about it like many do.' (Naga)

'He did not bad mouth anyone, according to most of the people we talked to. In fact, he disliked anyone making derogatory statements about others in his presence. He would simply ignore or say that he was not interested.' (Verma)

An example was given by Naga of an experience at MDI. He said, 'I once talked to a mess worker about the special sweet boxes being packed for distribution over Diwali. When I asked, whom are these boxes for? Are they for the Director? He said, "They are for guests; we dare not give any of these boxes to the Director, he will throw us out—we have been instructed not to give special boxes to the staff either." Everyone within MDI was given identical sweet boxes and that included the Director.'

He further added, 'The cleaning crew (contractual staff) at MDI were on a tea break one morning, when he chanced upon them. While chatting, one of the temporary staff said,

"As long as this man is the Director here, we are not worried. He ensures timely payment of salaries and takes care of us."'

It speaks volumes about the integrity and compassion of a leader when the lowest levels of workers—contractual staff—trust him.

'When needed he made tough decisions which were required for the institution despite the risks—the decision to acquire land for the Noida campus of IIM-L is an example.' (G. N. Pandey)

'He took the needed decisions for the benefit of the institution, even if they were sometimes unpopular with others.' (CNN)

'Above all, he backed his people to the hilt, he was there to take the blame and keep his people safe when things went wrong.' (Subir Verma)

'There was tremendous consistency and congruence in his every thought and action; his core values dictated his decisions.' (Naga)

'Dr Singh had strong values and convictions; he never compromised on his values and he worked with a high degree of integrity', according to R. V. Shahi who had seen Dr Singh on the boards of both MDI and IIM-L.

Even as a board member he was highly conscientious, doing full justice to his role, rather than being swept away by current practices on Indian Boards. For example, 'He would always come prepared—he would have read the thousands of pages and come prepared with questions to be asked; the pages used to be neatly flagged. Given his distinction and stature, he could have simply sat quietly and done nothing; he didn't take that easy route.' (Dinodia)

Impactful Person

The following statements indicate the type of impact Dr Singh had on people:

'If Dr Singh made a request—maybe it was his personality or my liking for him—but I could never say no to him. There was some magnetic quality in his personality, there was transparency, there was honesty. I am not using these words generously because Dr Singh is no longer there, it is just that, that's what I felt with him.' (Chauhan)

'He was very clear in his views—gently persuasive, never rammed anything down the throat. Very pleasant, very persuasive. Never jumped into an argument. Never raised his voice, disarming smile, persuasive approach. Did not need to push or argue.' (Damodaran)

'He was a charismatic person. He was charming and enchanting. People were attracted to him.' (Bakshi)

'He was charismatic, the way he dressed, the way he walked.' (Subir Verma)

'He had great dress sense and etiquette.' (Acharya)

'He impacted the whole class of 170 students at IIM-B.' (Dalmia)

'He always made an impact on anyone he met; they would not easily forget him. That quality enhanced his networking ability.' (Jauhari Lal)

'The diversity of knowledge, the richness of exposure helped in conveying his views with impact.' (Shahi)

Part 5 has dealt in detail about how people saw Dr Singh, his personality, values, attitudes and behaviour. The observations ranged from impact of interpersonal behaviour, relationship building, range of personal qualities which indicated authenticity and decency as a person. No doubt these qualities added tremendously to Dr Singh's acceptance, charisma and influence.

SUMMARY AND CONCLUSIONS

Chapter 2 mapped out findings from the research work conducted by the authors to identify the experiences and views of the sample group regarding Dr Singh as a leader and as a person. Findings have been organized in the following five parts for the convenience of presentation.

Part 1: Thematic Analysis of the Findings from the Study

Part 2: Architecting Institutions—Transformation Code

Part 3: Leaders Go the Way and Show the Way

Part 4: Guru in a Business Suit

Part 5: Above all, be Human

These five parts delineate the actions taken by Dr Singh to build institutions and the modes of influence as a leader and person.

Part 1: Thematic Analysis of the Findings from the Study

Part 1 presents a brief analysis of the quantified interviews (46) and Festschrift data (31) regarding Dr Singh as an institution builder, as a leader and as a person.

1. *As a leader:* Findings from the Festschrift data show that the key themes which emerged from the content analysis regarding Dr Singh as a leader are institution builder and leader (accounting approximately 50%); followed by talent shaper, stakeholder focus, and team, together accounting for 32 per cent of the themes. Indianness,

result focus and excellence focus together account for around 18 per cent. Interview data analysis revealed that leader, stakeholder focus and talent shaper account for almost 67.14 percent (almost two-third of the themes). Institution builder accounts for 12.39 per cent of the word count. Team builder, result focus, excellence focus and Indianness together account for 20.47 per cent of the word count.

It must be mentioned that in both kinds of data sets (write-ups and interviews), the same broad themes are evident. The order of importance of the themes has varied, probably owing to the sample composition, with the interview group consisting of a larger number of external stakeholders (see Table 1.1).

2. *As a person:* The Festschrift data on Dr Singh as a person, brought out that interpersonal style attributes account for almost 60 per cent of the themes, and impactful personality accounts for the rest (40.50%).

Interview data revealed that interpersonal style is the dominant theme with two-thirds mentioning these attributes, followed by one-fourth perceiving him as authentic and 12.32 per cent viewing him as an impactful personality. The interview-based data is similar to the Festschrift data, with one exception—a third unique category emerged in the Interview data—authentic human being. On the whole, however, there is a lot of overlap between both categories of the sample (Interview and Festschrift) and hence we can conclude that there is consistency in the way Dr Singh was perceived as a person, across both types of data sets—Festschrift essays and interviews. This is an unusual feat, reflecting tremendous consistency in speech and actions.

Part 2: Architecting Institutions—Transformation Code

This part answers the basic question about the strategies adopted to bring about transformation at MDI Gurgaon, IIM-L and IMI New Delhi, and the methods used to facilitate implementation of these strategies. This part began by mapping out the context of each of the three institutions when Dr Singh took charge, with a view to highlighting the type of context-specific response needed in each of these institutions. The view taken by this research is that sensitivity to the contextual factors is important to build an appropriate response, and develop a suitable strategy, which can then address the unique issues and challenges of that organization. The work also takes a view that there can be no single formula for institution building, although it is possible to codify the broad steps for transforming organizations.

Part 2 brought out the following two categorizations.

Strategy for Transforming MDI, IIM-L and IMI

Analysis brought out that in all the three institutions, a holistic approach was taken to redefine the primary purpose of the institution; and attention was paid to all stakeholders. This holistic approach translated into the following actions:

- Building holistic business schools, with focus on the key pillars of higher education—creation of knowledge, dissemination of knowledge, application of knowledge, achieved through emphasis on teaching, research, training and consulting.

- Developing future leaders (of management schools) by grooming people by providing them opportunities and grooming them.

- Spotting, attracting, retaining and shaping talent.

- Taking care of all stakeholders especially the staff who are typically neglected.
- Expansion and growth of organizational activities—so important for institutions to maintain their independence.
- Branding and positioning the institution through, accreditations and ranking, media presence and global reach.
- Building strong industry connect—a part of branding—a powerful way to apply knowledge via consulting as well as bring in practical knowledge into the classroom.

Figure 2.1 presents the strategies diagrammatically. All seven strategies in turn mutually influenced each other and created a virtuous cycle, resulting in the creation of synergistic outcomes for the institutions.

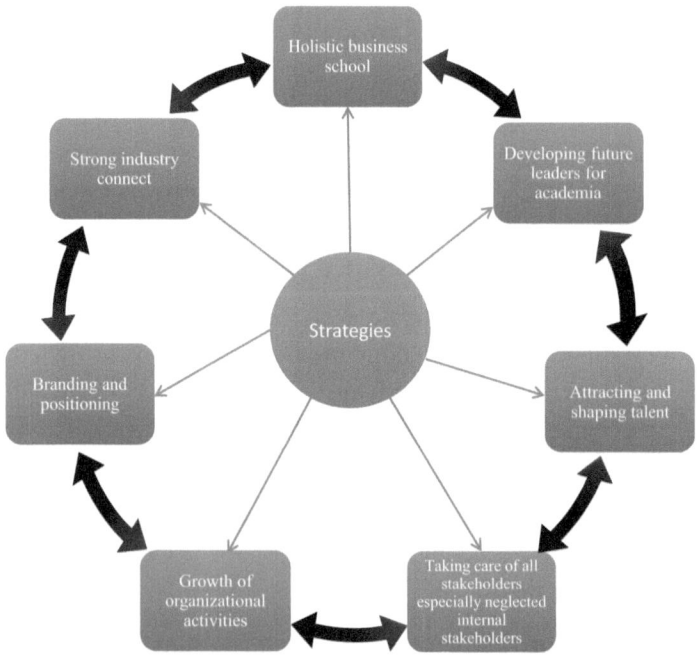

Figure 2.1. Strategies for Transforming and Building a Management School

The key to implementation of strategy is people and their level of engagement in the workplace. Leaders have to focus not only on strategy but equally on implementation. Findings indicate that Dr Singh placed tremendous emphasis on people power for building organizational transformation and an important way in which this was done was, among other things, by creating a conducive work culture as well as a conducive workplace. This has been one of the important keys to the transformation which took place at these institutions. The work culture built to enable organizational transformation is briefly presented in the following text.

Implementation Code: Building the Work Culture

A suitable work culture was created with focus on the following aspects (Figure 2.2):

- Exciting and inspiring
- Open and informal with high communication
- Motivating the team
- Performance and reward focus
- Empowering and supportive
- Speedy and result focused
- Diverse, inclusive and boundaryless

This provoked individual initiative, increased trust as well as comfort and satisfaction levels in the workplace, with clear focus on what was to be delivered. It became a great retention tool as well as helped create high performance in the institutions.

Figure 2.2 indicates that work culture emerges as a Gestalt outcome of the seven attributes mentioned. All the seven mutually interact and influence each other and generate synergistic effects which make the work culture unique. The underpinnings of the work culture are the various

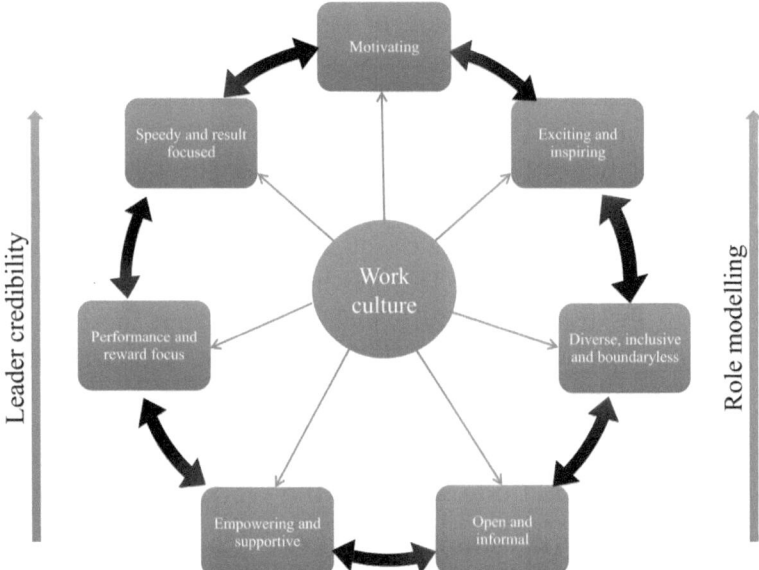

Figure 2.2. Work Culture Components

systems, processes, and leadership styles which were aligned to develop the above cited work culture.

Part 3: Leaders Go the Way and Show the Way

Behind every strategy and work culture is a good leader. Part 3 seeks to answer the question regarding the How? What was the type of leadership which enabled Dr Singh to transform these organizations?

It is the leader and the team who builds institutions and therefore understanding the leader and leadership is the key. Examination of the leadership characteristics and style of Dr Singh, which emerged from the observations, brings out that he displayed a range of leadership attributes—transformational leader and a scholar leader, a visionary dreamer, talent shaper and inspirationally Pygmalion. He brought people together, was accessible, open and patient, a creative thinker and persuasive communicator, outward looking, connecting horizon with ground and performance focused. These were the multifaceted leadership qualities he displayed according to the sample group.

He envisioned institutions and through the power of integrating strategy and execution he made them a reality. By instituting various policies and practices designed to strengthen research, teaching, training, and consulting; highlighting core values of merit, excellence and world class; valuing and taking care of both faculty and staff, he created a work culture suitable for academia. Through role modelling, consistency between precept and practice, he built trust and credibility. Like a true transformational leader, he raised the level of consciousness and aspiration of people by showing them what they can become, by grooming and shaping their thinking and by providing the relevant exposure to develop themselves. Figure 2.3 depicts the above, diagramatically.

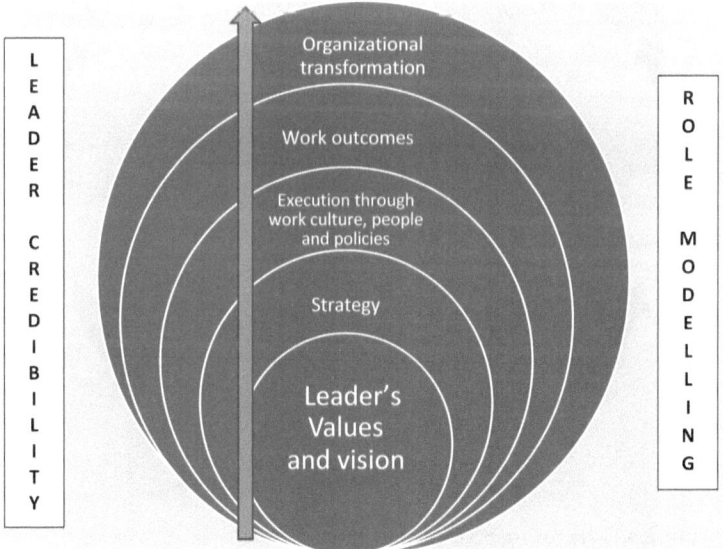

Figure 2.3. Comprehensive Model of Organizational Transformation Process

Part 4: Guru in a Business Suit

This part brings out Dr Singh's style as a guru and its impact on people; how he made Indian wisdom contemporary in the management world and his contributions to government departments, organizations and professional associations (see Figure 2.4).

Dr Singh wielded influence as a guru and a thought leader both within and outside the institutions he headed—corporate sector as well as in the government and on boards of companies he was part of. He balanced both the typical corporate values of business growth, wealth creation, excellence and result

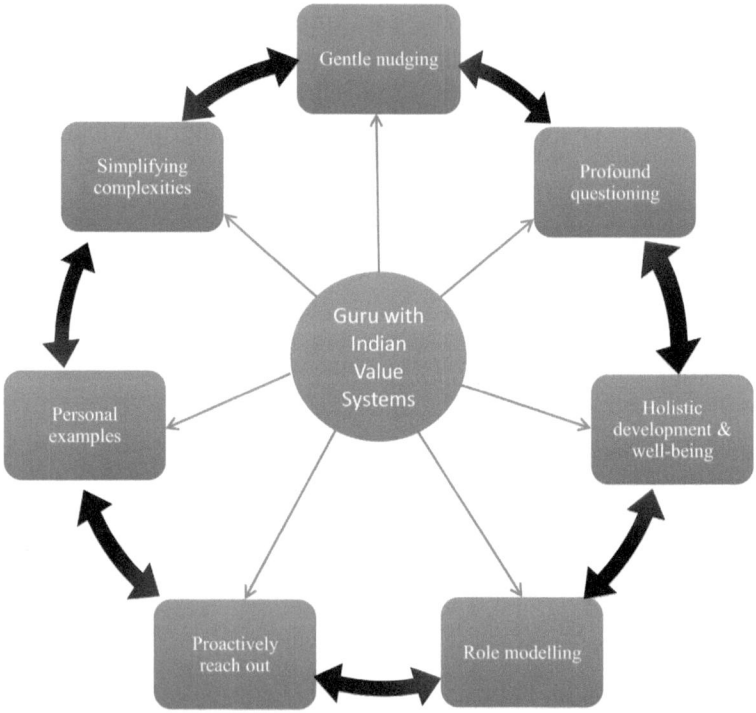

Figure 2.4. Mentoring Style of the Guru

focus as well as the monk-like spirit of detachment from self-gain, concern for the well-being of all and working for the greater good.

The style of advising and guiding appears to be an important part of Dr Singh's capacity to create a deep impact—gentle nudging, asking profound life-altering questions, which touched on one's identity, simplifying complexities, giving personal examples, proactively reaching out, showing concern for both professional and personal development, and above all exemplifying through practice rather than preaching. His forte seemed to be to give advice not like an expert, rather in the spirit of a guru with concern for one's overall well-being. The observations made by people seem to indicate that the advice was transformative—deep and life altering, touching on one's identity, making one look at one's own life in perspective.

Dr Singh's approach was that of an Indian Guru—literally the one who removes darkness. There was a strong experiential component, being gentle and indirect. The approach of using quotes in Sanskrit, stories from mythology and from one's own life, made the learning far more powerful because of its authenticity and its alignment to the philosophical and cultural context. People neither felt judged nor patronized, nor left feeling small. In fact, people felt validated, their self-esteem was enhanced because of the respect and positive regard they received from a distinguished person like him. They were thus more inclined to work on their non-strengths.

Learning also took place without teaching, through the power of role modelling—as there was little difference between precept and practice. He was a bridge between eastern and western philosophy and knowledge systems which he integrated so well. Dr Singh was unique in one sense—he brought together the capacity both to advise and guide like a guru, along with the quest for excellence and merit in both organizations. The guru facet of Dr Singh's personality has been an important source of influence in academia, corporate world as well as in the government; and in turn, it directly or indirectly had a virtuous impact on building the institutions headed by him.

Part 5: Above All, Be Human

At the core of the leader is the human being and it is important to understand this central facet. This part indicates that the influence which Dr Singh had on others was significantly influenced by his personality and values. Two facets which emerge are as follows:

1. *Personal and interpersonal qualities:* There are characterized by relationship building; being an excellent listener; good voice modulation; sense of humour; and being respectful, polite, and calm. Interpersonal attractiveness is a great start for any leader who can draw people to him through such behaviours.

2. *Authentic person:* Findings revealed that characteristics like being humble, genuine, positive, grounded; and being a man of honesty and integrity were evident. No doubt such qualities generate trust, credibility and lead to acceptance of the leader.

He was thus seen to be affable and humorous along with being humble. The absence of a hidden agenda and a genuine concern and helping nature not only professionally but also as a friend, made people admire him and seek him out for advice. Interpersonal behaviours characterized by relationship building; being an excellent listener; good voice modulation;

sense of humour; and being respectful, polite, and calm were highly appreciated. Above all, liking and respect as a person—contributed strongly to enhance Dr Singh's acceptance as a leader and as a guru.

Dr Singh's sources of leadership influence were at multiple levels: (a) interpersonal—listening, respecting others, transparency, (b) personal qualities—appearance, affability, positivity, energy, appreciation, accommodation and humane orientation. These interpersonal and personal qualities together made him highly acceptable, established his credibility and accelerated the acceptance.

Figure 2.5 brings out an integrated picture of Dr Singh's major sources of influence. The figure indicates that Dr Singh could achieve organizational transformation on the bases of three key sources of influence—Visionary and Transformational

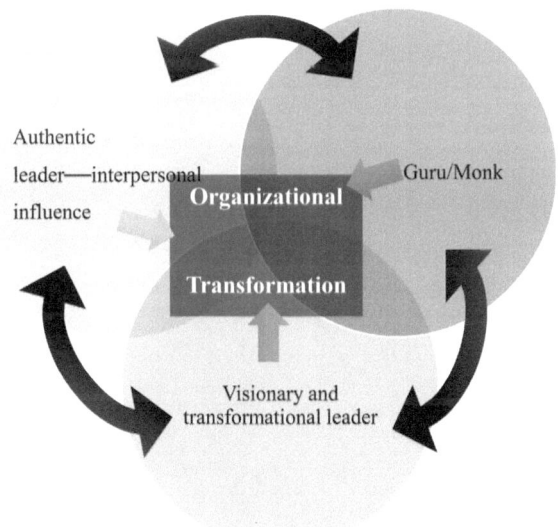

Figure 2.5. Influence and Organizational Transformation

Leadership (Part 3), Guru and Mentor (Part 4) and Authentic Leadership Influence (Part 5) owing to his personal and interpersonal qualities. This trifecta of qualities made Dr Singh a widely acknowledged, respected and liked leader.

CHAPTER 3
A COMMEMORATION AND REMEMBRANCE

This chapter consists of 31 invited write-ups by colleagues, former students and mentees—who were associated with Dr Singh at different stages of his career. An attempt has been made to present the write-ups in a sequence running in tandem with his career movements. The move to develop these write-ups came from a former student and it subsequently gained momentum and snowballed into this book.

The first essay is by Dr Anil Khandelwal, who was Dr Singh's student (and later a great friend) in the evening program at the Department of Commerce, University of Rajasthan, Jaipur where he was a young assistant professor (1969–71).

After University of Rajasthan, Dr Singh moved on for his Fulbright Fellowship to Indiana Bloomington, USA and on his return joined XLRI Jamshedpur (1975). We have write-ups by two colleagues who knew him from that phase of his life (Sharad Sarin and Rajan Saxena), followed by three persons associated at ASCI Hyderabad (1979–1992)—Rattan Sharma and Premila Verma his faculty colleagues and Rajan George who attended his sessions and then became a life-long friend.

We could locate three persons from Dr Singh's MDI-V1 days (1996–1998)—M. P. Jaiswal, his colleague, S. K. Bose and Sunil Mithas who were students in the National Management Program.

There are five write-ups from the IIM-L phase (1998–2003)—Ashok Banerjee, R. L. Raina, Debashish Chatterjee and Kala and Sridhar who were faculty colleagues there and one write-up is by the then Registrar IIM-L Dr G. N. Pandey.

MDI-V2 phase (2003–2006) has three write-ups by Nand Dhamija, Reeta Raina and Jyotsna Bhatnagar.

The IMI phase has four write-ups by A. K. Rath, Subir Verma and the then Registrar C. N. Narayana (CNN).

The remaining 11 essays have been written by distinguished academic colleagues and corporate Leaders. Six have been authored by academic leaders from India—Anand Prakash, Anu Lather, D. P. Singh, Nupur Prakash, Yogesh Singh, Sanjay Srivastava; and three from Europe—Alfredo Behrens, Davide Sola and Jyoti Gupta; two corporate leaders—Atul Sobti and Mamta Vegunta. They all have written based on their association with him. Incidentally, apart from being from the corporate sector, Mamta has the distinction of being Dr Singh's daughter-in-law.

The write-ups focused on Dr Singh as a person and as a leader, with examples and evidence.

A SCHOLAR WHO ROMANCED MANAGEMENT EDUCATION

Anil Khandelwal, Former Chairman, Bank of Baroda

On the early morning of 3 June 2020, when I received a cryptic phone message, 'Is the news about Dr Singh, correct?' This threw me into confusion; anxious, I phoned Dr Asha Bhandarker and she confirmed my worst apprehensions. I asked myself: How could it be? He'd talked with me only a couple of days back about his forthcoming book on governance in collaboration with his other colleagues.

My mind ran into a rush of memories: I first met Dr Singh in Jaipur about 50 years ago, in August 1970. I had just joined the University of Rajasthan's MBA Program. Singh was a newly minted Financial Management faculty member. We were overawed by this bright young Masters of Commerce gold medallist from Banaras Hindu University (BHU) with a doctorate (PhD). In his very first class with us, he charmed our group of 14 engineers, all curious to learn about management science and improve our careers.

For 90 minutes, without a word about the subject, he spent time learning about each one of us, our life stories and telling us his own. Those early days, we did not know anything about organizational behaviour (OB), HR or behavioural sciences. In today's parlance, it was clear that he belonged to the real world, and that he himself was on a journey to discover the meaning of this life. Some students of our class were seniors from the industry, and he always encouraged them to share their experiences.

Within a short time, he captivated us with his raw energy and immense passion for teaching.

For some reason, he and I clicked, so during our free time we'd have long conversations in the corridors of the Commerce college, and he showed a deep understanding about the university educational system. He shared about his modest family background in his village, his dreams for life, and his plans for going to the USA to do his MBA.

During our MBA program, he encouraged us to form an MBA association and on creating consensus among the students to nominate me as its president. With his help, we published a magazine. In my engineering college days, I had experienced a hierarchical and formal culture where teachers were task driven, mostly unfriendly with some degree of intellectual swagger. In total contrast, here was a person who always made us feel like colleagues and friends. Every one of us became very fond of him. His teaching was filled with vigour and passion, he made even the dull subject of finance so interesting for all of us.

In that year of close association with Dr Singh, I learnt a lot—his down to earth approach, humility, helping nature and above all, his relentless focus on thinking big.

My impression of Dr Singh in the 1970s was one of an explorer who had begun his journey in search of life with an open mind, a pure heart and feet firmly on the ground. His broad smile, occasional chuckles and unrelenting hunger to learn have been the hallmarks of his personality till he breathed his last. In transactional analysis jargon, his personality showed a strong combination of natural child (his spontaneity), nurturing parent (always supportive and confidence building) and confident adult (always taking a view after participatory discussions and listening to various voices).

I will describe Dr Singh through his qualities of a rare leader.

An Institution Builder

An incident that reminds me about his thinking big was when he willingly volunteered his services to Dr R. G. Sarin, then Director of the MBA program, to plan for a separate building for the MBA program separating it from the archaic environment of the commerce college. I was lucky to be included in the team, and three of us, Sarin, Singh and I, approached Dr Ram Nath ji Poddar, a successful industrialist from Rajasthan. Within a few meetings he was convinced to make a donation for a building within the university zone. The die was cast and the Poddar Institute of Management came to life. Singh's vision of thinking bigger and larger was visible early, right in his late 20s.

Dr Singh always used hyperboles to express his concepts and expectations. He often talked about Himalayan vision, change masters, transformational leaders, renaissance leaders, etc.

His concept of leaders and leadership was very different from the textbooks. He belonged to the real world and for him leadership meant change management and transformation. His two prominent books, *Corporate Success and Transformational Leadership*, and *In Search of Change Maestros*, deeply resonate with his philosophy. He was not an armchair academic but a true practitioner of his own philosophy.

One of the greatest contributions of any leader is to revive a moribund organization through his vision and passionate commitment, mobilizing every stakeholder to think afresh and deploy himself fully in its rejuvenation. This is truly reflected in his turnaround of MDI, Gurgaon. After a good start in 1976, MDI had lost its shine over the years and had become a lifeless institution. In 1993, when Dr Singh took over as Director, everything from the building to plants and people was infused with new energy and his arrival heralded a new wave of change.

MDI now occupies a very high-ranking place among Indian management institutions. He was a warrior who did everything to ensure that his goals were achieved. He knew that an academic institution is not created by a great campus alone, but by its good faculty. He attracted faculty from some of the prestigious IIMs and other leading institutions to join MDI. Rules were no barriers to him, toward a larger goal. A dear friend from the MDI faculty recounted an instance of Dr Singh's large heartedness even before he joined up—arranging family accommodation for a whole quarter in the plush MDI guest house, to simplify his children's school admission in time. His focus on bringing the best faculty and alliances with the corporate world to commit to executive training at the institute were but a few steps to rebuild MDI. His painstaking contribution in reviving MDI is undisputedly his greatest success.

Dr Singh laid great emphasis on the concept of space in management schools and this is evident in his architectural reorganizations at MDI, IIM-L and IMI New Delhi. He believed that physical space creates mental space to accommodate new learning and an intellectual space for learning together.

Dr Singh was a management doctor who curiously diagnosed organizational problems through research and studied his subjects clinically by observing what they do, how they do, what their mindset is and above all, whether they were passionate or not. During his training sessions, some of which I attended, I observed that he spoke with passion and laid emphasis on the need for transformational leadership from public governance to corporate board rooms.

A Quintessential Teacher

After I took over as Chairman and Managing Director of Bank of Baroda in March 2005, I requested Dr Singh to organize a three-day 'Vision' workshop for my top team. He and his colleague Asha Bhandarker readily agreed and designed the program with great passion. He was present on all three days guiding the deliberations. He spoke with unalloyed passion and great warmth, winning hearts everywhere. Over lunch or dinner, he'd share his impressions of each of my GM/DGM's potential. He would do away with the formal schedule of the program, if some topics required stretched discussions. This flexibility and adaptability to each participant's need made him popular with any group, including the one at Bank of Baroda.

One critical factor of his resounding success as a management teacher can be attributed to his constant interaction and learning from the corporate world. Though he was held high in the corporate community, he always listened to, diagnosed, experimented and avoided providing readymade 'Vicks-44' management formulas to all problems. His genius lay in his own openness in learning. Though he was not an Industrial Relations (IR) teacher, on a Delhi–Mumbai flight, he listened to our story of building a new paradigm of IR in my organization with rapt attention.

He was also a panel member with the government in the selection of Chairmen and Executive Directors, which led to interactions with many senior bankers. I know first-hand of several new ideas he brought to the banking industry. He was probably the first to introduce a learning module on overseas visits in the management training programs to develop a broader perspective in executive cadres. His innovative and creative mind had some degree of positive restlessness.

When the news of his demise came, all the executive WhatsApp groups in many banks carried moving tributes to him. He was a household name among executives of the banking industry on account of his deep association as Board member in Dena Bank, PNB and various financial institutions.

Dr Singh's world of peer reviewers was managers, corporate leaders, public servants, senior bureaucrats, teachers and HR fraternity. He learned from his own experience, research, corporate board rooms, colleagues, spirituality, and it was no wonder that he was such a darling teacher. Like an orchestra player, he would be in a rhythm that was eclectic and blissful.

The connecting thread in all his lectures on any topic was leadership. His leadership was a kind that, as Warren Bennis says, 'Commits people to action, converts followers into leaders and convert leaders into agents of change.' For him each day brought a new promise, a new agenda for change and a new challenge to make it happen.

A Talent Finder

Dr Singh celebrated talent. He would find his ways to pick, groom and nurture talent, going the whole way to help them.

So many academicians of repute attribute their success and career advancement to him.

He was vulnerable too, like any other leader, to his close relationships, to protect their interests and sometimes go out of the way to help. I once told him this and he smilingly said, 'Anil, I am a human being. My basic nature is to help and if it helps people, I do not feel guilty.'

I understand from his academic colleagues that he was a great delegator and listened to various viewpoints. This is the reason for his success in building an academic reputation like MDI in such a short period.

A Humanist

Dr Singh cared for everyone. I've listened to instances about his reaching out to connect with the maintenance employees, at the lower end of the ladder, such as gardeners, sweepers, peons and office staff. He was humane in his approach and he would go beyond protocol to help people in distress.

A Visionary

Most management institutions develop a relationship with the private sector or multinationals, whether in teaching, consulting, or case writing. Dr Singh was an exception. He relentlessly reached out to government sectors and especially public sector enterprises (PSEs). He always called PSEs as national assets and praised their managers for their passion and commitment, despite the poor compensation they receive. He built strong networking relationships with the public sector in general, and more particularly with the public sector banks.

In his role as Board member on bank boards, many of our common friends from these banks told me that Dr Singh contributed ideas for business and also for good HR practices and governance. He did not sit on any board as merely an

OB or HR expert but a completely involved board member. Probably his exposure in the field of finance and his MBA helped him understand business in a larger perspective.

His greatest contribution perhaps has been in building a vision for great management institutions. He contributed to this by being a member of innumerable committees of the MHRD, AICTE, Prime Minister's committee for identifying IOE, etc. He always wanted Indian institutions to be the best, and comparable to the best in the world.

A Scholarly Practitioner

In spite of his many preoccupations, Dr Singh kept in touch with new ideas in management across the globe and established an excellent network of relationships globally.

He would talk about these ideas in corporate boardrooms, with HR professionals in conferences. He never lost touch with the scholarly world, although his involvement with academic administration and engagement with the real world increased substantially. He wanted scholarly ideas to change our work organizations, he wanted the academic community to emerge from its ivory tower and work with practitioners. In this search, he actively associated with professional organizations like ISTD and NHRDN. He started a new course on MBA at MDI in collaboration with NHRDN. He was a friend and mentor to many HR professionals and academics.

Although he taught me for only one year five decades ago, our friendship matured like old wine. I cherish my association with him. I will miss his occasional Sunday calls with an affectionate, 'Hi Doc! What are you doing?' and then, an endless journey into the affairs of the corporate and academic worlds.

In his untimely demise, I have lost a precious friend from the field of management, a thinker, an institution builder and above all an affectionate friend, who always filled me with renewed energy. He was truly a fascinating academic. In the true sense he romanced management education. Maya Angelou, noted American poet, memoirist, and civil rights activist, said, 'I've learned that people will forget what you said, people will forget what you did, but people will never forget how you made them feel.' You made us feel as if we were you, and you were one of us. Rest in peace.

DR SINGH: THE MULTIFACETED PERSONALITY

Sharad Sarin, Former Professor, Xavier School of Management, Jamshedpur

My first impression of Dr Singh was as my father Dr R. G. Sarien's colleague. In 1968, my father was Head, Department of Commerce, while Dr Singh was a lecturer in the same college in Rajasthan University. When I joined the Indian Institute of Management (IIM), Ahmedabad for the MBA program, Dr Singh expressed his keenness to become familiar with the education there. He stayed with me in my hostel room for a week. I was awed by his humility, sleeping on the floor of my room due to the space constraint.

By mid-1975, I was keen to quit the corporate world and was looking for an opportunity to join academics. I did not hold a doctorate then, so getting a faculty position in the IIMs was difficult. This is when I got in touch with Dr Singh and expressed my desire to enter academics. By then he had joined the XLRI Jamshedpur as professor. Without losing any time, he arranged an interview for me at XLRI. I joined them on 1 May 1976 and stayed on till my retirement in 2016. The credit goes entirely to Pritam, on both professional and personal fronts, for my cushioned landing and settling down at XLRI. Dr Singh, I learnt later, had gone out of his way to help me!

At the XLRI, he had an excellent reputation as a successful trainer and consultant. I recall him sharing with my wife Mani, his desire to become a director of a well-known educational institution and he did fulfil that at a very young age, as the Director of MDI.

Dr Singh's contribution in the field of institution building is unparalleled and his tremendous leadership qualities and governing abilities recognized by an unending list of laurels he earned in his lifetime. Managing a business school requires tremendous tenacity and mental toughness, and this was so evident in Dr Singh.

His ability for research based on empirical data and their analysis is outstanding, as reflected in his books and articles. He never tired of writing and publishing. His work with Dr Asha Bhandarker is an outstanding story of partnership and joint ownership of intellectual property.

Reflecting back, I can identify many outstanding traits in Dr Singh: a personality rooted in the ground realities of India; readiness to help; networking capabilities; outperformance despite limited resources; tremendous persuasiveness; gentle assertiveness; phenomenal outreach; and humility with integrity and honesty.

I consider it fortunate that our families shared an intimate bond. Personally, I am certainly indebted to Dr Singh for having laid the foundation of my career as an academician.

A TRIBUTE TO A TRANSFORMATIONAL LEADER

Rajan Saxena, Former Vice Chancellor, Narsee Monjee Institute of Management Studies

In June 2020, with the passing away of Dr Pritam Singh, Indian management education lost a visionary, a transformation specialist, a change leader, a champion of institutional autonomy and faculty development, and an outstanding coach in leadership development. At a more personal level, I lost a friend whom I first met in 1980, at XLRI, where we were part of the faculty group and campus community. While he left his imprint on all those he came in contact with, through his warmth, affection and deep understanding of the Bhagavad Gita, I would always remember him as a transformation specialist and one who worked to bring out the best in every member of the team.

Change and Continuity

I was fortunate to have either worked with or observed from close quarters, a few leaders who effectively turned the growth path of institutions and made them India's most credible institutions. Dr Singh was one such leader. Two institutions that directly gained the most from his leadership are MDI Gurgaon and IIM-L. Before he took over as the Director of these institutions, they were 'just there', so to speak. In several of my conversations with him I mentioned that he was a visionary and one who could move the institutional mouse with vigour and energy that he drew from his team—very rare to come about in higher education. Unlike most of his contemporaries, Dr Singh believed in change and continuity not as an either/or choice, but as one where change could be brought about while still preserving the legacy.

Institutional strategy needs to be responsive to the environment and hence, change, over time. For example, the renewed focus on research and publication by faculty is in direct response to the requirements of accreditation agencies and hence the strategy to incentivize faculty appropriately, is of more recent origin. Dr Singh used this strategy effectively to create a research and publications culture in MDI and IIM-L. The outcome was Association of MBAs (AMBA) and South Asian Quality Assurance System (SAQS) accreditations for MDI—the first institution in India to receive international accreditation! Meanwhile, IIM-L rose considerably in its ranking among management schools in India.

When asked why faculty should spend time on research and publication and not consulting, which was financially more rewarding, Pritam's response was, 'In this process all gained.' Dr Singh did, however, ensure adequate compensation for his research faculty. It was a great motivational factor for faculty to join institutions he headed, besides encouraging everyone to deliver on the change agenda.

Passion for Change

Dr Singh would often mention that without vision and '*junoon*' (passion) to change, no institution can really grow and gain the stakeholders' respect. A firm believer in teams, he is known to have developed many faculty members who are today acknowledged researchers, teachers and leaders.

An excellent networker, he established connections not just within management education but also in higher education in India and the world over. Moreover, he also developed relationships with government bureaucrats, corporate leaders, and policymakers that helped advance the interests of his institutions and his team members. A quality that endeared him to many, including his critics.

Communicating a Compelling Agenda of Change

A good communicator and a visionary leader can usher a change only if he is able to effectively communicate a compelling aspiration for the future. This requires genuine conviction. Unless the leader himself is convinced of his own agenda of change, he cannot convince his team to alter their pathways. He has to be the face of change.

The powerful communicator that Dr Singh was, he could effectively navigate change in legacy institutions by selling aspirations and a future that promised credibility enhancement, making the institution and faculty relevant to the changing times. It *did* require people to get out of their comfort zone.

Making Everyone a Hero

A good leader always makes everyone in his team a hero. Recognition, reward and celebrating accomplishments are critical leadership skills, and perhaps the most underutilized skills in organizational leadership team management.

Often, leaders are quick to take credit for every accomplishment. Effective leaders share the credit of accomplishment with their team, while owning up any failure of the team. This is a critical factor in ensuring continued success and change management, and yet ignored by most. Dr Singh had a unique trait of making everyone who came in his contact feel important and make them a hero.

I firmly believe that the best tribute to Dr Singh would be to develop many more such leaders. Institutions, especially management schools, could launch a leadership program to develop transformational leaders for higher education institutions. Today, India needs leaders who are able to preserve legacy and motivate their teams to compelling heights, while pursuing the innovation agenda.

MY FRIEND—DR SINGH

Rajan George, Operations Consultant, Renaissance by the Creek

I have known Dr Singh for half of the 78 years of his life. He was many things to me; a multi-faceted man who touched my life.

A Wise Guru

I first met Dr Singh in ASCI Hyderabad, where I attended a team-building workshop in the early 1980s. I was in a T-group session where the young Dr Singh was in his jeans, t-shirt, sandals, a cigarette in his hand, as he gave us the ground rules of the T-group. In the next one hour we could talk about anything amongst ourselves, but what we talked about had to be 'here and now', and that he would only be sitting as an observer. I was really anxious, and I did not know what 'here and now' topic to speak of with a group that I had just met. In a few minutes I had an idea for a topic and said, 'Excuse me sir, may I request one thing? Can you please stop smoking? I have a problem with the smoke you are puffing out.' The topic I introduced worked; the group got a 'here and now' topic that fit the set norms. Dr Singh took note of me, my name and the journey of the next 38 years of our association thus began.

In the MDPs that he conducted in two of the companies I worked for, he led our CEO and top team workshops at Bayer and AT&T. Through management and leadership transformation process work, he built the people of these companies over a few years of interactions.

During my stint in HR at Bayer India, I worked very closely with him and had asked him to be one of the six evaluators of assessment centres at Bayer. His capacity to work as a team member and advisor with my German team members was revealed in these interactions. In fact, he gave the Germans such valuable insights on each person's behaviour and attributes that his wisdom became an asset for Bayer AG to tap into for future assessment centres.

I have seen Dr Singh growing from strength to strength in the academic world, in the corporate training world and as the author of many books and articles. He was proud of India, its values and rich traditions. His knowledge of Sanskrit shlokas and their apt usage fit the need of the hour and enamoured the audience. He would have the rapt attention of the audience as he recited the shlokas and drew out their meaning and relevance to illustrate the points he was making. Using his personalized style of storytelling, with strong content and powerful narrations of live situations, he would positively charge the participants to transform into value-based leaders. His teachings registered in the minds of participants beyond classroom level learning. His authority over Sanskrit and the Bhagavad Gita, stories from the Bible, as well the stories of Mulla Nasruddin, Zen Master and others, were received with rapt attention by his listeners. During workshops, he had the knack of remembering the names of all the participants and what they said—he brought this into his narratives, which helped the rich process work he carried out at CEO and other levels of the organization where he was consulting.

He was a good judge of people; he could spot high achievers and would do all that he could to groom them. He would praise them and get the best out of them. He could predict behaviours just by talking to people and using empathic listening and observation. He could identify what was being said and what was being left out.

In the mid-1990s, when my daughter was only a few years old, she had heard Dr Singh use the term *Bhaiya*. When he visited us later one day, she asked him if he was the *Dhoodh wala Bhaiya* (a term used for milkman in Mumbai). He was tickled by my daughter's innocent connection of the term *Bhaiya* to a milkman. Thereafter, he narrated this story in training programs to illustrate stereotyping and mindsets. Just as the way he was a great teacher he was also a great listener and a continuous learner.

A Loving Father

He was a proud father of four boys and two girls. Each one's achievements were important to him and he never compared one child to the other or judged them. Whenever he spoke about his children, he considered all the kids as the best, and that to me is the biggest learning as a father. Only once did he cry on my shoulders and that was when he lost his son Vivek. Vivek's untimely death broke his heart and from then on, I saw him physically aging faster. He carried that grief for the rest of his life.

A Loyal Friend

I have known him as a father, a guru and a friend. I owe my doctorate status to Dr Singh. He planted this idea in me and coached me on leadership, which was his forte. There were no cell phones and long-distance coaching was impossible, so, whenever he visited Mumbai or I visited Delhi, I got his time to review my PhD papers and research work. Even if he was in the midst of work, he'd make time to guide me at every step. He was ever passionate to walk that extra mile and invest in the growth of his mentees. I owe my PhD in leadership not just to Dr Singh's guidance, but also to the help from Dr Asha Bhandarker. This was a priceless contribution to my career.

One of my proudest moments was the chance to attend Dr Singh's Padma Shri award function in 2003. At the function, Dr APJ Abdul Kalam stepped down from the podium to pin the medal on each awardee as a gesture of thanks for their noble contribution. When Dr Singh's turn came, as a mark of respect and humility towards Dr APJ Abdul Kalam (whom he knew from the workshops conducted for DRDO during his stint at ASCI), he walked up to the President with folded hands on the podium. In a reciprocal gesture, the President spoke to him for two minutes, something unprecedented in such formal events.

I was glad to be one among the few, closest to him outside his immediate family, and will remember him till the last day of my life. May his soul rest in peace.

DR SINGH—THE WAY I KNEW HIM

Rattan Sharma, Principal Director, Vivekananda Institute of Professional Studies

I first met Dr Singh in 1984 at ASCI Hyderabad, just after I joined the college it feels like just yesterday. I was very nervous when I joined ASCI as it was my first assignment outside Delhi. Teaching graduates and postgraduate students in Delhi University is very different from training well accomplished and experienced executives in ASCI.

On the first day, Dr Kaura, the then Chairman of Finance & Control Area, talked to me about Dr Singh and spoke very highly of him. All my fears were dispelled later that day when I was introduced to Dr Singh over lunch. He was very friendly, very informal and made me absolutely comfortable. My respect and admiration for him began then and has kept growing since. We continued to meet during our lunchtime. In fact, ASCI also had a tradition of an 11 am tea break and Dr Singh utilized the time and opportunity to interact with as many people as possible, like a true people's person, delighting everyone with his charm.

Dr Singh was a great trainer and was always rated very high by participants attending the programs. There was hardly any training program where his professional/academic inputs were not sought by the course directors. Besides, he was excellent at attracting business for ASCI—training programs, consultancy projects from different organizations—public, private, governments, banks. In addition, I remember he brought several academic chairs to the college, something every institute vies for. He was a multi-faceted personality—a trainer, researcher, consultant, and business developer right from his days at ASCI.

One incident that stayed with me was when I was planning to leave ASCI for IIM-L. The then principal of the college asked Dr Singh to persuade me to stay on. In his inimitable style, Dr Singh played the role of a mentor and guide and helped me make a smooth exit. While this may appear trivial, personally, it was important and left a deep imprint on me. He became my role model and I emulated his style in my different administrative capacities at IIM-L.

When he joined MDI as Director, it was difficult to say no when he persuaded me to join the institute in 1996. Back then, MDI was best known as a training institute, and the first batch of PGDM students was set to pass out. Dr Singh's vision was to make MDI one of the most sought-after business schools in the country. He met everyone—industry, businesses, government, media—truly, with anybody who could help him actualize his dream for MDI. He brought in a lot of business and expanded MDI's service offerings in terms of training programs, research and consultancy projects. He turned the institute around and transformed it with all-round growth and development. He developed and nurtured a team that was strong, effective and result oriented. Dr Singh had great work ethic, worked selflessly, and was a great institution builder—an ability few possess. Whenever we met, we discussed plans for the growth and development of the institute. When he moved to IIM-L as Director, he left behind a deep and lasting legacy at MDI.

Dr Singh was a strategic thinker, a true visionary and a leader. I attribute his consistent track record of success to the values he held so close: he was a leader who valued people and relationships, nurtured talent, had an eye for detail, and a vision driven by purpose focused on outcomes. He was a leader who shared success with others.

We shared a personal bond; Dr Singh felt like a brother, friend, philosopher and guide. He would say that others remember you by your contributions and always encouraged me to contribute positively to the lives of others. Dr Singh—a true 'People's Leader',—is a legend.

THE CROWNING GLORY OF MANAGEMENT EDUCATION

Premila Verma, Ex-faculty Member, Administrative Staff College of India, Hyderabad

It is extremely difficult to summarize Dr Singh's contribution within the confines of these pages. My acquaintance with Dr Singh reaches back to when I was a faculty member on the Human Resource Management team of ASCI Hyderabad. My job involved training, research and consultancy. I had organized a fortnight long program on Human Resource Management. As part of the program, I had invited a guest speaker on leadership, who introduced the topic by stating that a good leader wears a crown comprising ten domes: winning attitude with fire in the belly; visionary; Midas touch—radiating positivity; sensitivity to the needs of the team; effective communicator; trusted mentor; inspiring role model; the power to empower; and high emotional intelligence.

When Dr Singh joined the ASCI as the Dean and Head of the Organizational Behaviour team, I had the privilege of being mentored by him. He guided me to go beyond what I thought were my capabilities. He encouraged me to participate in the training programs he conducted for senior executives at ASCI. The executives went through role plays and the process required interacting and giving them feedback. He trusted my handling of this extremely sensitive task and, with subsequent programs I grew more confident in this role. It's later that I realized he was helping me develop a skill that was in good stead in the corporate training field.

Dr Singh initiated and spurred me on to present a paper at the 33rd International Federation of Training and Development Organizations (IFTDO) world conference in November 2004. I was glad for his inspiring support through the conference experience. Despite his busy schedules during the convention, he made time to be in the audience applauding my effort at the end of my presentation—this was a thorough morale booster.

Dr Singh's contribution through his books, research, membership on the boards of institutions and organizations driven by his vision and long-term commitment provided valuable opportunities beyond social borders with an everlasting impact on the leadership ethos. The world, for Dr Singh, was not a parking space but a racing track on which to stay constantly on the move.

During the three decades of my career, my association with Dr Singh helped me delve into the profound treasure trove of divine wisdom—the Bhagavad Gita, the original ten domed crown crystallized into three basic tenets of the Bhagavad Gita:

Gyana—Knowledge, *Bhakti*—Devotion, and *Karma*—Action

I believe this three-domed crown aptly fits the Padma Shri awardee Dr Singh.

MY EXPERIENCE WITH THE LEGENDARY MANAGEMENT GURU

Mahadeo Jaiswal, Director, IIM Sambalpur

Dr Singh was a leader who created more leaders, who transformed organizations in turn, and created a culture of performance and celebration. The greatest leader is not necessarily the one who does the greatest things, they're the one that gets the people to do the greatest things, and that's what Dr Singh was all about. I met him for the first time in 1997 at MDI, where he was the Director. That meeting was so warm and welcoming, that I decided to join MDI, opting out of the IIM offer which I had at that time.

I shouldered the responsibility for building the IT infrastructure for MDI and work with him went so smoothly that I could finish my tasks successfully and before time.

Dr Singh praised me and even gave me the title of 'IT Czar'. His leadership style was so effective that within a very short period he created many 'Czars' in different functional domains and MDI became one of the top 10 ranked management institutes in 1998 and then the top 5 in 2000. The working environment was so conducive to success, that each and every one became professionally productive and personally engaged. The institute started growing vertically as well as horizontally as many new programs were added.

He introduced a very innovative performance management system for the faculty, based on work unit concepts—a system now followed in almost all the IIMs. Additionally, he created a performance and celebration culture at MDI that paid dividends to all the stakeholders of the institute. Dr Singh wasn't just a noted academician but also a great institution builder, transformation leader, management guru and empathic human being.

A true legend, Dr Singh played an unmatched role in shaping the management education and corporate management space in India. He was very well networked, counting top corporate executives, government and HR leaders among his contacts. His teachings were steeped in Indian ethos fused with a global outlook. With his deep understanding of Indian scriptures and their modern application, he was adept at helping leaders connect the dots to bridge the gap between thoughts and action, thereby establishing a strong business multiplier.

Dr Singh had many wonderful, unique leadership qualities which I was exposed to over all the years of our association. I wish to highlight some of them here.

His actions and communication inspired others and made me feel very appreciated—a great motivator. I remember how he introduced me to dignitaries and professionals by always highlighting my research and professional achievements.

His leadership style was also empowering. I remember when I went to him with a proposal to set up a centre of excellence in enterprise resource planning (ERP) in collaboration with an MNC at MDI, he immediately made me the Chairman of the Centre of Excellence, although I was the junior-most faculty member at the time. He provided all the support needed—financial or otherwise to set it up. As a result, I was able to contribute tremendously to the corporate sector in the field of ERP. I owe him so much for all my achievements.

Empathy and humility were his other prominent leadership qualities. Whenever I met him with my family, he used to enquire about every one of us in detail. These qualities transform people, making them more positive, resilient, persistent, healthier and happier—the kind of feelings that drive the commitment and loyalty leaders want. If someone is made to feel uniquely seen, understood, valued and appreciated at work, that will hook them into being committed to their team, leader and organization. He would highlight only our positive qualities and that helped all of us in directing our professional as well as personal endeavours in a meaningful direction. He persuaded me to buy a flat in Gurgaon and even helped in arranging financial support for the investment. In fact, even my father would often remember him, although he met Dr Singh only once.

He was so well respected that when he retired from MDI, the entire MDI community remembered him for his immense contributions and empathy. Dr Singh was very passionate about his work, and even after his retirement, he was fully engaged in academia, policy making, social, and scholarly work all over the world. I used to meet him in many such forums, and it was always refreshing and motivating listening to his deliberations.

Maya Angelou's wisdom that human beings are far more influenced by feelings than by rational thinking—'people will never forget how you made them feel', permeated Dr Singh's leadership practices.

THE MAKER OF LEADERS

S. K. Bose, Executive Director–Human Resources, Indian Oil Corporation Limited

I met Dr Singh in 1995 while I was pursuing my NMP-VIII at MDI Gurgaon. I was impressed by his leadership style and leadership talk. He had a vision for the institution and vision for everyone who came in close contact with him. He was a true institution builder, and this he had demonstrated in letter and spirit.

Besides our interactions at MDI, during the course of my journey at Indian Oil, we met at several forums, conferences, HR conclaves and in institutions. My interactions with Dr Singh were very intense when we worked towards creating a course framework for developing women leaders at Indian Oil with Dr Singh and Dr Asha Bhandarker in 2017. Under the stewardship of Dr Singh, Indian Oil designed the first ever women's leadership program, Arohi, to prepare mid-level women executives to take up higher leadership roles within the organization.

Dr Singh had always an eye for identifying and locating talent. He always believed that a leader's job is to get things done through encouragement and building confidence in those being groomed to lead. The ability to deliver results depends on how well and consistently you grow other leaders. The job of a leader is to see the person as a whole, over time, in a variety of situations, and work backward from what you observe to determine what that person's individual gifts really are.

He always nailed down the person's natural talents and tendencies first and then looked for situations that would allow them to develop and take off. During discussions, Dr Singh elaborated that a young leader should be able to see the big picture across functional silos. She should be able to break assignments down to manageable tasks and deliver on them. A leader needs to experience working in many geographies, in different functions and experience different cultures. She should have considerable financial talent, be a good teacher, a good negotiator and a strategic thinker. It also required her to grow in the job. Cultivate much broader thinking in qualitative issues, regulatory affairs and try to head several business functions in the country, and beyond the boundaries, in order to prepare her for the future. With this perspective of Dr Singh, a mid-course correction was made, several business and leadership modules were included. He insisted that we needed in-depth focus on fewer people zeroing in on the positives and drilling for specifics.

Dr Singh rightly said that an organization would continue to flourish because of its people, its timely adoption to technology and continuous focus on innovation. He added that when employees are engaged emotionally and psychologically and committed to the organization, the business, they perform more efficiently, and consequently, when business performs better, employees become even more engaged. Most of the Fortune-500 companies that still sustain their positions in the list through three decades, do so mainly because they engage their employees to feel a stronger sense of ownership of their company's success year after year. These successful companies also invest more in their people, creating an increased sense of pride or ownership.

These high-performing organizations have a high performing business culture which is a competitive advantage for them. The engaged employees in those organizations feel connected emotionally, socially and even spiritually to its mission, vision and purpose. Just as loyal customers are among a company's most profitable patrons and passionate advocates, engaged employees are a company's most productive and efficient workers. Dr Singh also believed that engaged employees see the big picture and see their contribution to organization as aimed mainly to build the nation's economy and infrastructure. An employer needs his employees and therefore needs to value their contribution. Frequent and immediate recognition for good work also creates beneficial positive emotions that broaden our perspective and stimulate creative thinking and excite us to contribute more to the organization and to society.

He said it was not enough to just have the right structures, processes, systems or policies in place to foster creativity and innovation. More importantly, there is a need for leadership at all levels to simply engage every employee to unleash their potential.

Applying teachings from the Mahabharata to management education was Dr Singh's special forte. His conversations and talks were peppered with wisdom from the book, and he could not emphasize enough on how important it is to teach human value in every stream of education.

I can go on, like a ride through a crooked street in San Francisco, and record his conversations endlessly, but let me stop here with a hope that learnings from Dr Singh reach students across the globe and immensely benefit them.

A CHANGE MASTER PAR EXCELLENCE

Sunil Mithas, Professor, University of South Florida Muma College of Business

I was shocked to wake up to the news that Padma Shri Dr Pritam Singh departed for his heavenly abode on 3 June. This was all the more shocking, for just a few weeks ago, he'd called to invite me to be on a webinar panel with Dr Alfredo Behrens, Dr Davide Sola, Dr Asha Bhandarker, and him on the impact of Covid-19.

As usual, Dr Singh was energetic on that call and told me about his upcoming book on board governance. He talked about his work related to the Prime Minister's Committee to identify 20 institutes of eminence in India. He was full of energy in preparation for this webinar. We had a rehearsal on 13th May and he was at his best on 14th May where he shared powerful lessons on what it will take to lead in the post-Covid era. Soon after the webinar was over, he sent a complimentary message. There was nothing to indicate that those would be my last interactions with Dr Singh.

As I reflect on the legacy of Dr Pritam Singh, I will remember him as a great academic leader who was an institution builder and a transformation leader par excellence. He touched many lives in significant and positive ways; I feel lucky to be counted among them.

First Set of Interactions (1996–1998)

My association with Dr Singh began when I went to MDI Gurgaon for my MBA when he was the Director. My first meeting with him was at the inauguration function of NMP in July, 1996. Dr Singh made an indelible impression in that meeting with his stories on leadership and organizational transformation. He narrated a story about why a new church never got built because some could not imagine replacing the old dilapidated church due to their fear of the unknown. That is how I remember the story; it was powerful and stayed with me for many years. Interestingly, Dr Singh made a brief mention of this in his 14 May, 2020 webinar as well, bringing that memory back to me.

I recall some other interactions with Dr Singh during my time there. He was very involved in creating a student-run signature event to publicize the MDI brand in those early years when the Post Graduate Program in Management was relatively new and not as well known. He advised the students on how to go about fund-raising and how to orchestrate some of the faculty-moderated panels that students were putting together.

Dr Singh's hands-on involvement in an event like that was remarkable and speaks of his ability to lead with action.

While at MDI, we heard stories of how Dr Singh personally recruited faculty members from other top institutions such as IIMs and IITs. He made investments in faculty members by providing them opportunities for participating in high-profile executive teaching in India and abroad. He gave significant responsibility to promising faculty members early on, and it's no surprise that MDI became well-known for grooming academic leaders who eventually headed other reputed institutions such as the IIMs. I graduated from MDI in 1998 and had the honour of receiving my degree from Dr Singh.

Second Set of Interactions (2005–2007)

My second set of interactions with Dr Singh started when I visited MDI Gurgaon in December 2005, where Dr Singh had re-joined as Director. Subsequently, I met Dr Singh again when he visited the Robert H. Smith School of Business in 2006 to meet the then Dean, Dr Howard Frank. He and Dr Frank had good chemistry, both shared traits that all great transformational leaders show.

Third Set of Interactions (2012–2020)

My third set of interactions with Dr Singh started in 2012 when he was the Director at IMI. The Dean of Smith School, Professor Anand Anandalingam, and I visited MDI and discussed quite a few collaboration opportunities, including joint executive education opportunities that Dr Singh proposed. Eventually, Dr Singh and I co-led an executive development program for Executive Directors and General Managers in 2013. Beyond professional interactions, I benefited and learnt quite a lot from Dr Singh in other settings as well. He was generous in creating opportunities that would have otherwise escaped me.

Dr Singh made tremendous contributions to management education in India by leading and transforming several institutions such as MDI Gurgaon and IIM-L. No less important, he nurtured and developed leaders who later became Directors of management institutions. He was a great communicator and made lasting impressions through his moving stories on leadership. He demonstrated through his actions some of the driving principles he identified in his book on Change Maestros: contextual sensitivity, compelling vision, winning streak, people connect and engagement, meaningful contribution with speed, creative destruction for transformation, evolving self, and culture architecture (Singh & Bhandarker, 2011). I count him among some of the most charismatic leaders that I have had the fortune of meeting or observing in various corporate or other settings. His actions transformed many lives and institutions, and his memories and kindness will continue to inspire many. I feel lucky that I had the opportunity to know him, learn from him and I will forever remember him.

THE DOYEN OF LEADERSHIP

G. N. Pandey, Advisor and Head of Department (HR-OB), Doon Business School-Group

The construction of the now famous IIM-L was fraught with problems of land dispute. In May 2000, for two consecutive days, a huge demonstration was held at the IIM-L main gate, comprising a gathering of villagers, led by leaders from various factions—the Samajwadi Party, Bharatiya Kisan Union (Tikait Group) and Gram Pradhans from most of the surrounding villages. The IIM had initiated some levelling work on a portion of the 85 acres of land the ownership and use of which remained a cause of dispute between the two entities.

Dr Singh took it up as a challenge, and ordered the levelling of this disputed land, leading to the villagers' agitation.

The agitators openly threatened the lives of those that dared to trespass on their land. In response, Dr Singh boldly offered his own life in exchange to the agitators. The problem was multi-faceted, with no apparent solution but to maintain the status quo. Through sustained efforts and negotiations, a historic Memorandum of Understanding (MOU), was signed on October 24, 2000, between the IIM and the aggrieved parties.

Finally, IIM-L got back its 85 acres of land and the villagers started viewing it as a partner, and not an obstacle, to their progress. The astute leadership and exemplary statesmanship exhibited by Dr Singh, coupled with cautious optimism and concern for the interests of all stakeholders, set him apart from the rest. Converting a dispute into a win-win for all highlighted his unique problem-solving ability. Courage and will power to persist were his typical attributes. Dr Singh disliked disputes, and yet, he addressed a series of them. He boldly impressed upon the Board of Governors that a premier management institution like IIM-L, could not afford to have continued disputes with everyone. Against a special approval obtained from the board he enabled settlements of all major disputes.

My association with Dr Singh dates to January 1988, while attending a one-month General Management Program at the ASCI Hyderabad. I saw him as a mesmerizing teacher, with his heart-searching explanations and pinpointed analysis of the responses to psychometric questionnaires that he administered to the class. Each participant was guided to carve out a leadership improvement plan for himself. This approach truly reflected his unique leadership development and nurturing capabilities.

My next interaction with Dr Singh was 10 years later, when he visited the ONGC, Delhi office for various strategic training and development meetings. He was the Director of MDI Gurgaon and as General Manager (Personnel & Administration), heading ONGC's Corporate Human Resource Group, I attended these meetings. The training contract for ONGC executives and Managers with the MDI had ended and tenders for inviting a new contract were initiated. Two rounds of talks had failed. But for the third round of negotiations, I had the opportunity to head the ONGC team. On reaching the MDI entrance, we were greeted by Dr Singh himself—'Welcome to Gurgaon, the place immortalized by Guru Dronacharya!' Impressed and touched by his humility, the ONGC team began negotiations with Dr Singh that extended to an untiring eight hour discussion. Seeing his unique negotiating skills, I discovered a lifetime learning opportunity. The negotiations concluded with a win-win situation and ONGC consequently awarded MDI a long-term contract for training.

In January 1999, when Dr Singh was asked by the Government to join as Director of IIM-L, he invited me to come on board as IIM-L Chief Administrative Officer. It was a hard decision to abandon a 36-year-long association with ONGC, and move to a job with nearly half the annual package. Dr Singh persuaded and motivated me to make the decision and join IIM-L. It proved to be a wonderful four-year opportunity to work and learn through active association with Dr Singh.

There was another instance of dispute that involved a 3.5-km stretch of road connected to Sitapur Road, the land ownership of which lay with IIM-L. The Government of Uttar Pradesh planned to set up a by-pass route to Lucknow city, diverting the inter-state and inter-district traffic. Dr Singh anticipated heavy traffic congestion over IIM road, and advised the State Public Works Department (PWD) not to go ahead with this plan unless they widened it to a four-lane road. This suggestion went unheeded by the government. In a courageous and bold move, Dr Singh sued the PWD and Government of

Uttar Pradesh in the High Court resulting in the government complying with the appeal for the four-lane road.

During the latter half of December 2000, the IIM-L Board of Governors proposed that the postgraduate intake be doubled over the next two years. This would require constructing facilities including an extra hostel, classrooms and other related infrastructure. Commissioning this with just five-month time in hand was considered an impossibility. However, Dr Singh always looked beyond the impossible. He believed in finding a way. The building contractor had refused to build within this time frame. Dr Singh persisted using his strong project management skills, and finally had the work got completed in time.

Dr Singh believed that the essential fusion of industry needs and academic expertise cannot happen without MDP and so, he introduced the IIM-L's MDPs for the corporate sector in August, 1999, by repurposing an abandoned building in the vicinity. Today, IIM-L is the largest, premier executive and management development centre in the country.

The Noida off-campus centre of the IIM-L, devoted exclusively to executive education (the only one of its kind in the country among the IIMs) is the brainchild of Dr Singh. He conceptualized the need for IIM-L to be nearer to the industry in NCR, as the Lucknow region practically had no industrial base. Dr Singh proposed a lease of 10 acres of land for the Noida Campus, and in due time, approval for 20 acres of land was accorded in September, 2000; this was at a time when no other IIM could get approval to have an off-campus centre within the country.

IIM-L's campus initially wore an empty and deserted look. But Dr Singh had envisioned an academic institution with MDP inter phase to have a friendly, inviting and inspiring campus. He worked hard to ensure this transition. As soon as one enters the IIM-L main gate, highly motivating statues of Mahatma Gandhi's 'Dandi march' and Lord Krishna and Arjun's chariot (both depicting the speed of action and philosophy of management) steal the view. The roads are lined with flower beds, buildings are reflected in water bodies containing beautiful fountains, lush green lawns with pop up irrigators invite the visitor to relax. Beautiful mango orchards fill the campus today, planted two decades ago during his directorship. Each building has an inspiring and meaningful name—the administrative block is named 'Samadhan', houses the non-academic staff and conveys that they are meant not to administer but to strive to explore solutions to the problem areas of core academics. The Library building is named 'Gyanoday' (the rise of knowledge) with murals depicting Lord Buddha in meditation and enlightenment postures. The Faculty block is called 'Chintan' (aim to become thought leaders). The academic PGP block is known as 'Bodhi-Grah' (the house of wisdom). The Management Development Center itself is known as 'Manthan' (MDPs are meant to stimulate the churning of body, mind and soul). The Community centre is 'Samanjasya'. When queried on the Director's house named 'Samanvay', Dr Singh explained that the Director's role is to integrate diversities. Being on the campus one truly feels that poetry flows through this place.

I have shared only a few examples of what Dr Singh personified. He continues to be revered as a visionary evangelist, effective manager of execution, as well as a strong relationship builder. He was the doyen of leadership, in every sense.

DR PRITAM SINGH—AS I KNEW HIM

Ashok Banerjee, Professor, IIM Calcutta

It was a late December 1999 evening in Delhi and winter was in full force. I received a dinner invite from one of my close friends at the MDI, for the next day. When I met him, he took me to see Dr Singh, who had recently taken charge of IIM-L as a Director. We had a long discussion that evening and at the end of which, he invited me to apply for a faculty position at IIM-L.

I joined IIM-L in the mid-2000. What struck me the most in our first encounter is Dr Singh's friendly greeting like a long-time friend. While seeing me off after the meeting, he walked with me for a while and narrated his journey as an academic thought leader. It made me feel important and I left my friend's house with fond memories of Dr Singh. Several years later, one of my faculty colleagues at IIM Calcutta met Dr Singh in a seminar and sure enough, Dr Singh enquired, 'how is Ashok doing?' and continued to share his fond memories during our time at IIM-L. I again felt very important!

I have closely observed Dr Singh and his administrative style during my days at IIM-L. I try, in this piece, to highlight my take on Dr Singh as a leader and a human being.

Effervescent

I have encountered two types of personalities—exhausting and effervescent. Exhausting personalities are those one wants to avoid meeting. These persons generate negative energy, make one feel exhausted or drained and derive pleasure by belittling others. They feel happy in finding faults in the other person's arguments and demand unquestioning obedience. An effervescent leader exudes positive energy and encourages the listener to come up with ideas. They do not highlight faults in the other person's arguments even when that becomes quite apparent. Rather an effervescent leader lets the other person 'discover' the flaws or gaps in arguments by herself. Pritam is an out and out effervescent leader. We would love to meet him whenever we felt low on motivation and self-belief. Even when he would not have any concrete suggestions to offer to address our problems, what he would leave us with is a sense of positivity. I remember one such incident. I was handed a course to teach within a month of my joining IIM-L. Along with it came the course outline to follow. I wanted to change some of the course reading materials and case studies but was advised against it, the matter landed on Pritam's desk. He called me and the area-chair to his chamber. He had an interesting approach to the issue—he was all for innovation and experiment and added that students would be the best judge for adapting to an experiment and we would have to accept it. He subtly nudged the area-chair to provide some freedom to experiment and if my teaching feedback was not up to the mark, the changes would be reversed. When we left his chamber after the meeting, none of us felt bad and the area-chair later became one of my good friends.

Persuasive

Dr Singh had the enviable style of persuading people to embrace changes and urged his colleagues to venture out of their comfort zone to experiment with new ideas. Once he was convinced with an idea, he would leave no stone unturned to help the idea's implementation. He would not wear a 'control' hat, rather patiently listen to all perspectives, and reserve his comments for the end. I recall one instance in a faculty council meeting. The main agenda was curriculum review—a hugely challenging task in any academic institution. The curriculum review exercise happens once in a decade and requires a fine balance between the internal choices and market demand. People are normally reluctant to change, and academics are no exception. So, Pritam knew that it would be difficult to satisfy everyone in that exercise. Of course, he was privy to the changes proposed by the curriculum review committee before the same were presented to the faculty body and offered his comments to the committee. Thus, the committee members and Dr Singh were on the same page before the proposed curriculum was shared with the larger faculty body. Dr Singh started the faculty council meeting with his opening remarks, 'Curriculum review is a very important and serious affair and we should be in no hurry to adopt the proposed changes as presented. I look forward to your suggestions and for this purpose, if we cannot finish the deliberations in one meeting, we will continue with the meeting for the next few days till we have heard every opinion and suggestion. Please remember our goal is common—we need to revise our curriculum. Once we agree to this goal, the rest is easy.' The meeting went on for five consecutive days and Dr Singh did not utter a single word during the deliberations. He painstakingly listened to every argument and took meticulous notes. On the final day, he broke his silence after lunch and said that 'it is time to close the loop and come up with a revised curriculum for the MBA. I'll go by the consensus.' Finally, the faculty council meeting ended with an approved revised curriculum. A majority of the faculty members felt happy that their voices were heard and suggestions incorporated. Little did they realize that during these five days of intense discussion, Dr Singh would meet the members of the curriculum review committee every evening in his chamber and analyse the deliberations of the day. He would chalk out a strategy for the next day and the stance that the members of the review committee should take next during the meeting. So, he steered the deliberations in the faculty council meeting without making it obvious. Nobody felt his imposing presence and yet the final outcome was what was desired.

I remember another incident to demonstrate Dr Singh's persuasive nature. He pursued a matter only when he was convinced that the proposal is beneficial for the institute. IIM-L was about to launch a two-year full-time residential program on agri-business. He had a meeting with the Secretary, the Ministry of Agriculture, Government of India, to make a presentation on the proposed program and seek the Ministry's support. Members of the program committee accompanied him to New Delhi for the meeting and the Chairperson of the committee made a formal presentation to the Ministry. The secretary was impressed and mentioned that the curriculum was very relevant and there was a need for such a program. At that time, only IIM Ahmedabad had a similar program. Dr Singh did not interject during the entire presentation and listened quietly. After the remarks by the secretary, Dr Singh said IIM-L is grateful to the secretary for sparing his valuable time and blessing the program for its success. And then he said, 'I have also come to you with a hope that goes beyond blessings. We need your financial support to run the program.' Going forward, IIM-L received the needed support.

Relationship Matters

Dr Singh was one of the rare directors of any IIMs who could pick up the phone and call a CEO without a prior appointment. He carefully maintained a fine distinction between personal friendship and professional needs. That may perhaps explain why Dr Singh had easy access to corporate leaders which helped him secure endowment for chairs and sponsorship for various events of the institute. I recall one such incident.

The Director, HR of a large public-sector bank invited Dr Singh to discuss how IIM-L could help in the bank's recruitment of probationary officers. The bank's existing practice was a written test followed by a personal interview to select candidates for the position. Could IIM-L design and conduct the interview process for the shortlisted candidates based on a written test performance? This assignment could draw in much-needed revenue to the institute as the bank normally interviews thousands of candidates nationwide for the positions.

Dr Singh proposed the bank use innovative tools in the selection process to target the 'right' candidates. 'We could help do more efficiently what you have been doing so far. There has to be a good reason for coming to a premier institution like ours for a solution, and we must be able to offer you some more value for the job.' Thus, he suggested that the shortlisted candidates go through a three-stage selection process—(a) psychometry test, (b) group discussion and (c) personal interview. He argued how a psychometry test would enable the bank to identify candidates who would have qualitative traits to emerge as future leaders for the bank. The new approach would help the bank look at the new recruits as future leaders rather than mere employees. The Director (HR) of the bank was convinced and for the first time the selection process for the probationary officers changed. Undoubtedly, Dr Singh leveraged his personal rapport with the banker, though what is noteworthy was, he helped his friend with a suggestion that was immensely valuable for the bank and at the same time ensured more revenue for IIM-L.

Driven by Intuition

Dr Singh took many decisions based on intuition. Data used later supported the credibility of his intuition. Not all decisions are driven by cold, hard numbers—one needs to trust one's gut. Unless one has experience in a particular field, it is extremely tricky to decide based on gut feeling. Also, one needs to have self-confidence to rely on one's own judgement without necessarily depending on data. I once approached Dr Singh with a proposal to organize a conference. I had no prior experience and his approach was completely unconventional. He did not ask me the usual questions on the theme of the conference, expected number of participants, and how many faculty colleagues would provide organizational support. Instead, his said, 'Are you convinced that the conference is going to make some impact?' and I said, 'I think so.'

He asked me to leave the proposal on his table and said, 'the institute will give you a matching financial support equivalent to the amount of sponsorship that you raise!' His statement had two implications: (a) he approved the proposal without going through the details; and more importantly (b) he hinted that one should be entrepreneurial in any new endeavour and he was willing to support such efforts.

Always Available

A busy man always finds time, goes an old adage and it fits Dr Singh perfectly. He was busy flying between Lucknow and Delhi almost weekly and yet easily reachable whenever there was any urgency, even at odd hours. Once I had to discuss a project proposal with him urgently as the deadline was just 24 hours away. I called him to seek an appointment and told him about the urgency. He agreed to meet right away as he had two hours to spare. I was surprised as I was looking for just a few minutes of his time. I accompanied him to the airport on his way to catch a flight. We discussed the proposal and he was all ears during the hour's drive from the campus and gave me valuable suggestions.

Great Enabler

A desirable quality of every leader is (s)he should be an enabler—encourage people to take risks and urge them not to fear making mistakes. I close with this final anecdote about Dr Singh as a facilitator, an eternal enabler. I had, working with one of my colleagues, developed a framework for operational risk management for financial institutions, at a time when the industry was struggling to come up with a model for estimating loss due to operational risk. We met Dr Singh with a plan to present our research to a few bankers, seeking feedback. He picked up the phone instantly and called the Chairman cum Managing Director (CMD) of a public sector bank. The meeting was arranged within a fortnight. Although the CMD could not attend the presentation, he spent a good part of an hour with us to understand our model, after the presentation. I still recall him say, 'Dr Singh has spoken to me about you and your work; and hence I was interested to see what you guys have done.' Though we couldn't pursue the research further, it helped to understand the industry's perspective on this issue. Dr Singh would provide similar opportunities to many of my colleagues and once he had openly said, in one of the faculty council meetings that 'I would like to see my faculty members interact more frequently with the industry and try to understand their challenges to come up with research ideas that make sense to the industry.'

Even as I was coming to the end of this essay, a message popped up on my WhatsApp—a link to the breaking news that Padma Shri Dr Singh 'leaves for his heavenly abode'. I was shocked and couldn't believe the news for a moment as I had spoken with him only ten days ago. I decided to finish the piece today (3 June 2020) and pay my homage through this essay to the great soul—Dr Singh!

WHO IS A TRUE LEADER?

R. L. Raina, Vice Chancellor, JK Lakshmipat University, Jaipur

My association with this great guru of gurus began the way associations do between a sincere and hardworking, but dissatisfied professional, and an acclaimed guru who had mastered the craft of understanding people—in and out. My personal as well as professional progress over the last 30 years was nurtured by my role model, inspiration, guide, philosopher and family member—Padma Shri Dr Singh.

One morning in 1997—1998, I switched on the TV for the morning news bulletin and found a bearded middle-aged person being interviewed on management education and leadership. He was speaking about a few time-tested books on leadership and holy scriptures like the Vedas, the Bhagavad Gita, the Ramayana, the Guru Granth Sahib, the Bible, and the Holy Quran, to illustrate his views on management and leadership. After listening to him for only a few minutes, I said to myself that this is a leader. People would be fortunate if they got an opportunity to work with him. That evening, I shared this experience with my wife, quoting him, 'leading from the front', 'others interest over self', 'walk the talk,' 'credibility and visibility makes one successful', 'belief in giving', 'selfless sacrifice', 'commanding not demanding leadership', and more. She was derisive and said—characters like those only exist in books! I, however, hoped to someday get to meet him and remarked that our institution would certainly benefit with a Director like the guru I had heard that morning on the television.

Dr Singh joined IIM-L and during the first three weeks, he met each and every faculty member, activity head, officer, as well as all other non-teaching employees of the institute, individually, and in groups as per their work areas, over a cup of tea, either in his office or at their workplaces. In this exercise, apart from exchanging welcome and introductory notes, he asked one question to each and every one of them—while I appreciate your role and contribution to IIM-L thus far, what would you like the institution to be like in three to five years from now? Asked to elaborate on that he would cite the contribution, credibility and visibility of the other three IIMs (Kolkata, Ahmedabad and Bangalore) at that time.

What upset me during this entire time was why I hadn't gotten to meet him yet. I finally called Dr Singh, and once I had introduced myself, he said, 'Doctor, I know I haven't met you after my joining but I will soon, once there is something worthwhile to share with you!' In the short conversation we shared, I was surprised at how much he knew about my performance at IIM-L for more than 15 years, my personal and professional life, my struggles and achievements, my potential and my aspirations. His sincere interest in the people he worked with was amazing. He'd then connect the dots from other sources to have a well-rounded understanding of them, and take it from there to encourage their aspirations!

One day he asked me how I felt about taking on some additional core responsibility. I was very pleasantly surprised when asked to step into the mainstream teaching at the institute. I immediately agreed. My decision received mixed, predominantly positive, responses from various quarters: a few senior faculty colleagues, officers and a couple of area chairpersons. Dr Singh then advised the Dean, Academic Affairs to include my application for processing as per the institute's norms. I joined as Professor in Communications at IIM-L with a clear undertaking that I will manage my existing responsibility without any compromise. Later, I gathered that he had announced the decision on my appointment to all other key stakeholders, including the Chairman of the Board as well as the Ministry (HRD, Government of India) officials.

While handing me the appointment letter as a Professor, the Dean asked me to start teaching within a month. In a system where faculty are normally given a term or two to understand the teaching-learning process of the institute, I was asked to teach a class within a month's time! It felt hard on me, particularly given the subject was 'Communications for Management'. I did have years of experience of teaching postgraduate students although the subjects spanned a variety of courses and the students were different. In this backdrop, I went back to Dr Singh with a request to get some preparation time. 'You should start teaching tomorrow', was his response to my plea, then he spent an hour motivating me on how to go ahead. I left, highly encouraged and inspired. I put in my best, studying and preparing for the classes. I delivered the course with a student feedback of over four on a scale of five. Dr Singh commended me, 'I am sure, you will do even better, going forward.'

He then added that since I had begun working with students directly and understanding them better, I would also then have to handle student affairs. Minutes after this discussion, I received an official order stating that I shall be the Chairman, Student Affairs at the institute. Gradually, Dr Singh gave me the additional responsibility of taking on alumni, corporate communications and media relations. In less than two years, our bonding with the alumni went from almost nothing to a level where our alumni became a part of the institute's entire activity-mix—teaching, research, consultancy and training—gaining widespread appreciation.

Leaders Lead from the Front

On one occasion when I was having lunch with him, Dr Singh received a call; I gathered the caller was the Secretary, Ministry of Human Resource Development, Government of India, who was calling regarding the promotion of a faculty member and a representation vetoing it by other faculty at the institute. Dr Singh replied clearly in three lines:

1. I have already taken a thought through decision on the matter and the communication to that effect has since been accepted;
2. I never go back on my decisions at just the wishes and whims of someone; I have a blank signed paper (of resignation) in my pocket to be submitted when the situation so warrants; and
3. I have never compromised on my values and will never ever do so.

The discussion lasted for a few minutes and immediately after, he asked me to accompany him to his office to complete the unfinished action in the point 1 above. Only leaders like

Dr Singh have the courage to stand by their decisions for colleagues, even at the cost of their own careers.

Even after leaving the institute, Dr Singh stayed connected with me. One morning, when I was vacationing in Jammu, I received a call from him letting me know about a vacancy for the Director's position at Lal Bahadur Shastri Institute of Management (LBSIM), Delhi. He encouraged me to apply since I was doing well in my role as an academic as well as in institution building at IIM-L. I applied and joined the institute on a two-year extra-ordinary leave from IIM-L.

Life at LBSIM was not that rosy to begin with, particularly since I was transitioning from an IIM to a private institution. Constant coaching and mentoring by Dr Singh helped me excel at LBSIM. I must add here that his coaching and mentoring was very unique. To begin with, he listened patiently to me till I was completely done explaining my problem. Crisp would be his advice, 'Yes, that is the way to go ahead normally, but can you look at it this way also?' armed with his fresh inputs, I would then go on to find the best solution to the issue at hand.

I pray that this great guru of gurus lives on in our hearts and lives, in our goals and ambitions, and in our thoughts and deeds.

HE LED, SO WE LEAD

Debashis Chatterjee, Director, IIM Kozhikode

Dr Singh's reputation preceded him when he joined IIM-L as Director in 1998. The turnaround story of Management Development Institute, Gurgaon was still buzzing in academic circles. There was an air of anticipation about his vision for IIM-L.

My first memorable conversation with him was about IIM-L's very successful campus placements that year. All our students got placements; several students got multiple job offers in a year of recession. I was expecting the newly appointed Director to claim credit for our institutional performance. Instead, I was surprised that he gave me all the credit as Placement Chair, and the Lucknow Times of India's first page carried a very flattering headline that read: *There is no Recession this Side of the Gomti River*. This was the beginning of the shift in perception about IIM-L from an inward-looking academic institution towards a very visible brand that meant business.

Dr Singh taught me that leadership was all about the triumph of aspiration over scarce resources. I never saw him economize on his dreams, never witnessed him losing that ray of hope in the gloomiest of circumstances, except that one day—the premonition of his own death with the untimely passing away of his son in the United States.

The world of perceptions was more real for Dr Singh than reality itself. His leadership signature was about shifting perceptions. I remembered as part of one of my courses in IIM-L, I asked the students to raise funds for on-field leadership projects that would help shift perceptions about the institute. One of the projects was about re-defining 3.4 kilometres of a stretch of road that connected the National Highway to IIM-L. The students and I agreed to raise funds to put up eight billboards containing quotes from great leaders and achievers of the world including Einstein and Tagore. The idea was to claim the road as an inspirational drive for visitors to IIM-L. There were murmurs and vetoes from the Dean and some senior faculty of IIM-L who complained to Dr Singh that I was looking to advertise my course through these billboards. Since, the institute did not officially fund it, Dr Singh argued, the faculty concerned, and students should not have a problem in putting these billboards up. Empowered by this, I got the quotes painted in blue, the institute's brand colour, on white billboards. During his convocation speech, the Chairman of Tata Steel made a passing mention of those billboards. Dr Singh lost no opportunity to talk to a large number of the faculty stating how the billboards that were my project, had resulted in the mushrooming roadside liquor stores giving way to several emerging educational institutions. Dr Singh's support helped many positive changes.

A significant element in Dr Singh's leadership signature was his clarity about an institution builder's mandate. He saw the Director's role as primarily expanding the boundary of the institute and brand building. He invested in his faculty as his primary brand ambassadors. He always took and made an opportunity to showcase his faculty before the corporate world. Dr Singh had the uncanny ability to redefine people and kindle their inherent potential for high performance. Contrary to the Western academic world's preoccupation with their anti-hero stance in leadership, Dr Singh believed and lived the Great Man view of leadership. He was unapologetically Indian in his speech, thought and world view.

The final aspect of Dr Singh was exercise of autonomy in execution. I found myself inspired by his autonomous style of work. At IMI New Delhi, Dr Singh led the way before me as Director General. I ensured that I neither imitated his style of work, nor did I listen to his advice on how to run the institution. He was happy that I carved out my own path. That was Dr Singh's true gift for me—the privilege of being my own man.

Dr Singh, Padma Shri, leaves behind a glittering array of management institutions he helped shape as a teacher, scholar, Dean and Director: XLRI, ASCI Hyderabad, IIM Bangalore, IIM-L, MDI Gurgaon and IMI New Delhi. His access to corporate corner rooms and the corridors of power in the government was based on the Midas touch of his personal chemistry.

As a leader he owned his people, loved them, and nurtured them until they became leaders themselves. Like an indulgent parent, he gave me a shirt always a size larger than my fit. He dreamed that I would someday grow into it.

I now stare at a pair of huge shoes that he leaves behind as legacy for his countless admirers and followers. It would require real daring to even consider stepping into them. He will be dearly missed but his life and work will never be lost. Take a final bow Dr Singh!

THE BUILDER OF INSTITUTIONS

Kala Seetharam Sridhar, Professor, Institute for Social and Economic Change, Bangalore

V. Sridhar, Professor, International Institute of Information Technology Bangalore

We have known Dr Singh since 1999, when we were in Washington, DC. After our PhDs in the United States, we were actively looking to return to India. When we applied to IIM-L, much to our pleasant surprise, Dr Singh called us in Washington. I (Sridhar) remember one sentence he said over the phone, 'all roads lead to IIM Lucknow'. He then gave us an overview of the things that were happening at IIM-L and persuaded us to accept his offer to join the institute. We accepted his offer and relocated to Lucknow.

When we joined IIM-L in August, 1999, Dr Singh did everything possible to enable us to carry on our research and teaching at the institute. Two specific instances come to mind, when he referred me (Kala) to meet Professor A. M. Khusro, then Chairman, Eleventh Finance Commission (EFC) and his team. He said that the EFC wanted to meet with eminent economists and named me (Kala) as one. The second instance was when he referred me (Kala) to meet with the then Finance Minister of UP, who was inviting suggestions from eminent economists to reduce the revenue deficit of the state. The second instance specifically demonstrated his keen engagement with top policymakers in the state of UP.

Early on, in a move to inculcate the culture for research at IIM-L, Dr Singh introduced monetary awards for papers published in national and international journals, which incentivized many of the faculty to publish.

Dr Singh was a great institution builder, and a leader with extraordinary out-of-the-box ideas. Many criticized him as someone who bypassed bureaucratic procedures, but he always did what he believed was in the best interests of the institution. For example, when Hari Shankar Singhania, the then Chairman of the IIM-L Board visited the institute, he asked us to go meet him to demonstrate that he had young faculty like us with PhDs from leading universities in the US.

We owe it to Dr Singh for inspiring us to start writing articles based on our research and ideas for policy, for financial dailies such as The Economic Times. This not only served to enhance the institution's name in the minds of the public, but also gave us academicians a reality check on our work. Dr Singh was an institution builder and we still recollect the many instances during our tenure at IIM-L where he would go out of his way to motivate and nurture faculty to bring out the best in them.

I remember at our daughter's second birthday celebration in IIM-L's community hall, Dr Singh stayed back and kept us company for dinner after all the guests had left. He said that 'everyone has their dinner and leaves. Nobody stays until Kala and Sridhar have their dinner, I will stay and give them company!' Dr Singh holds a special place in our family, including our parents who held him in great regard, particularly thankful for being instrumental in bringing their children back to India.

Dr Singh was a great scholar and eloquent speaker; he knew the entire Bhagavad Gita. A frequent phrase which he used in his speeches was from Chapter 18, Verse 78 of the Bhagavad Gita:

यत्र योगेश्वरः कृष्णो यत्र पार्थो धनुर्धरः ।
तत्र श्रीर्विजयो भूतिर्ध्रुवा नीतिर्मतिर्मम ॥

(Wherever there is Shree Krishna, the Lord of all Yog, and wherever there is Arjun, the supreme archer, there will also certainly be unending opulence, victory, prosperity, and righteousness. Of this, I am certain.)

Even now, when I (Sridhar) visit IIM-L, I cannot but recollect the wonderful moments that we spent at the institute under his stellar leadership. The last time I (Sridhar) communicated with Dr Singh was on February 29, 2020, while on a visit to IIM-L. It was only during his tenure that the Fellow Program in Management (now made equivalent to PhD) was set up at the institute. The statue of 'Dandi March', which was installed at the entrance of the institute during his tenure, reminded me of the golden times we spent at the institute. At that instant I sent him a WhatsApp message about my recollection, and immediately Dr Singh responded. It is the supreme human quality and respect that he had for us that brings tears in our eyes whenever we think of Dr Singh.

After IIM-L, my (Sridhar's) relationship with Dr Singh continued at Management Development Institute, Gurgaon. I (Sridhar) was about to join the Department of Management at IIT Delhi. However, due to the typical bureaucratic bottlenecks at large institutes, I could not join at the last moment. In fact, we spent close to one month in the IIT Delhi hostel with our parents and our five-year-old daughter waiting for the appointment letter from IIT Delhi, which, to our utter disappointment, took a long time to come.

Then I went to MDI to see Dr Singh about the possibility of joining MDI, along with our parents and daughter. He warmly welcomed me and enquired about our well-being. When I told him about my dilemma, he immediately said 'Sridhar, this is your office. You can come and join tomorrow.' The room which he showed me was his own, before he moved to the Director's office at MDI. I was dumb struck. Here I was, struggling to prove my bonafides to IIT, while I was welcome to join MDI with open arms by Dr Singh. On my way back to Delhi on that day, I indeed received the offer from IIT Delhi which I politely declined, thanks to Dr Singh's benevolence and his appreciation of my scholarly work. I joined MDI in 2003 and stayed there until 2008.

The other notable event that I (Sridhar) cannot forget happened on 9 August 2014. On that day, the launch of my book on spectrum regulation was scheduled for launch at the India International Centre (IIC), New Delhi. While I invited some friends from my professional network, I somehow missed out inviting Dr Singh. I hurriedly called him when I was on my way to Delhi from Bangalore on the morning of the launch. To my utter surprise, Dr Singh was there at IIC promptly at 5 pm for the book launch. The humility of Dr Singh just overwhelmed me!

More recently, I (Kala) was recommended for the Fulbright Nehru Academic and Professional Excellence fellowship, and I remember Dr Singh served on many selection panels in the past. I wanted to call and give him this news, and seek his blessings for the same, but never got to, before he passed away. We miss Dr Singh not only as a mentor, but as a close family member.

We are immensely thankful to Dr Asha Bhandarker for this initiative, and invitation to us to contribute to the volume in Dr Singh's honour, as this is the only way we are able to express our grief on the passing on of one of India's leading and greatest management thinkers and leaders.

IN GRATITUDE TO MY GURU

Nand Dhameja, Dean and Professor FMS, Manav Rachna International Institute of Research and Studies (MRIIRS)

Padma Shri Dr Singh was my guru, guide, mentor and philosopher. He was a doyen of management, an inspiring role model for me, for alumni, for corporate heads, and for those involved in policy making. Above all he was an outstanding institution builder, groomed hundreds of CEOs, and a consultant to multinational corporations in India and abroad.

My association with Dr Singh goes back about five decades when he was Senior Research Professor, at XLRI, Jamshedpur—an association which started between two teachers developed into a deeper and stronger guru-disciple, guru-guide and mentor-mentee relationship. As Director of Management Development Institute, Gurgaon he inducted me as professor. This was a good learning opportunity for me to work and grow under the guidance of Dr Singh. He was a big motivator and hardworking, fast decision maker, always reminding us of the approach he followed, 'Raise the target to a higher level whenever you have achieved or are nearer the target.'

Dr Singh had a strong willpower, was a people person, had strong networking attributes, always ready to help and thus guided many mentees. He always started his classes by reciting a shloka from the Bhagavad Gita or by narrating a story and kept his audience spellbound.

He emphasized that in every course, 20 per cent of the teaching must be by an industry expert and one-fourth of the course reading material/cases for each paper contributed by the faculty member. The objective was that each faculty member could publish a book on their subject within three or four years. As a result, a good number of faculty members were self-published authors of reading material for the courses offered.

Dr Singh was a strict disciplinarian, known for his punctuality; he believed that 'work is worship' and had the same expectation from his colleagues. He developed a system to reward faculty members for their contribution in research, consulting and teaching, and instituted annual awards in these three areas.

He brought several research projects and encouraged faculty members to contribute research papers with an incentive system of rewards being in place. As a plan to develop and diversify, Dr Singh had a structure for developing a portfolio of MBA programs with specializations to answer the market needs and sponsors' expectations. MDI was the first institute to develop leadership programs for defence personnel which went on to become a regular feature.

Dr Singh worked closely in designing and organizing programs at the institute. Besides the flagship PGP, MDI has made its mark with industry associations and is recognized for its MDPs as well. He would take a personal interest in promoting and developing MDPs as per the expectations of the client organizations. Dr Singh encouraged the faculty to meet the client organization and gauge their training needs so that the programs could be tailored to their expectations.

It wasn't uncommon for Dr Singh to retain outgoing faculty by offering them an incentive, in anticipation of the approval from the board. On being asked how he managed it, his quick response was that so long as it is in the interest of the institute, why delay in rewarding the deserving ones? MDI has provided a large number of Directors to other well-known business schools, which stands testimony of their grooming at MDI and its facilitation by Dr Singh.

Dr Singh's working style is highlighted by the following shloka from the Vedas:

ओम स्वस्ति पंथा। मनु चरेमा सूर्या। चंद्र मसाविवा।
पुनर्वास। घनता जनता सम गमाहि।

(May we ever unswervingly follow the path of duty as do the Sun and the Moon.)

Dr Singh's contribution of award-winning books and writings has enriched management literature. I would end by quoting the last verse of the Bhagavad Gita (78th verse of Eighteenth Chapter), this verse was very dear to Dr Singh and I quote it here in gratitude to my revered guru:

यत्र योगेश्वरः कृष्णो यत्र पार्थो धनुर्धरः।
तत्र श्रीर्विजयो भूतिर्ध्रुवा नीतिर्मतिर्मम

(Wherever is Krishna, the Lord of Yoga; wherever is Arjuna, the wielder of the bow; prosperity, victory, happiness are imminent; such is the conviction.)

'LEADERSHIP IS THE CAPACITY TO TRANSLATE VISION INTO REALITY' (WARREN BENNIS)

Reeta Raina, Associate Professor at FORE School of Management, New Delhi

The above quote aptly sums up the persona of Padma Shri Dr Singh who stood tall amongst other luminaries in the academic world. When I was approached to make my contribution towards this book, I felt deeply honoured, yet more than a little apprehensive of whether I have the bonafides and the stature to write about the larger-than-life personality that he had become within his lifetime. Nevertheless, I felt this would be a great way of paying my tribute to the mentor and guide that he had been for me ever since I shifted base to Gurgaon.

It was December 2006 when I first met Dr Singh in his office at MDI to be interviewed for a faculty position in the Communications domain. Dr Singh was then at the helm of affairs and in the course of my many visits to MDI campus then, what struck me most as an outsider, was the distinct architecture of the institute and the intellectually stimulating atmosphere which could be felt in every corner of the beautiful, green campus. During these visits I would often get an opportunity to engage in conversations with faculty, students or staff visiting the library. During my interactions with them, I felt that each one of them was excited, charged up and working in tandem with the lofty vision and mission of MDI, 'Be the Thought Leaders and Change Masters' and 'Value-based Education & Best Global Practices', which their visionary leader had set for them. Well, every institution starts with a lofty vision and mission story but more often than not, I have seen that these visions and missions end up as mere rhetoric, empty words that are reduced to just serve the purpose of decorating institutional walls.

Here, at MDI, the story was different; I observed that their leader Dr Singh—was not only subsumed and passionate about translating this vision and mission into reality but he would never fail to applaud innovation as also motivate and drive his team to share that passion and dedication towards realization of the dream. The stamp of this missionary leader becomes apparent as soon as you set foot into MDI campus. I noticed how the faculty kept itself updated about the new paradigm shifts happening in the business world—innovation, business practices, skill-sets or leadership—while interacting with industry leaders, practitioners or partners from their collaborating international business schools.

One of my colleagues, while I was still new at MDI, once shared with me that albeit Dr Singh was a generous boss who would ensure that his faculty was well taken care of, their demands and their needs are met generously, but at the same time he expected high standards of performance and commitment from them. He expected them to share the same passion for excellence so that, together as a team, they would be able to translate their vision and mission into visible symbols of excellence. It was stressed upon the faculty that they were to prepare and train students not as managers but as future leaders with a global mindset, rooted in their tradition and culture.

By the time I had joined MDI as a faculty member there already had occurred a change of leadership and I unfortunately did not get the opportunity to work directly under him.

Nevertheless, as is wont in such cases of people of high stature, while there were people who were very critical of his style of functioning, there were others who simply could not reconcile to the fact that he was no longer heading the institute. The latter section of people outnumbered his critics and I found even his detractors, though grudgingly, would acknowledge that he was an exceptional institution builder. Their only complaint was that he would mostly, not comply with the laid-out systems. Maybe they had a valid point. However, personally speaking, I believe that systems also choke one's initiatives. Systems are important but at the same time they can become roadblocks in the development and growth of an institution. Dr Singh, who has been in the forefront in the field of management education in India and already had by then many achievements to his credit, could not have possibly been able to achieve as much had he been bogged down by the so-called rules and regulations. I think it demands courage, conviction and pioneering instincts in a leader to sidestep systems in order to aim at bigger goals in the quest for institutional excellence. Obviously, Dr Singh was not the one who for the sake of compliance would have settled for a spinney when there were lush forests to aim at. He could not be a 'pawn' when he was meant to be the 'king'.

Nothing small or average worked for, or was acceptable, to Dr Singh; it had to be big and exalted. I vividly remember after having been selected in MDI I once escalated to Dr Singh that

I had not got the second increment I was promised; prompt came his reply, 'Reeta Ji, you will certainly get what is promised to you, these are small issues, come to me for bigger things, bigger ideas or bigger projects.' I felt rather small when I realized the level at which Dr Singh was thinking—big people obviously think big, it was a lesson learnt. Here, I am reminded of that beautiful quote by Israelmore Ayivor: 'If your thoughts are as tall as the height of your ceiling, you can't fly above your room.'

Another admirable and noble facet of Dr Singh as a leader is that he did not subscribe to the philosophy of creating followers, to the contrary, he believed in creating leaders. He inspired and empowered his people to dream big and work hard to expand their capacity to take up leadership roles in future. Today, many of his protégés are successfully heading leading institutions in India and while others occupy eminent, senior positions in various institutions. This could be attributed to Dr Singh, unlike many leaders, never fearing the competition from his high achieving performers. He would rather take pride in the accomplishments of those he helped along the way. He belonged to that class of true teachers who 'use themselves as bridges over which they invite their students to cross; then, having facilitated their crossing, joyfully collapse, encouraging them to create bridges of their own.'

Dr Singh was a man who dared to dream big and visualize what he could achieve on an audacious scale, without allowing anything to circumscribe or limit his thinking. It indeed is not an exaggeration when people label him—the Man with the Midas Touch.

REMEMBERING DR PRITAM SINGH

Jyotsna Bhatnagar, Professor, Human Resource Management, MDI Gurgaon

It was a cold February morning in 2004 when my phone rang, I did not recognize the number. I answered and heard a voice addressing me as 'Ma'am', and then went on to introduce himself as Dr Singh, Director, MDI. What followed was a most unusual interview and induction process. Meetings with senior professors, discussing my thesis, then a research seminar I was invited to attend, and finally a faculty retreat. All this before I actually joined MDI's faculty in 2004.

Academics Are Kings and Queens

I was welcomed with warmth into a personalized office space. Later, in the tea lounge at MDI, Dr Singh welcomed the few of us who had joined the institute and he said, 'all my professors are kings and queens.' He gave us the freedom to choose our domains of expertise. We were not rushed into teaching or training or research but given a couple of months to settle down. We were all nested in the Scholars building, with the statue of Swami Vivekananda in front of the library, reminding us to 'stop not till the goal is achieved'. The message was clear, you are here to teach and learn and grow as scholars!

Action Paced Visionary Approach

In 2006, MDI was the knowledge partner for the NHRDN Conference. I was involved right from planning each session, to inviting research papers for the book, *Future of work-Mastering Change*. At that stage, I learnt micro detailing from Dr Singh and Dr Bhandarker. When it came to the book, I was given full freedom to invite research papers based on the theme of the book, from scholars around the world. We had received a humongous response. This was my first book experience and Dr Singh was able to sense my nervousness. One evening after work during a team meeting, Dr Singh said, 'Weaving each chapter of the book is like stringing pearls into a beautiful necklace. Now you go weave your version.' I liked his soft, but firm approach, and burnt the midnight oil, as it were, to bring the book to life. On the first day of the conference, Dr Singh invited Dr Udai Pareek to inaugurate the book, and as a surprise, told me to present the book to Dr Udai Pareek to unveil for the conference. What an astounding moment that was! In just that instant Dr Singh built a path for the young scholar I was.

As a Teacher-Leader, Know the Unknown

We were often invited to attend training sessions in MDI Gurgaon in our early days. We attended Dr Singh's sessions. His sessions would always stand apart. He would enthral senior bankers and senior leaders from the public sector with his wisdom and his analyses. He would never tower over us in a class, but would sit in the middle, among the participants and discuss the challenges. We would work on projects late at night with the participants and be back again at half past eight in the morning for a cup of tea with the participants. I had never experienced such an immersive approach. He was very kind and inclusive and he built us juniors up in his team, never intimidating nor displaying his greater knowledge, and always inviting us like a father figure into a class, reassuring us in our hesitancy and instructing us to observe. I remember how he propelled the participants with his experience and his stories. He would also enthral with stories of Chanakya and Mahabharata, drawing on everyday wisdom from these parables, reciting shlokas from his memory and linking the Indian scriptures to leadership lessons.

A Genuinely Warm Human Being

I remember a day, on our way to a class, we passed a staff member who was walking slowly. Dr Singh immediately stopped and enquired about his family and then about his health. The gentleman looked down and his eyes were filled with tears and thanked him for enquiring. Dr Singh told him that if he needed any help, to let us know, and that we would support him. We were amazed at this simple humane interaction with the staff. He knew the entire faculty and staff—their challenges and issues and remembered in his own authentic way to enquire. He just reflected the humble, down to earth person that he was.

THE TEACHER OF A LIFETIME

Arun K. Rath, Professor, IMI and former Secretary, Government of India

I knew Dr Singh for nearly two decades. Our first meeting was in the year 2000 in an international conference at Ashoka Hotel Bengaluru. I was the Joint Secretary in the Department of Public Enterprises, Government of India in New Delhi. At the conference, I made my presentation and came down from the dais to be greeted warmly by Dr Singh with his benign smile. I had not met him before, but was immediately struck by his pleasant personality exuding warmth and affection. He introduced himself and appreciated my talk given I was someone without formal association with a business school. I shared that it was all self-study on the subject, with an urge to learn more. Dr Singh invited me to MDI, Gurgaon where he was the Director, to share my experiences in the classroom with students and management trainees. I was impressed with his unique capacity to strike an instant rapport with a stranger in whom he could perceive some talent.

Many who know Dr Singh know of his generous praise and happiness to see people succeed and rise. His mission was to motivate people to grow to full capacity! Like a Guru!

Soon he invited me to speak to top corporate executives on the subject of corporate governance in MDI, where my presentation was very well received. Thus, began my initiation into the field of management. I was invited several times to give lectures and talks not only in MDI, but also in other fora. Dr Singh would organize events for training and capacity building of manpower from different levels, both in public and private sectors. Often, he would invite me to join. He inducted me as a Visiting Faculty of MDI Gurgaon. Soon after, Dr Singh suggested that I do my PhD in management. I said I would pursue a doctorate if he agreed to be my guide, and he readily agreed. I was elated—I had never thought of doing a PhD nor knew how to proceed and why. He asked me to choose my topic; I selected the topic of Contribution of Independent Directors in the Boardroom in 2004, which was promptly approved by Dr Singh. It was unique to work for a doctorate on your own subject of work under the supervision of a renowned professor like Dr Singh!

Initially, I thought it would be easy for me to do the doctorate with such an affectionate guide. Little did I know that Dr Singh would not be soft in the matter of quality! We had originally planned for responses from 50 Chairmen, Executive Directors, Government Directors, Independent Directors and Company Secretaries of blue-chip companies of the country to collect primary data for my research and analysis. It was an impossible task to get handwritten confidential responses to a 12-page questionnaire from some of the busiest corporate executives of the country. Soon, I realized my folly of selecting a topic and methodology of such nature. With great difficulty, I collected the required number of 50 responses. When I discussed this with Dr Singh, he was very happy but he told me in his characteristic manner, 'Sir, you are not doing research for a doctorate degree! If the name of a person like you is to be associated with any work it must be the best ever. It would be a great experience to work with you on such pioneering and reliable research work. So, could I get 100 responses in place of 50, which would lead to a unique and exemplary research work?' I almost gave it up as an impossible task. But the guru did not give up. He pursued, visited me and made me continue the work. It took me about two years more to collect the data. When Dr Singh saw the result, he was very happy, like my success was his own.

I superannuated from the IAS as Secretary Ministry of HRD in the month of January 2009. Like many members of the IAS, I was planning to join up an assignment under the Government of India. But Dr Singh thought otherwise! He invited me to join academics; I received an offer from MDI Gurgaon to join as Professor of Public Policy and Chairman, School of Public Policy and Governance in MDI Gurgaon. I was happy to receive the invitation, but was not sure if I should accept. Dr Singh rang up and convinced me that I can set up a world class School of Public Policy in MDI. There was really no looking back. I decided to join MDI. I have very fond memories of my association with Dr Singh in MDI Gurgaon.

Often, we had lunch in the faculty dining hall and walked back to the faculty building. We had ample time to chat on the way. I remember one such chat: Dr Singh asked me to define a great man. In response, I requested him to give his definition. He gave a simple and profound definition—if you meet a man and he makes you feel great, then he is a great man, if he makes you feel small, then he is a small man. I am yet to get a better definition! Indeed, he was a great man himself. He would always make you feel great!

Dr Singh left MDI to join as Director General of IMI New Delhi. Soon, he invited me to join. I joined in 2012 and had the joy of working with him for nearly three more years.

Dr Singh was a great leader and an institution builder par excellence. He transformed IMI, New Delhi to a world class B school just within three years. He overcame all hurdles including funds and statutory clearances with speed and decisiveness. He would invite me to visit many government offices to expedite the clearances. I have never seen a person who would implement a project with so much commitment and zeal. IMI New Delhi owes its present stature as a global B school in large part to Dr Singh.

Dr Singh was a master of management development programs. In fact, MDI Gurgaon was shaped by him as a global hub for MDPs. Inspired by him, I conducted many specialized MDPs in MDI which were highly successful in terms of the attendance and ratings. Dr Singh asked me to take up pioneering MDPs in IMI New Delhi. I proposed a training program for CEOs, Directors and Independent Directors of leading companies, provided he joined and supported me in view of the high-profile groups who came to be trained. He readily agreed and we conducted three highly successful Directors' Conclaves with more than 40 CEOs and Directors of blue-chip companies across India. Soon after the third Directors' Conclave, Dr Singh left IMI, at the end of his tenure. That was the end of the conclaves.

During the three Directors' Conclaves, he would stay for all the three days at each of the three venues. He not only participated in all the events, but also interacted with each participant, with the same respect. During the first conclave one civil servant who had joined the program as an Independent Director, was unnecessarily impolite to Dr Singh. The incident upset me and I wanted to fight back but Dr Singh was unruffled. With his characteristic benign smile, he patted me on my back to cool down and handled the ill-behaved participant. I was amazed to see his cool disposition in the face of provocation. He spoke to the hot-headed participant with respect and the fellow was a different person! He apologized profusely and became a fan of Dr Singh.

I organized a mega MDP on the MOU system for senior executives of central public sector enterprises in the United Service Institute of India, New Delhi. Dr Singh meticulously helped me in planning for the program including preparation of the brochure but had to leave for Europe for a few weeks and was to return a day after the program started. However, I was pleasantly surprised by Dr Singh present at the venue half an hour before the start of the program to boost my morale. Later, I learned that Dr Singh had cut short his foreign trip and returned to keep his commitment to join my program. One can always depend on a kind and supportive leader like Dr Singh!

Dr Singh wanted to introduce a pioneering MDP on Risk Management in IMI New Delhi. When he realized that nobody he had initially entrusted would take the risk of pioneering a training program on Risk Management, he looked at me and said, 'Sir, now you have to take the lead.' I almost fell off my chair and told him that it was not my domain of expertise. He replied calmly, 'Sir you can do it by combining risk management with corporate governance. The two subjects are correlated.' That was brilliant motivation from the guru of management! I had no alternative but to say yes. Thus, began my MDP on Corporate Governance & Risk Management. After I floated the ambitious program, I told him that I have taken a chance that may backfire; he smiled and said that he would share the blame with me if the program did not get sufficient nominations from companies. The first program, however, was a resounding success with 44 paid nominations, while the second one in IMI Bhubaneswar received 48 nominations. Dr Singh was a great judge of a person's potential and placed all his trust and confidence in them once he was convinced, supporting all efforts to the hilt.

Dr Singh was a true friend, philosopher and guide to me for the last 20 years. Like a guru, he recognised my capabilities better than I could and would always guide me on the path to success. He was ever willing to help, support and inspire. I wish he had stayed with us longer to motivate and guide us in our lives ahead. I pray to God Almighty for peace to his noble soul.

KRISHNA MY FRIEND, PHILOSOPHER AND GUIDE

Subir Verma, Director, Nirma Institute of Management

I don't know what made Dr Devi Singh, the then Director at MDI Gurgaon, send me to escort Dr Singh from the hotel in Delhi to MDI for his felicitation on the award of Padma Shri in 2004. The 18-km car ride with him was an unforgettable journey. I was in complete thrall of the man and his persona. He had a presence that went beyond his handsome looks, elegant dress sense and generous laugh. It was the eyes. They were gentle, warm, smiling and knowing. He was aware of himself and the impact he was creating. By the time the ride was over, he had gently walked me through my professional journey, my personal life, my idea of MDI Gurgaon and my take on the current situation. That was the beginning of an unforgettable and very fulfilling association of 15 plus years—an association I began as his junior colleague and culminated in becoming his co-author in his last book on Corporate Governance.

The news about Dr Singh's return to MDI as its Director in 2004 was met with tremendous enthusiasm, optimism and hope among the faculty and staff of MDI. There were colleagues who had worked with him in his earlier stint, and they had stories to tell about his awe-inspiring network with the corporates, his ability to swing MDP and consulting contracts and above all his concern and care for the faculty. Folklore abounded. Today, I can only say that these stories do only modest justice to the man who was instrumental in transforming MDI Gurgaon and IMI New Delhi. In fact, for me Dr Singh was a lesson in leadership, and I had probably one of the best seats for learning.

The first lesson for me was his unwavering orientation towards transforming the institute amongst the top management institutes of the country. When he returned as the Director, MDI, it was a good institution; but not great. If placements were the benchmark, then it was rated right after FMS and IMT and was marginally ahead of IMI. It was all about purpose. A purpose that flowed from the big dream. Jim Collins and Porass called it BHAG. Dr Singh would say it is a Himalayan dream that leads to a Himalayan contribution. It was this that made him passionately committed to outcomes. Of primeval concern was the ranking of the institute. This required making students and the corporates the centre of the institute's universe. Customer centricity meant commitment to the students and the corporates and therefore the need to mobilize the levers of corporate relations, placements, industry-relevant academic programs, and rigorous program delivery and training and development programs for the corporates. This was his architecture for institutional greatness. As the Faculty Coordinator of Placements at MDI, I experienced his commitment to outcomes. Dr Singh told the placement committee to make a presentation on our placement strategy. The meeting was an eye opener. We were swamped with questions, which we had never before encountered: the ABC list of companies, our contacts both at the gatekeeper as well as decision making levels and our strategy to convert them. Questions were asked about our brochure and CD and our placement pitch. We were queried about our corporate connect activities and how closely we knew our recruiters and our summer and final placement dates. More importantly Dr Singh wanted to learn about the expectations of the batch and more. In fact, till the time Dr Singh came in, these criteria were not part of our mental model. He enquired about our existing resources and what our future requirement was; about any challenges we were facing and the office we were operating from, and what kind of support we required to succeed. At the time, the placement office was located behind the academic block, at the notch in the basement neighbouring the coffee vendor. We had a rusty and noisy air cooler during summers, a heater in the winter, one dedicated phone line, a fixed budget and for every little event, like scheduling a corporate visit, a long winding process. And then in a matter of days, we were out of the hovel and situated in the largest office on the ground floor of the academic block with a dedicated placement officer, two domestic lines and access for international calls in his office. Instead of giving us a budget, he told us to create our budget, given our placement calendar.

He converted placements into an outcome of good and strong corporate relationships. He demanded that all letters and greetings that went out on his behalf be signed personally by him. We would leave bundles of 400–500 letters and cards that he signed with utmost alacrity. The message passed on to us was: build relationships, develop personal rapport and connect frequently. Placement visits by faculty members to corporate houses, creating and fostering relationships became a recognized and significant institutional activity. The investment in relationships saw a substantive return in terms of placements, corporate visit to the campus, training and consulting assignments. He made all the right investments including sending me to Singapore, Dubai, Australia and when I dithered, he argued that he had no expectations that companies would arrive in droves to recruit students from MDI. So long as I succeeded in creating a relationship, I was doing good. That, for him, was progress in the right direction. He believed that investing in people and investing in relationships, some day you will harvest the results. MDI harvested! Companies came from Australia, UAE and Singapore to hire from MDI. Our cup was overflowing. This was the beginning of what I called his most significant contribution to the notion of Great Management Institutes: co-partnership with corporates and the government. His was not the mind of an academician alone; it was also the mind of a CEO of a business organization. During his tenure, MDI became the place where the principles of modern management were being practiced in their most evolved form.

In fact, it was not that all the faculty members at MDI were easily sold on Dr Singh's thoughts. There were a handful of faculty members who protested that the purpose of an education institution was to teach and not place students. For them, placements ran secondary and were a follow up to academics. It required some enlightenment from Dr Singh to help these faculty banish their conventional approach. There were three watershed moments in making corporate relations and placements a critical pillar in MDI's push towards transformation and the next orbit.

The first was when the then Chair, PGP raised an objection to the rescheduling of first year examinations that would enable the batch to place the second-year students. In MDI, the norm was that the entire first year batch would help in placing the graduating batch. Since we had planned the final placements to be completed in three days (including the proverbial Day Zero), it meant that classes would be suspended on the said three days. The then PGP Chair strongly refused to do so. Subsequently in the meeting set up to break the deadlock, as the Placement Coordinator, I was told, in no uncertain terms, that academics were a priority and classes would not be suspended or rescheduled. In case the placement coordinator went along with the scheduled dates, the administrative staff would take on all the responsibilities that were earlier earmarked for the students. During the meeting, the Director was in consensus with the Chair, PGP's argument. After the meeting, I felt like a miserable loser before my placement committee members, and dreadfully anxious about the capabilities of the clueless administrative staff, to pull off the placements with the finesse of the students—students who had been selected and trained by the senior placement team to conduct the placements.

After the meeting, I was preparing to take my first year PGDM class. All of a sudden, the pantry in-charge in the academic block rushed in to tell me that the Director was on the phone line in the pantry, asking to speak with me. I was anxious and miserable expecting to get an earful from the Director. Instead, Dr Singh began by asking me as to how I was feeling. I told him that I am down in the dumps. He then asked me what would happen if the placement dates were moved out. I told him that we would lose the recruiting companies to our competitors and also suffer a huge loss of face, as the companies were already informed that they will be the first on the MDI campus. Finally, he asked me if the dates remained the same and the classes were suspended, how confident was I of placing the entire batch? I replied, 'a 100% placement!' He then told me to go ahead to confirm the recruitment dates with the companies. The classes will be deferred. Even though the PGP Chair felt slighted, the placements got a leg up. We were able to place the entire batch as promised and the quality of placements went up by several notches and MDI was counted as the best B-School in Delhi-NCR. I passed Dr Singh's test. Now, I was anointed as one of his Generals. This was another lesson in leadership for me. Great leaders are those who believe in teamwork and people power. I got a lesson in the management jargon of empowerment, responsibility, trust and good faith.

The second thrust came next year (2006) when MDI was able to place the entire batch in just six hours, on the very first day of Final Placements. 'Gone in Six hours' was the headline in the Times of India newspaper. Soon after, MDI was able to pip IIM-L and became the third ranked institute in the Outlook-Cosmode B-School survey. Year 2006 was a landmark one. There could not have been a more telling story of MDI's transformation under the inspirational leadership of Dr Singh. I think the quality of placements went up significantly because he instilled in the students' supreme confidence in their abilities with an optimism about desired placements. He took time to address the students, communicating to them the importance of preparation, understanding the context of their job and the need to display a positive attitude, and resilience in the face of failure. More telling was his arousing in the students the warrior spirit: Gurgaon is the land of Guru Dronacharya. This is the place where he trained the Pandavas. And when students asked him where the Kauravas trained, he said it was in the competitor school. This one telling comment showed his remarkable faith in the excellence of his faculty, the rigor of the academic program and the students' proficiencies. More importantly, he transformed each student into a warrior ready to ace the talent combat. The students of MDI were more than ready. The placements that year proved it.

The third thrust came in 2007. In this year the first batch of PGPM-HR students came up for placements. Day Zero saw only one HR student getting placed. At the end of the day, the students retired to the hostel, absolutely demoralized and tired. The moment Dr Singh got to know about the debacle on Day Zero, he called up the HR heads of few legendary companies in India requesting them to take a look at the students. I remembered his famous words to them, 'Do not hire Institutes; Hire Talent.' Then he called a meeting with the students and gave an inspiring talk. At the end of his address, each student had a spring in their step and looked forward to the next day. The next day was epochal in the annals of MDI as big-ticket companies came in waves to hire students from HR as well as from the General Management stream. The last student in HR had three job offers in hand. The placements were completed on the second day itself. A complete turnaround was scripted by Dr Singh, with his magic wand. The impossible had happened. That day, the entire MDI fraternity celebrated.

In the mindscape of this great leader, corporate placements were only one pillar. Another pillar in his grand vision was accreditation. MDI had sent its application for the AMDISA-SAQs accreditation. Very fortunately, Dr Singh gave the responsibility of preparing the Self-Assessment Report and coordinating the visit of the Peer Review Team (PRT) to me. What was remarkable was his eye for detail. He knew everything about what was in the Self-Assessment Report and even though MDI was presumably the first institution to go for international accreditation, he knew the exact steps in the process. To ensure all faculty members had the same understanding of MDI's vision, ownership and commitment to it, he had organized a vision building workshop conducted by the legendary doyen of Indian Management, Dr Dharni Sinha. And when the PRT visited the institute, the story of MDI was so beautifully and persuasively articulated. It was not surprising that MDI received the AMDISA-SAQs accreditation as well as the AMBA accreditation under his leadership. His amazing quality to visualize, inspire, mentor, express and lead stood out more starkly when, despite the presence of every component required for EQUIS accreditation, MDI failed to be awarded. It is the greatest 'if' in the history of MDI when his absence at the helm was so sorely missed and had such disastrous penalties.

His perennial optimism and faith in goodness of human beings, undying commitment to the institution, his courage of conviction and his strength to pick up cudgels against untruth and unfairness has been for me the most remarkable image of his personality. 'The Just gives punishment, even to his own', and so, whenever anybody crossed the line of honesty, ethics and justice he would take up the matter and make it his own. I have seen him do this several times even with those who were closest to him. This was a great learning for me.

There is no leadership without followership. This adage is true about Dr Singh. His transformation of his subordinates into his associates and then his followers was almost seamless. The realization that I was not just an associate but a follower happened for me rather magically. It was not just about his formal position. In my 17 years of association with him, he was Director for just four years. For 13 years, I like some others who associated themselves with him, his leadership was inspirational, moralizing and ennobling. He elevated all of us. The loyalty was to his ideals, his beliefs and his commitment. He never looked upon his team as his subordinates. Everybody was a peer and a subject of his venerable introduction. He remembered the smallest achievement of each one—the most unforgettable vignette in their life, the most insignificant happening in their family. He gave everybody a name, an identity and a dignity. He was a prophet who sought glory in the success of his institution and derived happiness in its purest and pristine form in the achievements of his followers.

A SOULFUL LEADER

C. N. Narayana, Senior Professor and Director Pune Business School, Pune

Exceptional leaders can go beyond role models, mentors, coaches; transcending to the level of touching the souls of those whom they meet. Dr Singh is the rare leader who created that kind of aura in my life.

My journey with Dr Singh began when I joined IMI as the Registrar and Professor and he was appointed as the Director General of IMI in 2011. As I got to know his credentials—his contributions to Administrative Staff College Hyderabad, IIM Bangalore, IIM-L and MDI Gurgaon—I realized just why he was referred to as the academic leader with a magical touch in transforming every institution he had been associated with.

As the registrar of IMI, I don't remember a single day not talking to him, even if he was travelling on official purpose. We normally spoke every evening, discussing matters about various institution building activities for IMI. As Director General, he was responsible for developing and growing all the three institutes—IMI New Delhi, IMI Bhubaneswar and IMI Kolkata.

I would describe Dr Singh as a leader free from fear, ambition, and greed. He was focused on reaching the vision for the team and the organization and worked tirelessly like the calm waves of a settled deep blue sea. Dr Singh had one ambition—building IMI to greater heights in terms of brand, self-sufficiency and sustainability. The focus, therefore, was on the four engines of growth for a management school—teaching, research, MDP and industry connect.

Being located in South Delhi, IMI New Delhi had lots of restrictions in terms of vertical expansion. The growth of this institution has been affected because of the lack of physical infrastructure to support growth in activities. No previous Director had fathomed going vertical. The first meeting with the architects of the existing buildings indicated that it was going to be a difficult task as the Municipal Corporation of Delhi (MCD) and Delhi Development Authority (DDA) would refuse to give permission as it was a 'fly' zone for aircraft and that we could not go beyond six floors. Dr Singh decided to take a second opinion by inviting another architectural firm and we quickly started working on the plans, while simultaneously chasing nearly seven different government authorities for various permissions.

Dr Singh said, 'We need to get this thing done CNN and you are capable of making history for IMI. You have my full support in every single thing you decide to do, to connect with concerned authorities. You need to focus like the Mahabharata character, Arjuna.' Amazingly enough, he himself came along with me many times to meet the DDA, MCD and Architecture Committees, tirelessly putting our case to the top-most authority of every such regulatory authority that mattered. Motivated by Dr Singh, together, the team worked to make it a reality.

MDP at IMI grew in geometric progression, while enrolment numbers in the long-term programs more than doubled; new PGDM courses in Banking and Finance were added. Suddenly, IMI New Delhi climbed several rungs of the business school rankings based on the criteria of teaching, admission quality, research output and MDPs. Dr Singh's dream was making the business school global. He brought in resources from various reputed institutions and started preparing for the toughest international accreditation—the AMBA. The formation and nurturing of the academic and research team resulted in achieving the milestone of success to IMI being the first business school to get a five-year accreditation by AMBA. IMI was also the first institution to achieve the feat of triple accreditation namely, NBA, SAQS and AMBA.

Dr Singh inculcated the research culture in IMI by introducing a point system for research outputs. He was instrumental in introducing a very successful Fellow Program in Management (which is equivalent to University PhD) and is recognized by AICTE. I refer to this as the golden period for IMI. Today, the three eight-storey towers at IMI New Delhi campus and the 22-acre lush green campus of IMI Bhubaneswar stand for the magic created by a humble leader.

Dr Singh's informal way of teaching, guiding and mentoring transformed people for life, not just for one's career alone. Despite all my experience, I learnt a lot from him in the nearly four years of association, and this took my career to newer heights.

Dr Singh was more a facilitator for people around him to grow. He had a meticulous eye for detail and surrounded himself with like-minded people to follow his lead. This was clearly a driving force in IMI's success story.

He always encouraged people to listen to all the stakeholders carefully before responding. He gave freedom to Deans and Area chairs, apart from the Registrar, in taking decisions in the interest of the institute. He built teams and capability instead of creating silos in the system. He ensured that all decisions were taken in consultation with all the stakeholders. His leadership also reflected more of a personal touch rather than a system where one person commands and others merely follow. He recognized and valued everyone's opinions. Unlike most others, he would consider and implement good ideas, irrespective of the position and cadre of the individual who suggested it, in the larger interest of the institute.

His command over details from Hindu epics, to Chinese stories, and classics always astounded me. He even delivered impromptu speeches with such ease that I always wondered how he was able to remember so much. Every single mantra he gave to management was Chanakya Nithi. He would tell me, 'CNN, sometimes we need to go through the grind of stress for a selfless cause of institutional interest. We need to sacrifice our personal comforts, sometimes listen to people who you know are not right—it will build resilience in you to become a great leader in the long run. People may make mountains out of your mistakes, but in the end, truth will survive. IMI will always remember and recollect the contributions you made.'

Dr Singh led the team by example and established trust with candour and transparency. He travelled beyond sceptics to create curiosity in us to perform better and faster. He ensured not only seeing a vision but living and breathing it every single day. He also had the courage to take some unpopular decisions sometimes in the best interest of the institute. Most importantly, he ensured that the community celebrated every small success, which was crucial in aiming for and achieving a bigger goal. He always created a winning team rather than just building a team. His inspiration, aura, and fiercely positive and persevering personality will light the way for all the leaders who follow in his footsteps. Like a good leader, he let you explore your way through the challenges that the work presented, even allowing you to make your own mistakes, and he was always nearby to ensure you had someone to count on when you needed motivation.

I am indebted to him for having been my mentor. One thing he said will always stay with me, 'Contribute as much as you can to the organization you are associated with.'

A CHAMPION OF CHANGE

Anand Prakash, Professor and Head of Psychology Department, University of Delhi

When asked to write about Padma Shri Dr Singh, I realized that it was not an easy task to capture the shades of his work and personality. Being former Director of IIM-L and MDI Gurgaon he had created a niche for himself in the field of management studies and professional sphere in the context of the developing world. I first met him when he was Director General of IMI New Delhi. I had heard a lot about the charisma of his personality from a variety of sources. His recent books including *In Search of Change Maestros* (with Dr Asha Bhandarker), *The Leadership Odyssey: From Darkness to Light* (with Dr Asha Bhandarker and Dr Snigdha Rai), *Millennials and the Workplace: Challenges for Architecting the Organization of Tomorrow* (with Dr Asha Bhandarker and Dr Sumita Rai), all provided glimpses of his creative acumen as a scholar par excellence to me. Known as a management guru and leader of management education in the country, Dr Singh left an indelible mark with visible milestones on the landscape of management education in the country. I found him a person with the rare quality of integrating contemporary knowledge with ancient wisdom. He always impressed by leveraging appropriate quotes from the Bhagavad Gita and the latest writings and analysis from articles published in academic journals like the Harvard Business Review. The integrative approach of synthesizing ancient wisdom with modern management practices is a unique distinction that created a great deal of attraction and appeal toward him as an academician.

It's bewildering that a person who got his first job at the Reserve Bank of India (RBI) moved to the domain of education. As a psychologist I was curious to understand his making as a professional, and more as a person. His early socialization experiences must have indoctrinated the values and preferences that helped him blossom later in life. Quite a traveller, literally and metaphorically, from BHU to the most prestigious institution in Hyderabad, the Administrative Staff College of India, Hyderabad, a premier institution for training industry leaders and bureaucracy personnel. His subsequent moves attest to his capabilities as a true institution builder and champion of negotiating the difficult turns of an institutional journey. They figure as a few of his strengths that are worth reflection.

I have read Dr Singh's work on leadership with interest and was quite influenced particularly, by his notion of toxic leadership and its dimensions. His observations and conclusions with data, both qualitative and quantitative, were extremely fascinating. The researcher in him was driven more by the passion of creating a research driven solution and that was his uniqueness. A much sought-after management guru on the Indian landscape, Dr Singh had the rare distinction of bringing ideas, thoughts and strategies of implementation onto the same page, clear evidence of a unique holistic thinker. More often than not, he was a strong believer in setting high standards for the teams and presenting those standards in a manner that appeared doable. Following the golden rule of reciprocity in human interactions, he took along people, and demonstrated how one could solve problems in life and avoid being exploited by those who use reciprocity against you. He was a strong believer in the adage, 'if you know what your mind is up to, and why you so easily see the world through a distorting lens of good and bad, you can reduce your righteousness.' His shared perspective had always been that one should reduce the frequency of conflict with others who are equally convinced of their righteousness. I gathered all these precious experiences through numerous interactions that I had with Dr Singh.

His ability to manage a team of highly accomplished individuals was par excellence. Dr Singh's remarkable command over three languages, Hindi, English and Sanskrit gave him the necessary intellectual edge over others in harnessing the group synergy. The ease and effectiveness with which he quoted from the Bhagavad Gita, the relevant Sanskrit verses to drive a point home, was quite an experience.

I found Dr Singh to be a strong believer of data driven research and building understanding over the edifice of evidence for dealing with and understanding management issues in general, and human resource management in particular. While working with him on a book project, I realized several other dimensions of his genius. The genesis of this work began over reflections that HR professionals in our country have not been understood in the right and adequate perspective. There is a need to carry out a knowledge management process in a manner that helps readers know the biographical journey of celebrated and accomplished HR professionals of this country. The methodology agreed would remain qualitative and quantitative in a balanced way. Dr Singh proposed that the best methodology suited as far as this kind of work is concerned should be 'lived reality details'. We looked at each other's faces in bewilderment. 'Stories of people must be understood if professional nuances are to be understood,' he said. For me, as a psychology researcher, this felt like a breath of fresh air. Generally, the management world is full of numbers, statistics, graphs, intricate statistical jargon, and tables. This statement drove home the point that Dr Singh was well anchored in the traditional knowledge system and at the same time quite open to work with the latest trends and developments in the discipline. The famous phrase that life is what we deem it, and our lives are the creation of our mind is what I found in my interactions with him on numerous occasions. But these claims are not helpful unless augmented by a theory. The book entitled, *Odyssey of Leadership*, where he discussed 'toxic leadership' propounding that an understanding of negativity bias and effective style clearly drove home the point as to why change is so hard in organizations.

I found during my interactions with Dr Singh that he considered reciprocity an all-purpose relationship tonic. I saw on many occasions that his style of reciprocity rejuvenated social ties. He was a great champion of building social capital through reciprocity and genuine engagement with people. Dr Singh expressed genuine concern in an effortless' simplistic way. His cultivated reputation for being fair to all human transactions took him to several high-powered policy and decision-making bodies of national and international institutions.

During a discussion on bringing ethics and ethical discourse into the teaching learning process of Indian education, he mentioned that every culture is concerned about the moral development of its members, and we find texts that reveal its approach to morality and ethics. There is more than enough in our cultural repositories about virtues that should be cultivated, and many of those virtues were, and still are, valued not only in Indian ethos but also across cultures. He expressed his views that there is an urgent need to introduce a curriculum focusing on this aspect, across all the centres of higher learning in India. The courses must highlight practical strivings to inculcate virtues that would not only benefit the person who cultivates them but also the culture frame within which these are lived.

Dr Singh opined that the wisdom of the Bhagavad Gita, Buddhism and Confucius, are timeless and relevant even today for learning, pleasure and guidance. Aristotle used a similar metaphor, and it would not be out of place to quote it in the context of ethics and moral education. As 'men become builders by building houses and harpists by playing the harp. Similarly, we grow just by the practice of just actions, self-controlled by exercising our self-control, and courageous by performing acts of courage.' I have heard, on several occasions, Dr Singh asserting that 'you get what you demand.' He believed that virtues reside in a well-trained mind. A strong believer in training and education in all his pursuits in a career spanning more than five decades, he contended that ethics-related education must also impart tacit knowledge skills of social perception and social emotions so finely tuned that one automatically feels the right things in each situation, knows the right things to do, and then wants to do it.

Sharing my understanding about Dr Singh was a revelation of its own kind. I find him cognitively resourceful, emotionally balanced and behaviourally effective in most of his intellectual pursuits, like governance, institution building, research activity, consulting and interpersonal dealings.

A TRAVELOGUE: JOURNEY WITH THE INGENIOUS MASTER

Anu Singh Lather, Vice Chancellor, Dr. B. R. Ambedkar University, Delhi

'We must all have a purpose in life, human-kind lives with a purpose. In the Mahabharata, reflecting upon each and every character of the epic, and on this Karma Bhumi, Kurukshetra, where I stand today to address you all, I pay my respects to the great Karma Yogis. Kurukshetra is called Karma Bhumi since the battle of the Mahabharata gave a great purpose and lessons of life for generations to come. Does anyone know what happened to Arjun or his kingdom after the battle ended, because not a single line has been written about it, as the purpose was achieved.'

This was my introduction to the great Master, Dr Singh, in 1995 at Kurukshetra University, where he addressed a gathering of university teachers. Such was the wisdom of this great man who envisaged the purpose of life through the ethos derived from the great epic. His words continue to inspire me in my life's journey as a teacher and a human being.

As luck would have it, I moved to Delhi 20 years ago and had the opportunity to meet him again as a management professional in an HR Conclave that I organized. Afterward, our interactions were more frequent, with my active participation in various management professional bodies and fora. I got to hear him speak more often and he left a lasting impact on my ideas on teaching management. The wisdom he imparted became 'a song, a philosophy, a thought', that I applied to every discipline—social sciences, humanities or technical and professional education.

He was original, creative and ever ready with an action plan for corporate solutions. His corporate workshops pioneered a new era for multinational corporations.

'A teacher can never truly teach unless he is still learning himself. A lamp can never light another lamp unless it continues to burn its own flame.'

These words of Rabindranath Tagore apply well to Dr Singh—the quintessential believer in life-long learning. He truly advocated the precept that if education has to be meaningful for the larger society, it has to transcend the orbit of abstraction into the realm of practice. As the founder of a host of institutions of management, Dr Singh nurtured them as his own, with determination and trust in the possibilities of applied knowledge framework of teaching, learning and research in a country like India.

In the early 1990s when India embraced a new economic regime, the country clearly needed a massive expansion in the management education sector and very few people had the requisite experience, vision and more importantly the courage to think out of the box. In those watershed moments of transition, Dr Singh showed extraordinary imagination for alternative management pedagogy that stressed upon the best from both worlds—local as well as global.

Over the decades he generated a sizable pool of young leaders who went on to become the movers and shakers of the new corporate India in the 21st century. It would not be an exaggeration to say that he has been an institution in himself, portraying the best of public moral conduct while solidly entrenched in the vocation of teaching, research, and consultancy as a true professional.

One dare not pigeonhole his expertise into any specific knowledge domain. He had a vast depth of knowledge in history, politics, philosophy and religion. All this came from his hunger for knowledge and his child-like curiosity. His courage to venture into uncharted territory led to his unique theorizing on HR practices that blended the micro and the macro, global and local, economic and cultural, cognitive and experiential. This made Dr Singh a legend, and his journey a folklore among the management academic circles in India and abroad.

As Vice chancellor of Dr B. R. Ambedkar University, Delhi, I was asked to plan the design and layout of our two new campuses at Dheerpur and Rohini. I knew Dr Singh as the only one to aptly chair the jury for the selection of architect for this job—the flourishing campus of IIM-L with its grandeur and lush green spaces, his gift to the country, came to mind. He surprised the jury members with his creative insights for designing a futuristic campus for Ambedkar University. Ambedkar University will be ever thankful to him for his time, vision and insight.

His brilliance lay in taking the ordinary and creating something extraordinary out of it. The innumerable people whose lives he touched, moulded and shaped, epitomizes a classic example of a teacher-cum-mentor.

In writing this tribute to this legendary man, I am reminded of his presence everywhere in the country. Dr Singh worked on the edifice of the higher education system in our country and shaped higher education institutions into humane institutions. He emphasized metaphorization as an effective organizational strategy, in which the organization needs to transform itself completely for survival and growth. The change must be induced from within, to enable the organization to command the change process.

MEMORIES WITH DR SINGH

D. P. Singh, Chairman, University Grants Commission

I have known Dr Singh for a very long time. I had the opportunity to interact with him closely on a number of occasions during my tenure as Vice-Chancellor, Banaras Hindu University (BHU), as Dr Singh was one of the illustrious alumni of BHU. Recently, as Chairman, University Grants Commission (UGC), I had been collaborating with him on creating world class institutions. True to his reputation I found him to be visionary, dynamic, awe inspiring and yet humble and genuine.

He mentored innumerable entrepreneurs and top executives for global business and corporate houses, and also served on the boards of a large number of companies. Similarly, his contributions in shaping government policies pertaining to higher education in general and management education in particular, deserve special mention. He was a member of the Prime Minister's Empowered Expert Committee, constituted for the selection of Institutions of Eminence in India, where he played a pivotal role.

Dr Singh was truly a thought leader, a legendary personality. Till his last breath, he remained active and contributed to the growth and development of this great nation. He has left behind a legacy, which not only ought to be preserved but expanded—a tall order for us all.

THE LIVING LEGEND

Nupur Prakash, Professor, University School of ICT, GGS Indraprastha University, Delhi

As I pen down my thoughts and experiences for the Festschrift of our beloved Dr Singh, my mind is filled with many cherished memories I made during my association with him. I met Dr Singh when he was appointed the Chairman, Board of Management of the University, to which I was the founder Vice Chancellor. It was way back in 2013, when I was nervously preparing to greet a towering personality—a highly acclaimed person, a Padma Shri awardee and a celebrity in management circuits—but to my delight, he came across as a soft-spoken person, with a comforting presence and a calm demeanour.

It couldn't have been a better start for a new university to be under the guidance and stewardship of a stalwart like Dr Singh. He was a quick decision-maker and a caring listener with tremendous humility and a positive disposition. His unique empowering style combined with a people centric approach made even my task much easier. At this point of time, Dr Singh mentored and guided me to provide value driven governance to the University with a well-defined vision and mission in place. He insisted on the branding and positioning of the university and encouraged me to strive for excellence.

During our frequent interactions, I observed that he always maintained a great connect with people around him and steered meetings without ruffling any feathers. His approach was always to build consensus in the most difficult decisions and help people arrive at a win-win solution. He enabled people to realize their full potential and achieve their desired goals in a collaborative manner. He was instrumental in helping me build a robust organizational culture with sensitivity and care towards its people.

He radiated positivity, hope, kindness and affection through his calming and soothing presence during any casual or formal interactions. While discussing various issues and pain-points related to the university with him, I experienced his intense concern for the well-being of the masses, especially people working at the bottom of the pyramid. I remember when the time arrived for the promotions to faculty members and staff in the newly formed university, he insisted that everyone should get their due in a timely manner.

One of Dr Singh's favourite quotes by Swami Vivekanand was, 'Thought without action has no meaning and action without thought is meaningless,' which enlightened many of us and paved the way to our success. His Vedic Indian wisdom inspired and propelled us to engage with people with both heart and head and gently nudge them towards constant growth and development of the organization.

Dr Singh was not only an institution builder, but he nurtured many institution builders like me with his value-driven guidance. He enabled me to achieve many important landmarks and propelled the university into a constant growth trajectory. He always focused on having a long-term vision for the organization without losing sight of the short-term goals for the betterment of all stakeholders.

During my tenure as Vice Chancellor, I would often come across difficult situations and a phone conversation with him provided unconditional support and strong backing to help me navigate through the dynamics of the organization by saying, '*Raj kaaj mein aisa hota rehta hai*' ('This happens in ruling the kingdom'). These words coming from him used to unburden me and helped me bounce back with renewed energy and enthusiasm. After my term as VC got over, he motivated me to move to the next orbit, define the purpose of my life and set new goals to serve mankind.

On a personal front too, I learnt a lot from him. The biggest learning came from his handling of personal grief after losing his son based in the USA. He sailed through the most difficult time of his life with immense grace and poise.

His book, *In Search of Change Maestros,* co-authored by Dr Asha Bhandarker, was one of the best gifts I received from him. The book reflects a magnificent understanding of what leads to building great Indian organizations.

Dr Singh was to the academic world, what Amitabh Bachchan is to the film world—A Living Legend. I pray to God that through his legacy he continues to touch the lives of many more people and help them realize their full potential, enabling them to achieve their aspirations and dreams for a better world around us.

A TRIP DOWN MEMORY LANE

Yogesh Singh, Vice Chancellor, Delhi Technological University

> 'Management is doing things right; leadership is doing the right thing.'
> —Peter Drucker

A true testament to what Dr Singh stands, an embodiment of progress and efficiency.

I had the pleasure of meeting Dr Singh for the first time in 2014. I was the Vice Chancellor of Maharaja Sayajirao

University (MSU) of Baroda, and Dr Singh was invited by the faculty of Management Studies to impart knowledge to the students. I was aware of his prominence in the field and was delighted when I was invited to a dinner that was organized for him at Surya Palace, Vadodara.

As I approached him to thank him for taking the time to come to MSU and guide the students, my first thought was, 'India needs many more Dr Singhs.' An educationalist and institution builder with such grace and people skills is rare. The Indian education system needs more progressive scholars like him, who are more than willing to voice their opinion for the betterment of the system. He has an intellectually enhanced mindset with one goal—evolution of the education system.

That meeting with him was impactful enough for me to seek his counsel and wisdom on numerous occasions. He is not only a well-wisher and a trusted mentor but also a wonderful being who saw the best in people.

He has done justice to both being an eminent leader as well as a management guru. His experience in shaping institutions to not only be productive but also be inspiring is appreciated by many. His zeal to create better management institutions made him a prominent expert in his field. His success is a note to great leadership and an even greater mindset. I have admired him for the unconventional steps he took for the betterment and progress of the institution.

He firmly believed that 'Great B-schools are ones which are in the business of creation of knowledge, application of knowledge, and dissemination of knowledge. Yet another very important component is quality of teaching. Management teaching is different from other subjects—understanding the ground realities is important. Integration of experience and thought is important. One may have great strategic thinking, but one needs to have a structure in place. Teaching in isolation does not have meaning. Global integration is important.'

True to his words he has helped build policies that do just that. Policies that facilitate a better environment. He was a key member in many of the policy making committees. He emphasized not just on teaching, but also research and innovation. His stand towards research is clear, 'that the quality of faculty and research is the hallmark of a good B-school.' He has been instrumental in advancing the rank and stature of every institution he has been a part of including IIM-L and MDI Gurgaon.

The Indian express newspaper featured a profile commending Dr Singh for his impactful journey. They represented him perfectly, 'An outstanding institution builder and an academic turnaround leader, Dr Singh is regarded as a man with the Midas Touch. During his tenure at IIM-L, he succeeded in positioning it among the top 5 B-schools and as a truly world-class management school having MoUs and collaborative linkages with around 20 European, Canadian, Australian and Asian Management Schools.' He played a vital role in facilitating and collaborating patterns into workable theories and strategies.

When he was awarded the prestigious Padma Shri, a first in the field of management education, it was a proud and well-deserved new chapter in his life.

He dedicated his time for the future generation, so that they are taught by the best and learn the best.

His books have made an impact on the lives of so many students and researchers. His work has been cited by many national and international scholars. He gifted one of his outstanding books, personally signed, to me. I was deeply touched when I saw his message inside, 'to Yogesh: A great human soul'.

His work speaks for his brilliance with such clarity. When worded right, a sentence can motivate, inspire and encourage someone, they are an endless source of power. I was motivated to make changes in how I functioned and have recommended it to many of my colleagues.

Dr Singh might mean many things to many people but to me, a never-ending source of inspiration.

THE SOJOURN OF A LIFETIME

Sanjay Srivastava, Vice Chancellor, Manav Rachna International Institute of Research And Studies (MRIIRS)

I had the opportunity to meet Dr Singh in early 2015—the very conversations with him during his many visits to the Manav Rachna Educational Institutions (MREI) campus in Aravalli Hills gave me ample food for thought to ignite a series of transformational moments in my life—both personal and professional. In the many years that I knew him, he became the fatherly figure I would reach out to in times of distress and dilemma. He enjoyed the same respect and affection from several others who he had led by the hand in corporate, industry and academia.

On June 3, 2020, I could barely contain the shock that jolted through me. The medical bulletin announced the tragic passing away of a global luminary and my mentor for several years—Padma Shri Dr Pritam Singh. During the melancholy that obviously followed, I witnessed the impact that the man had left on people he taught, mentored, and interacted with.

If they say that leadership is about making others better through your presence and making sure that the impact lasts in your absence, Dr Singh's life is a testimony of an individual who was the epitome of leadership. He was one of the finest management teachers and global gurus to have blessed our nation. A builder of people and of the nation, an academician par excellence, a leadership nurturer, a celebrated author and scholar, Dr Singh was often considered a person with the Midas Touch. He was a constant on India's management education scene for more than four-and-a-half decades and was one of the most important mentors to several Indian B-schools in their growth to prominence. He taught and guided several individuals who went on to hold important positions at the top of their organizations—building for himself a huge pool of followers among CEOs, CMDs, Directors, Deans and Vice Chancellors.

Dr Singh's vision was to prepare institutions of higher education in the global arena with a process-oriented approach. His contribution to the field of management education was duly honoured when Dr Singh was awarded the Padma Shri Award in 2003 for turning the fortunes of institutes in the field of management education. Dr Singh received acclaims galore, including being nominated as a member to the Empowered Expert Committee (EEC) for the Indian government's Institutions of Eminence (IoE) program.

His life and times have spelt inspiration and motivation for me, as I always found myself humbled by his simple but great ways. From the time he became associated with Manav Rachna till the time he breathed his last, he had been a guiding light not only for me but also to so many of my colleagues at MREI. In the honour of his memory, MREI instituted the Dr Pritam Singh Gold Medal for Leadership Excellence to personify character and competence.

Early in 2016, Dr Pritam Singh institutionalized his guidance to Manav Rachna as the Honorary Director General and a Strategic Mentoring Board was formed under his Chairmanship. He exuded an air of magnanimity, took up ground realities, touched people's lives and stood tall. Dr Singh's guidance ushered in a direction for progress at MREI. Bolstering industry connect and gratitude, he put in place the Manav Rachna Excellence Awards (MREA)—an annual event that recognizes contributions of people from various walks of life.

In exploring the essential traits of a great leader in his literary works, Dr Singh would often reference Hindu mythology, like the epic Mahabharata, quoting Bhishma Pitamah's view on leadership issues. According to me, Dr Singh's most powerful contribution to the field of leadership is the concept of Krishnaization. Lord Krishna has been a perfect example of a friend, philosopher and a guru. Dr Singh always talked about the usefulness of Krishnaization in building leaders, and often expressed discontent at Indian corporate culture being devoid of this. He said that leaders must be coaches who can inspire to excel. Dr Singh often told me that as a teacher, one can make a positive difference in the lives of students, irrespective of the courses they teach. It really is awe-inspiring to now understand the depths of what he sought to teach. So rich was his experience that his every word was sheer expertise.

It is a difficult task to pick the tenets of Dr Singh's inspiration. He drew to centre stage certain aspects which we either consider as obvious or which we even overlook. He was very clear about rewards for honest performance and alignment with organizational purpose. Although he ensured this, he also cautioned that with every responsibility should come accountability. Dr Singh's meticulous focus on action and outcomes was contagious. The data which businesses are fuelled with today was ingrained in his style of functioning for years. He would always talk about targets, quantifiable performance assessment and strong follow up for definite results, which would ensure no efforts miss the impact.

To continually drive good people towards their best performance, the culture of the organization must facilitate them. Dr Singh not only valued people but worked with them to understand their competencies, enabling them to grow from strength to strength, step by step. Every member of our team of FMS at Manav Rachna experienced the cohesion with him. For our students at Manav Rachna and especially at FMS, Dr Singh's association was a lifetime experience. He had a firm belief that for every successful academic institution, we must put students at the core, the pivot. While he advised students to strive hard, he also emphasized sensitizing them to the rationale behind hard work and rules, not just enforcing discipline.

One of his favourite quotes was, 'Look Within, Look Around, Look Beyond,' which he'd share with students and admirers, to encourage them to introspect and nurture a visionary thinking.

'What will a faculty member teach, if they have no experience of business,' was a question Dr Singh would often ask. It was his insight of bringing practicing business leaders into postgraduate business education that put us at MREI on the road to formalize systems for 'Professors of Practice'. He said academia may have limitations to go to the industry, yet industry can surely come to academia through this route. Dr Singh's thoughts were always ahead of their time.

As a practicing guru of human behaviour, Dr Singh said that the future belongs to those who understand, learn, adapt, unlearn and further learn. Faculty mentoring and student mentoring are two important aspects of learning development. Senior professors mentoring faculty members and in-turn training them to use student mentoring as a transformational tool was practiced by Dr Singh. He believed every faculty member had untapped potential, only waiting for the right mentor to release and channelize it towards a developmental process. He believed that faculty members can be trained for consulting assignments, research work and administrative insights using mentoring as a tool.

He understood the critical importance of public and private institutions partnering to offer the best education in the country and was pivotal in bringing international accreditation to India. He organized internationally acclaimed conferences for management and leadership, promoting exchange of ideas in the field of management. In the last few decades, not only was he on the board of 20 private organizations, but he also worked as a consultant with more than 200 CEOs in India and abroad.

Dr Singh was often requested to address the top management of MNCs and public sector organizations as a leadership coach. Showing tremendous faith in his academic and leadership prowess, he was appointed to several policy making committees and other statutory bodies for the government, when it came to higher education. He was the man chosen to organize and direct the first retreat of the central ministers as part of Late Shri Rajiv Gandhi's initiative to develop ministers as transformational leaders and change masters. Dr Singh is credited with transforming the landscape of management education and leadership development in India over the last 45 years by shaping higher education and uplifting institutions, inspiring lakhs of people in academia and the corporate sector, and bringing international accreditation to India. He especially played an instrumental role in transforming various educational institutions as a mentor and guide.

It is not so common at this stage of our careers to have professors who shape our intellect, interest, and life in general. But my mentor did that while we were initially brought together for academic purposes. I learnt immensely from his views, perspectives and wealth of knowledge. These learnings and mantras will always be fundamental for my understanding of the world. I find it fitting to conclude my thoughts about Dr Singh with Verse 21 of Chapter 3 of the Srimad Bhagavad Gita, for the way he managed to change the world, of which he was a part:

यद्यदाचरतिश्रेष्ठस्तत्तदेवेतरोजन: ।
सयत्प्रमाणंकुरुतेलोकस्तदनुवर्तते ॥

(Whatever actions great persons perform, common people follow. Whatever standards they set; all the world pursues.)

TELL ME, WITHOUT WORDS, TO UNDERSTAND YOU BETTER

Alfredo Behrens, IME, University of Salamanca, FIA Business School, São Paulo

I first met Dr Singh when I organized a field trip to India from my business school in São Paulo to figure out innovative management thinking being developed elsewhere. Dr Singh enchanted my Brazilian colleagues and me during a small seminar kindly organized by Dr Asha Bhandarker at the MDI Gurgaon in January of 2010. It was a great treat in the way of a morning seminar for less than a dozen Brazilian scholars and MBA students and such an enlightening experience for me that I continued to collaborate in any way possible with initiatives by Dr Singh and his team since then.

MDI's facilities, largely built under Dr Singh's direction, were quite imposing. When he entered the seminar room that day, with his usual smile and gentle demeanour he began by telling us a story: halfway through it, he had the dozen Brazilians in tears. It was not a particularly sad story and yet the Brazilians wept upon it, responding to the wisdom filling the room, to Dr Singh's soft body gestures, and to his soothing tone.

The next day, Dr Singh humbly asked me in private why we had cried. I did not know either, perhaps I still do not fully understand today what happened a decade ago, but I tried then to translate our reaction. Brazilian management scholars are steeped in the stark American one-way tradition that serves well only a small minority of Brazilians but feels intimately inadequate for a people unable to bridge large intractable societal chasms.

During his moving talk, Dr Singh's message suggested not only that an alternate way of thinking was possible, but also that it was even beautiful and worth following because it was free from the deadly embrace of the American 'What went wrong?' and the 'Who dunnit?' Our response as Brazilian listeners was not only to what Dr Singh said but also to how he said it. Dr Singh's overall message was an encounter with beauty; it suggested a path to truth, forgiving of all real life's imperfections, distortions and fateful confusions. It was deeply moving then, as it is today, remembering the moment.

Dr Singh's superb storytelling ability inspired me to change my teaching style. I am now teaching at the Universidad de Salamanca, where students also must fill the customary teacher evaluation forms after classes. Upon reading one of the students' recent comments, I remembered Pritam most gratefully. My student had written that during my classes they had the pleasure of learning as if I were telling them a story!

Yet, there is more to leadership stories than the setting. Dr Singh once suggested to me that 'Cross-cultural research should de-emphasize figuring out what makes us different from one another and bring to the fore what we have in common.' He even suggested following up on 'good king' stories, because those stories teach us what we like, and expect, from benevolent virtuous leaders.

I attempt to pay homage to Dr Singh by blending into the interpretation of stories some of Pritam's most insightful contributions to organizational leadership. I chose to frame my argument around the role of stories because great storytelling is one of Pritam's best talents. Besides, Dr Singh's overarching endeavour, to awaken by communicating effectively in India, and across cultures, requires that we retool our profession to contribute to the path he has opened for us. I believe that telling leadership stories through wordless fables, told in silent films through animals, may hold the secret. I still have to follow-up on Dr Singh's wise suggestion to delve into 'good king' stories, to bring to life the goodness that people expect of their leaders across the world. God permitting, I will continue to reverentially follow his path.

WALKING THE TALK OF LEADERSHIP: MY LEARNINGS FROM DR SINGH

Davide Sola, Professor of Strategy and Management, ESCP Europe

What is leadership? We all tend to believe we have a good idea of what it means to be a leader, but when we try to define leadership, things often become less clear.

The question of defining leadership led to my first experience of the teaching of Dr Singh. In 2006 I was invited by Dr Singh to visit MDI Gurgaon in New Delhi, where he was the Dean. At that time, I had just been appointed Director and Dean of the ESCP, Europe–London campus. I had recently left McKinsey for a sabbatical which turned out to be permanent, and I was very interested in strengthening ESCP's presence in India. Arriving on campus with my colleague Professor Gupta, a distinguished scholar in the field of finance, we were warmly welcomed by Dr Singh. He introduced us to many of his faculty and drew us all into fascinating conversations about how we could collaborate in research, teaching and executive education. Immediately, I knew I was among people who I could not only work with, but whose company and conversations I would enjoy and find stimulating. It was the start of a long-lasting relationship that continues to this day.

That evening, Dr Singh organized a dinner for Professor Gupta and me. We were also joined by Professor Asha Bhandarker who was heading two of their graduate programs—PGP-HR and PGP-International Management. Dr Singh sat next to me and as we sampled the excellent and spicy Indian cuisine, we regaled each other with stories and anecdotes. I was enjoying our conversation, so I asked him this question, 'I've just been appointed Director at ESCP and although I've had good training in problem solving, I'm not sure how well prepared I am for leadership. You have successfully led academic institutions and you are now an eminent Professor of Leadership. I'm sure you could help me understand leadership?' I was half joking, but the Professor replied, 'of course, let me tell you a story'. The story he told has remained with me.

There was once a chairman of a very important Indian corporation, one of the biggest in the country. He was about to retire and one of his final duties was to meet his successor. They met over tea and after some polite discussion the new Chairman asked him if he had any advice on how to lead such a massive organization. The outgoing chairman was reluctant to give advice, but the new chairman persisted. Finally, he agreed, but asked for a few days to consider the matter. When they met again a week later, after welcoming the new Chairman he explained that his advice would be in the form of three envelopes, numbered one to three. He further explained that the envelopes had to be opened in strict numerical order, and only if and when the new postholder was under such extreme pressure that he did not know what to do. The new Chairman was slightly bemused but agreed to the conditions and went away holding the three envelopes.

The new Chairman began his tenure with great fanfare. He visited every single office from the North to the South of India, and from the East to the West. He met thousands of employees, engaging in countless discussions with engineers, administrators, and sales staff. The Chairman, keen to make a good impression, listened carefully to the many suggestions of how the company could do things better. Expectations ran high as people anticipated their suggestions being implemented. The problem was that, inevitably, many of the suggestions were mutually contradictory. The Chairman began to feel under pressure. He wanted people to think well of him, but he knew that whatever changes he decided on would disappoint a number of people. He was therefore very reluctant to make any decisions. As the months went by, he continued to hesitate, and the situation worsened. Employees started to agitate about the slow speed of change and the financial position of the company started to deteriorate. At this point he suddenly remembered his conversation with the previous Chairman and rushed to get the envelopes from a drawer in his desk. He selected the envelope marked number one and quickly opened it. In it was a short letter, which read, 'If you are opening this letter, it is because you feel the pressure to take decisions, but you are torn. All the trade-offs seem negative. Furthermore, the financial situation is getting complicated, and the numbers are starting to go south. If this is the situation you find yourself in, I recommend that you blame your predecessor. You have inherited a complex organization that lacks clear direction, and this is obviously none of your fault.'

The chairman was delighted with such profound advice and quickly started to use it on every possible occasion. It seemed to work. The majority of people agreed that the new Chairman should be given time. After all, he was new and most of the issues he was dealing with were not of his making. For a little while all seemed well. Soon, however, problems started to re-emerge, while the deteriorating financial situation fuelled further discontent. Many of those close to the chairman were now pressuring him to take decisions, but the chairman was still unsure. As the pressure grew intolerable, he decided to open envelope number two. He reasoned that the first was such a godsend that even if the second letter could just help to relieve the pressure for a few days, it would be worth it.

The second letter started in a similar vein to the first one. 'You have now been in the post for some time. Blaming your predecessor gave you some breathing space to decide what to do, but it wasn't enough. You need more! The financial situation is rapidly worsening, but even more importantly, people are starting to doubt your ability to make decisions and move the company forward. Here is my recommendation: announce publicly that now is the time to act but you want to do so with the support of as many people as possible. Therefore, you will now appoint committees to evaluate all the key issues and come up with recommendations about the way forward for each one of them.'

The chairman leapt from his chair. What a great idea, he thought. He quickly summoned his assistant and asked him to organize a meeting with all the company's managers to announce this new approach. Two days later the managers, who had travelled from all over India, waited expectantly for the Chairman to speak. He announced the list of the committees and their membership. He also asked the chair of each committee to organize a meeting as soon as possible to set deadlines for completing their recommendations. The committees began their work but, predictably, it took days and sometimes weeks just to agree on deadlines. Then, over several months, the committees debated each and every issue at length, frequently going back over issues they thought they had decided. Eventually, one or two of the committees started to produce recommendations, but then as more came in, a problem emerged. Many of the recommendations contradicted each other and would force the Chairman to take a position and decide between two conflicting resolutions. What was he to do?

The Chairman's anxiety levels were going through the roof, exacerbated by the still worsening financial results. His position was critical. He had to make decisions, but he had run out of time. Then he remembered that he still had one more envelope left. The other two had worked so well that it was with a feeling of renewed hope that he rushed to his desk to retrieve the last one. After a moment of contemplation and a deep sigh he opened envelope number three. The letter started in a similar way to the other two. 'You have now been in power for quite some time. You have already used the other two letters which helped you but now the situation is worse than ever. The organization is on the brink of revolution; the finances are in dire straits and you are deeply anxious and very tired. Here is my final recommendation: prepare three envelopes for your successor!'

Dr Singh used this story to let me know what leadership is not. Often understanding what something is not is the first step towards understanding what something really is.

Over the next 15 years I continued to meet and work with Dr Singh in many different parts of the world, not only India but also China and back in Europe, in particular London and Paris. We worked together to deliver executive programs to leaders of Indian and international companies as well as collaborating on publications developed jointly with Professor Bhandarker and other Indian scholars.

All these occasions provided opportunities for me to learn more from Dr Singh about leadership. It would be impossible in one short article to share even half of these insights but let me outline the ones that impacted me most.

First, I began to understand that leadership is the accomplishment of a goal that requires people beyond just the leader. The man or woman who successfully inspires their followers to achieve such a goal is a leader. A great leader is one who can do this day after day, and year after year, in a wide variety of circumstances.

Second, great leaders understand their followers and how their individual goals and aspirations relate to the leader's goals. Understanding their followers means understanding their internal motivations. It is often said that leaders can motivate others, but this is not true. No one can motivate you but yourself. Great leaders create environments and situations where followers become motivated because they can achieve their individual goals while at the same time contributing to the achievement of the leader's goal.

Third, leaders succeed when they understand two fundamental principles: people are complex, and people are different. We respond not only to the traditional carrot and stick approach but also to ambition, the desire to win, love of goodness and beauty, boredom, self-doubt, and of course, fear. But the strength and importance of these motivating factors are not the same for everyone, nor is the degree to which they can be satisfied in their work. Some are motivated to follow because of the intellectual satisfaction involved in solving complex problems, others because it gives them an opportunity to work with someone they admire and respect. A great leader is able to adapt to the context and their approach to allow each and every follower to give their best.

Fourth, leaders care, and they take care of the team. By knowing and caring about their follower's goals and inclinations they make sure that these objectives are achieved and if things do not go as planned, they intervene by steering the projects in ways that enable both the project and the employee's goals to be met.

Fifth, leaders inspire confidence in their followers. A leader must seem to know exactly where the company is and where it is going. Leaders must seem to understand the implications of their actions and always be able to explain their reasoning. They must always seem to be consistent and clear in their decisions. The word 'seem' is important here. It is the impression leaders make that determines their influence on their followers. Great leaders can inspire confidence even in situations where deep inside they are experiencing doubt or insecurity. They know that betraying their insecurity will have an exponentially negative impact on their followers.

Last, leaders are great teachers who love helping people learn. They enjoy teaching people how to solve difficult problems, but they do it by letting their followers learn to find the solutions to these problems. Rather than simply announcing the right answer, they always first challenge people to think things through for themselves. They do this by asking a sequence of challenging questions that lead their followers, step by step, to a solution. Not only does this keep people engaged, it increases their commitment to implementing a solution which they themselves have devised. If the solution does not work well, the good leader will help them reframe and rethink the problem. And rather than talking of failure, the leader helps people see that learning what does not work is a step towards learning what does.

You may be wondering how Dr Singh delivered all these leadership insights. He did it in the same way as happened during our first encounter. Every single time we met there would be rich learning on leadership by way of compelling stories, like the one about the three envelopes, as well as through the way Dr Singh modelled good leadership and the way leaders love to help people learn. His stories were always captivating not only for me but also for the many different audiences he addressed. He was always able to contextualize stories which he may have used many times before, making them freshly relevant for his listeners. And it wasn't just his stories and the entertaining way he told them which communicated a compelling message. His behaviour as a leader reinforced the message of his stories. This is what I mean by 'walking the talk of leadership.'

MY FRIENDSHIP WITH DR SINGH, FULL OF JOY AND LEARNING

Jyoti Gupta, Professor Emeritus, ESCP Business School

My first encounter with Dr Singh was in 1993, when I was posted to Thailand at the Asian Institute of Technology (AIT) as the Dean and Director by ESCP of the School of Management (SOM), and he happened to be visiting. I was immediately impressed by his charm and simplicity. We soon established a friendship which lasted ever since.

We talked about his projects, and he asked me about the vision of SOM and its Mission. What impressed me at that first meeting, was his immense knowledge of Indian Philosophy, which he considered as an essential source of wisdom for the new generation of managers. He had a very human approach to the role of a manager.

One could see that here was a person who has a vision for business schools and a zeal to build institutions that have a lasting impact on management education. His idea was to radically change the business world through a new generation of managers who would think differently, not only making shareholders richer but also contribute to the nation as a whole. He also told me that business schools should integrate all that was happening in the different parts of the world, but not necessarily copy them. He insisted that business schools should internationalize and benchmark with the best schools in the world. We discussed how we could achieve these goals. Since then, we stayed in touch, and worked together on different projects.

When he joined as Director of MDI in Gurgaon, he showed his real talent as an institution builder. MDI has a very nice campus and is very well located in Gurgaon, but it was not recognised as one of the top business schools in India. Internationalization of the institution was not at all on the horizon.

He began by carrying out a Strengths, Weaknesses, Opportunities, and Threats (SWOT) analysis of the school. One of his great forces was that he never overlooked details. He started first by looking at the campus and the programs it offered. I remember him talking to me about the different steps that needed to be taken into account to make it one of the top business schools in India. He met all the stakeholders, including the faculty, the students, and most important of all, the board. He was very involved in the governance of the institution. This is where he showed his strong belief that proper governance is of extreme importance to build an institution of international reputation. We often discussed these issues.

His first step was to enhance the campus facilities. He did an excellent job. He transformed the campus into one of the best in India. He built new buildings that included residential accommodation, lecture halls and dining facilities which were of world class. His attention to detail was really incredible. He told me that every morning he took a walk through the campus to ensure that everything was maintained as it should be. He ignored nothing.

He renamed the buildings, plucking names from our historical past, of great leaders who were our role models. He then decided to get international recognition through international accreditation. He was the first Indian to think of international accreditation and he applied to the AMBA, a London-based international accreditation agency. One could see the visionary aspect of an institution builder. He realized that this would give visibility to Indian business schools at the international level, and also show that the Indian management style is something that the managers from all over the world can learn from.

This was a major step towards the internationalization of Indian business schools, and he also realized that Indian managers must have international exposure, as most businesses in India were going international. This also contributed towards attracting foreign investment in India. MDI under his guidance was the first Indian business school to get an international accreditation. What a great achievement! While he was in MDI, he developed Executive Education Programs for senior managers of a large number of Indian firms (which included both private and public sector companies) with an international component.

During his period at MDI, a collaboration agreement was signed between MDI and ESCP. This agreement was a sign that ESCP recognized the quality of MDI in all spheres of management education. The agreement included double degree, exchange of faculty and students. This led to the real internationalisation, as MDI students came to Europe, and at the same time European students came to MDI. The courses followed by European students at MDI, were recognized by ESCP as equivalent to credits obtained at ESCP. This meant that recognition was mutual. This indeed was a great step for MDI, in terms of international recognition.

We worked together on many management projects, which included designing new programs both for the PGP and short-term ones for senior executives; and how the vision of an institute should allow for the idea of bringing ethics as a fundamental principle of all management education. The great aspect about Dr Singh was that he was always ready to work with all the stakeholders.

When he finished his term in MDI, he moved on to be the Director of IIM-L. IIM-L was among the top business schools in India, but it lacked vision among the IIMs. This again was a new challenge for him. When he took his appointment at IIM-L, he saw the opportunity to build it as one of the top business schools in India and also get global recognition. I visited him several times. Once again, he made great changes to IIM-L. He renamed the buildings to emphasize the Indian tradition of management and at the same time started to globalize the school. IIM-L was awarded the AMBA accreditation.

We once again signed a collaboration agreement between IIM-L and ESCP. In my opinion, he showed his visionary approach to management education, when he opened a new campus in Noida, which is in the NCR region, not far from the big industrial belt around Delhi. This enabled IIM-L to enter executive education, a field where Indian business schools were absent, which was a real feather in the cap. He was the first one to recognize that the business schools senior management needed to revisit their strategy and the new developments taking place in the business world. I visited IIM-L after his term and could see his mark everywhere. Everyone I met, talked about the 'Dr Pritam Singh era'.

After his term at IIM-L, he took over the Directorship of MDI and furthered the good work done in his initial stint as Director there. In 2011, he took over as Director General of IMI in Delhi. He once again revolutionized the institution to become a leading business school.

In addition to these institutions, he has been involved with a whole range of academic institutions all over India. His advice was sought by these institutions to build them up as credible management schools, with a clear vision and global recognition.

We always worked together, once a friend, a friend forever. He never expected anything in return. Every time I visited India, he made it a point to meet me no matter how busy his schedules were. He always had new projects in view. He constantly detected opportunities for development in management education. Not surprising then, he was the first person in management education, who was awarded the Padma Shri by the Indian government in recognition.

I would say, Dr Singh was an institution builder par excellence, a thought leader and guru in the real terms. But above all, I would like to add that he was really somebody who believed in friendship, a generous human being.

A FRIEND, A PHILOSOPHER, A GUIDE

Atul Sobti, Former CMD, Bharat Heavy Electricals Limited

My association with Dr Singh started when I joined the BHEL Board in 2013 and continued when I joined SCOPE as Director-General in August 2019. I first met him at IMI New Delhi (which was also my alma mater) and I was in awe of the vision he had for the institute and his enthusiasm to take it into the premier league. Through all those years we were in regular touch and he always gave me valuable advice. In fact, we were exploring the possibilities of organizing a program for senior executives of PSEs at SCOPE under his guidance. His absence will be deeply missed and has left a vacuum in the management domain.

It is difficult to identify a singular adjective to describe Dr Singh. His was a motivating personality that inspired many managers and leaders, and I fortunately count myself among them, with the privilege of close interactions. He created an atmosphere of comfortable camaraderie and put one at ease.

Dr Singh was a true mentor. His zeal for management led many to incorporate little details into their work ethic, leading them to evolve from better to the best. He had an experiential teaching style that helped many institutions grow and thrive. As a teacher, his ability to communicate across all ages with ease was unsurpassable. He wasn't just a teacher, he coached and counselled, nurtured confidence, and gave direction to his students.

I remember his words, 'The ability to succeed comes from your thought of doing the "undoable".' This tenet has inspired and motivated many, be they entrepreneurs or from the corporate world, to go beyond their own perceived abilities, to succeed. He was also adept in imparting a lot even in a short conversation.

He taught students but also trained managers to excel in their management skills. In his five-plus decades as a Management Professor, he mentored many to succeed as heads of organizations or to hold instrumental roles. His leadership workshops have been sought after across the corporate world. Dr Singh's fearless views and perspectives on policy, governance and education earned him respect from many. His excellence and dedication to the management field earned him the most coveted award—the Padma Shri for his outstanding contribution to the field of management education.

He has left a pair of shoes that will never be filled. His mythological quotes during his addresses shall continue to ring in my ears and motivate me. I have lost a friend, philosopher and guide.

THE WISDOM OF BEING

Mamata Vegunta Singh, Director and Head HR, INVESCO, India

On that day in April 2003, the regalia of the imposing Durbar Hall in the Rashtrapati Bhavan was resplendent with the collective radiance of the Padma awardees. A recognition of the excellence in striving, creating and living for others, for the country, and for their own souls.

Receiving the Padma Shri that day was a striking gentleman, in a pearl-white *kurta* set and an off-white jacket. If one could be distinguished and humble at the same time, he was that. But of course, he was made of many things that are near opposites—erudite and conversational, intellectual and gracious, cultured and playful.

'Dr Pritam Singh...' His name announced, the gentleman made his way past the Prime Minister and the powers that be. Waiting for him was the President of India, Dr APJ Abdul Kalam. Presenting him his medallion and the certificate, was the people's President. Receiving the Padma Shri was every leader's guru. In that freeze-frame picture of the smiles shared by the President and the guru in those few moments—history was made. Not by chance but by choice, hard work, a desire to illuminate and an immense love for the country.

The journey to the Rashtrapati Bhavan began in the remote village of Kachhwa in Mirzapur district in Uttar Pradesh. It was before independence and freedom was a dream, as was India. For many, life was incomplete, and living was difficult. For Dr Singh, dreams were launched in his mother's songs. Songs of heroes, songs of valour, songs of dignity and achievement. For Sibabrata, the petite mother who adored her first born, what was possible for heroes was possible for her little Pritam. And more. Perhaps she knew she had borne a genius; she was only kindling his ambition.

With Independence, 'possibility' and 'potential' took on a new meaning not just in the context of the nation but at an individual level. And so Pritam went through school until it was time to leave the village for university. Ramdev Singh, his father and an astute community leader, knew that there was a price to staying, and in the long run, this was much more than the cost of going.

Married to the beautiful Saroj very early, on a financial tightrope, and away from home, Pritam made himself an instrument of scholarship. Earning a gold medal from Banaras Hindu University, a Fulbright fellowship for MBA studies from Kelley School of Business from Indiana University, Bloomington, were accomplished with the effort of discipline but with the ease of gravity. The USA was the preferred destination for many Indians even at that time, and Pritam had the opportunity to continue to work in the USA. Young Pritam's choice to come back to India was a defining one—a choice that showed up in many decisions that he was going to make in the coming years, both at personal and professional levels: impervious to money but devoted to his people and the nation.

Returning to India was easy but providing for the growing family was still a struggle. But love and young blood were the magnetic forces for the young couple who did not allow any problem to limit them. The idealist husband, Dr Singh educated the world, while the pragmatic wife Saroj did the same at home, keeping the home together and managing the everyday life of her world. Theirs was a partnership of magnetic forces that needed their polarity to keep their world humming.

Finishing his Doctorate in Management from Banaras Hindu University, Dr Singh embarked on the journey that made him an expert in the areas of leadership, economics, education and governance. His pursuit of excellence defined his path—creating not just IOE but also inspiring students of excellence. Dr Singh had the ability to envision what was difficult to fathom, and the wisdom to pursue what is of value. Pragmatism and principle were the two wheels that complemented each other on his journey.

'People don't care how much you know, until they know how much you care,' goes a saying. Embodying humanity and inspiring everyone—Dr Singh was pure joy when with people. Whatever the age or disposition of the person—curious or scholarly, Dr Singh genuinely cared for each one. He knew that the travails of daily life were an impediment to the journey to a higher life, so he had words of wisdom and motivation that would inspire people to endeavour, strive, achieve, give and be worthy of life. Everyone who crossed his path was transformed by his presence, and in turn, his happiness was nourished by his friendships and relationships.

The home would bustle with the energy of their six children—Savita, Vikas, Vidhan, Vivek, Vipul and Alka—playful, intrepid, intelligent and questioning. It was also home to many students, professors and business leaders who just dropped by. A steaming cup of the delicious ginger tea was always there to accompany a rich conversation. Like the river that takes everything with it, they became a part of a flowing river: Friends became family, daughters-in-law became daughters, students became family members and business leaders became *sishyas*. For me, he was Papa from the time Vikas and I married.

After his mother's songs, it was the Bhagavad Gita, the Song of God that made an indelible impression on Papa. His spirituality was a powerful dimension and a strong inner life. Equally conversant with the holy texts of all major religions, Papa's teachings were rooted in Indian thought, with the Bhagavad Gita being his spiritual dictionary. Papa's commentary on themes in the Bhagavad Gita—moral dilemmas, purpose, meaning-making, action focus, ethics, renunciation—are transcribed for the board rooms and governments.

The synthesis view of the Bhagavad Gita promotes the 'both-and' view instead of the 'either-or' view. Why renounce, when a dharmic householder can achieve the same goals as the renouncing monk through 'inner renunciation' or 'motiveless action'. Papa was a true Karma Yogi.

Ekla Chalo Re, a song by Rabindranath Tagore that deeply influenced Gandhi, was also one of Papa's favourite songs. It was a protest song, but for Papa it was the path of a leader. A leader often needs to walk alone because his vision is not yet shared by others, and he needs to walk that path alone, softening it, lighting it and showing that a path can be made, before it becomes the beaten path.

So much of his life was in the public and so much of his life is shared, that a legacy like his is truly and fully revealed in the narratives of each life he touched. We bring it together and make sense of it in retrospect: in moments of inspiration, the questions he asked, the truth he was devoted to, and his tough love that was crucial to catalyse change. Papa's noble qualities of generosity, work ethic, energy and wisdom have always inspired me, our family, his students, leaders in the government and corporates, and countless others. It is said that we only live as long as the last person who remembers us. Papa is going to live in many hearts and for generations to come.

In the busyness of everyday living, we tend to ignore the impermanence of life. More so, when we think of one so dear to us. It is my one regret that I have not had the opportunity to read this out to Papa. If I did, he would have probably told me about another song that he likes, and I would have told him that his life is a beautiful song, and to have been a witness to that is an honour in itself. And he would have smiled his angelic, benign smile with the sagely sparkle in his eyes.

SUMMARY AND CONCLUSIONS

The essays in this chapter present voices of the various authors, which bring out the unique perceptions and interpretations of events as well as experiences of working with Dr Singh as a person and as a leader. They are a great source of rich material regarding Dr Singh and his actions which contributed to building institutions—MDI Gurgaon, IIM-L and IMI New Delhi. By and large, most of the authors in this chapter have had a long association with Dr Singh. Actual episodes have been written about, and this validates and authenticates many of the points made in the interview data presented in Chapter 2. The uniqueness of the write-ups lies in their being first-person accounts of various aspects of Dr Singh's style of working and this adds immeasurable amount of depth to our understanding of the approach and style.

A detailed analysis of the essays has not been done here as it would have been too repetitive and would have significantly overlapped with Chapter 2. A cursory analysis brought out the following commonalities across the write-ups:

- None of the writers have written from hearsay. All have had direct experience of interacting with Dr Singh in different capacities.
- The authors have shared a unique set of memories, events and experiences to buttress their views.
- They acknowledged him as a transformational leader.
- They admired him for his pivotal role in building institutions.
- They spoke about his contributions and expressed awe at all that he had done, by providing actual examples.

- Most of them felt that they have gained immensely from the association.
- Most of them considered him a guru and mentor, as someone they look up to.
- They emphasized his focus on developing others.
- They highlighted his humility, ever learning orientation, strong people orientation and people skills, laying special emphasis on his strong networking skills.
- Most of them lauded his visionary, 'Think Big' approach in navigating the various professional roles he played.
- They highlighted his warm, approachable presence as being conducive to his people centric leadership style.
- They noted that while his unique outlook was rooted in Indian tradition, it was complemented by mastery of western management ideas.

CHAPTER 4

A HOLISTIC PORTRAIT

> *He was the Dhirubhai Ambani of Indian Management Education.*
>
> Sharad Sarin

This chapter attempts to bring together findings from the Festschrift essays, the interview findings and the conversation with Dr Singh, to arrive at a holistic portrait. The findings and conclusions are influenced by the long experience (almost four decades) of the senior author working with Dr Singh. The case study method was utilized where Dr Singh's leadership has been studied using multiple data sources (see Chapter 1 for methodology). Apart from the perceptual data, the objective data on improvements in ranking, growth in revenues, expansion of activities have been presented (see Chapter 2), which bear further testimony to the transformation which Dr Singh achieved in the institutions he headed.

The following four main theme-wise conclusions are now discussed. These are in line with the questions which we raised at the beginning of this work.

INSTITUTION BUILDING AND ORGANIZATION TRANSFORMATION

Dr Singh had a holistic and organic approach to institution building whether at MDI, IIM-L or IMI. There was a clear context sensitive approach (Hailey & Balogun 2002) which is the reason why the change was largely successful.

The strategy was to focus on top-line growth by introducing new activities—developing new long-term and short-term programs, encouraging research and exploring new avenues for consulting. The bottom line was also paid attention to and those activities were selected which contributed to significantly improve revenues. Focus was also given to invest in the future of the organizations. This is a great example of the leader who takes responsibility for the organization's future rather than focusing only on delivering immediate results. Doh and Stumpf (2005) emphasized three important dimensions of responsible leadership: value-based leadership; ethical decision-making and quality stakeholder relationships. Dr Singh demonstrated these aspects very well while transforming institutions. The goal was institutional self-sustenance, an important requirement for academic institutions in the long term. Such a strategy is relevant both in private unaided institutions in India, as well as in the government sector where institutions are fund starved.

Another aspect of the holistic approach was to reach out to all stakeholders and build win-win relationships for the organization. If we use the definition by Bhandari and Yasunobu (2009), it appears that Dr Singh focussed on developing social networks with relevant stakeholders and deepening engagement with professional bodies. This in turn led to reciprocity and such entities mutually helped and supported the institution and contributed to build trusting relationships.

By focusing on getting accreditations (national and international), as well as giving due importance to ranking, efforts were made to enhance the quality of the long-term programs. This further contributed to developing awareness about the institutions among the stakeholders—both students and recruiters—thus leading to improved quality of incoming students and better placements for graduating students. That he was a pioneer to initiate the process of international accreditations in India (specifically AMBA) speaks volumes about his vision, commitment to quality of education, global focus and developing a USP for the institution among other top schools. For quite a while MDI was talked about in the same breath as IIM-A, B and C.

At the core of the transformation of these institutions was the focus on faculty quality and faculty development. All the above efforts would have come to naught if faculty quality was weak. Getting good quality faculty was and continues to be a challenge in the field of management education, owing to supply side issues. This was handled by Dr Singh, by recruiting from good quality institutions and recruiting less experienced people with good academic performance; then grooming them and providing them developmental opportunities. Faculty were inspired and motivated by sharing the vision for the organization, introducing many systems and processes which went on to build a vibrant work culture (a pattern of shared values and beliefs that help individuals understand organizational functioning and thus provide them with norms for behaviour in the organization; Berson & Linton, 2005). The work culture was characterized by transparency, respect for faculty, building a collaborative spirit, fairness, and rewards and recognition.

Leader's vision and articulation—among other things—contributes to the development of a shared culture and norms (Jacobsen & House, 2001). Dr Singh regularly addressed organizational members (faculty and staff) and directly contributed to vision sharing. It was not only a one-way communication. Feedback and suggestions were taken and where relevant, they were incorporated. Khazanchi and Owens (2018) highlighted the importance of work culture to implement strategic intent. They add that the culture should inspire people to perform, both of which are well illustrated in this case. Dr Singh ably displayed both vision and grasp of ground realities, which richly facilitated implementation.

Taking care of the needs of staff and faculty, by and large, contributed to handling the typical resistance to change in such situations. As they experienced success and visibility, a self- perpetuating effect was created within the organizations, generating pride and goodwill among most of the internal stakeholders and building momentum for the change process.

A key finding in this part of the study was the extent to which both strategy and implementation were carefully crafted. In fact, it is a great lesson to all leaders that being in a position at the top, does not mean that one can afford to lose track of ground realities. Second, all stakeholders were brought on board influenced by the sheer personal qualities of Dr Singh and the relationship of mutuality with them. The decades old relationships which Dr Singh had cultivated indicate that people were valued and respected long after the institute related requirements were over.

AS A LEADER

This part consists of the following two broad facets of Dr Singh as a leader.

Transformational Leader

Dr Singh dominantly used the transformational leadership approach to changing organizations as well as a transformational leadership style. As research indicates, transformational leaders involve people in decision making (Bass, 2000), and are motivating and appreciative of their subordinates (Burns, 1978). The transformational style was combined with being an authentic leader as well as a scholar leader to bring about change in the institutions which he headed. The finding that not one but multiple leadership styles have been used is a unique finding of this work. We could capture this only because of our approach of using qualitative research, rather than using questionnaires. The profile of a scholar leader is an important requirement in the academic context because scholarly excellence (domain expertise and teaching excellence) is critical to earn the respect and following of peers. It is important to mention that transformational leadership was built on a solid bedrock of effective administrative capabilities.

Dr Singh had a vision for the institutions which he headed, which was widely shared and worked upon. Speaking about his vision and courage, Anadi Pande reminisced, 'He dared to go to uncharted territories, almost like Star Trek. He dared to take the path which none had taken before…. He was the master of executive action, not only developing strategies but working out ways to implement the same.' Studies of outstanding leaders, both charismatic (Conger & Kanungo, 1998) and transformational (Bass, 1985) have stressed the importance of leaders articulating a viable and engaging vision. The leader's vision and articulation contribute to follower satisfaction, motivation and performance (Lowe et al., 1996), and contribute to the implementation of the strategy.

Dr Singh not only operated at 36,000 feet and viewed the horizon but could also hover two inches above the ground and have a good grip of the nitty gritty details. Thus, he not only had a vision for the institution, he was also a hands-on leader, who ensured its implementation through the team. One of the key approaches used was to inspire people by enabling them to paint a vision of their own professional growth trajectory. This approach has been supported by the work of Klein and House (1998).

In many ways, he was a role model, visionary and inspirational and some even said charismatic. Numerous researchers have highlighted that leaders must be models for their followers (Bass & Avolio, 1990; Burns, 1978; Har-Evan, 1992; Hunt et al., 1990; Kouzes & Posner, 2002).

His interpersonal capabilities, relationship building and encouraging collaboration within the organizations he headed, further enhanced his credibility. Publicly giving credit to colleagues for work done is an exceedingly rare leadership trait, which Dr Singh demonstrated numerous times. Giving credit is not only about generosity, it reflects one's integrity. Besides, he showed genuine concern for the needs of the followers which helped in developing the followers' leadership potential (Bernard & Riggio, 2006). By showing respect to his colleagues, addressing subordinates respectfully, being polite and friendly, giving them due recognition in public, he was in turn able to help people feel elated, valued and important, resulting in voluntary participation and involvement in the institution. Thus, at the core of Dr Singh's influence was his integrity, credibility and the trust he could generate because of his focus on the larger cause of institution building.

Consistency between preaching and practice has been an important element of Dr Singh's style, which significantly contributed to his acceptance and credibility, resulting in trust and organizational commitment.

An overlapping style evident in the study findings is authenticity in the style of Dr Singh—positivity, open, transparent sharing of information and a genuine focus on the wellbeing of the organization and the people. In the research literature, this has been defined as sharing transparently, exuding positivity, demonstrating positive behaviour and fostering positive self-development among others (Avolio et al., 2009, p. 424). Effective leaders have been found to act in a transparent manner (Walumbwa et al., 2008) which has been true in the case of Dr Singh as well. All the actions which Dr Singh took were centred around result focus and excellence focus but the manner in which this was executed made it acceptable to people. The uniquely Indian element—citing Sanskrit quotes while communicating, the distinctive style of using stories and humour, addressing people by their names, giving nicknames in jest—for example, 'IT Czar', 'Oil Sheikh', or 'Don',—appears to have also had a positive impact on people at the interpersonal level.

As McColl-Kennedy and Andersen (2002) said, transformational leaders help improve follower's performance as well as help organizations to succeed (Waldman et al., 2004). Taylor et al. (2014), opined that 'leaders play an integral role in an organization's effectiveness.' Dr Singh has clearly demonstrated how the followers' performance can be improved and how an academic institution can be transformed, made more effective and gain in reputation.

The ultimate compliment was given by Maheshwari who said, 'Even in the toughest of situations Dr Singh would sense an opportunity and work for the growth of the institution. That's why, wherever he went, whether it was IIM-L or other places, within a couple of years, the institution would have grown manifold because he looked at things positively, optimistically and with great hope. With that kind of perspective, the leader has to make choices that are growth-bound. That's where he was a great institution builder and leader.'

Leader Guru and Mentor

The surprise finding in the study was the importance which people (both within and outside the institutions—MDI, IIM-L and IMI) attached to the mentoring which they experienced with Dr Singh. According to Kram (1983), mentoring leads to support from the protege, intrinsic satisfaction from helping a younger person as well as gaining recognition and respect from others. When leaders take on the mentoring role, it no doubt deepens their influence on the followers. Using the Pygmalion approach, setting high expectations from the followers and at the same time, making followers feel more efficacious (Eden, 1992) further contributed to building Dr Singh's leadership influence. While he no doubt groomed and mentored his team members, he was respected both in the corporate world and in the government for his wisdom and wise counsel where he impacted not only individuals but also top teams and institutions.

Manoj Kohli lucidly captured what made him an unparalleled guru in the management domain, 'He had the intellect which could convert Indian philosophy into modern leadership, and business management on how to run the business,…this is actually the rarest of the rare skills; he was able to bridge the two because he understood both. He would go from macro to micro very fast, and from micro to macro equally quick. I think his mind was so fertile. Frankly, I have met many good teachers, but I haven't met anyone like him. It is this distinction that made him superior to everyone else.'

Tripathi summed up his influence by saying, 'You know we have a picture of a teacher right from childhood, what an ideal teacher should be: somehow Dr Singh did fit that image, so, I was always very respectful to him and I always used to feel that he deserved all the respect for how he conducted himself, because of his knowledge and how he treated people.'

Thus, apart being both a visionary and transformational leader, Dr Singh has also been acknowledged as a guru and mentor, and someone with authentic leadership influence, owing to his personal and interpersonal qualities. Thus, this triumvirate of qualities, perhaps rarely seen in any single leader, made Dr Singh not only a highly influential leader, but also one who was highly respected and liked.

AS A PERSON

It is important to examine the characteristics of the leader as a person—'a being with attributes such as reason, morality, consciousness or self-consciousness (Oxford Bibliographies, n.d.) and a holistic set of human characteristics.' It is important to make such a distinction because both are separate categories in their own right; this is also important because both overlap within a person's psyche which is the totality of the human mind, conscious and unconscious (Amoroso et al., 2018), and behaviour. The use of the term 'person' in the broad question, which was asked in this study, helped us to tap into a much wider range of behaviours and attitudes than would have happened through the questionnaire approach. Findings of the research indicate that Dr Singh had a winning interpersonal style which increased his acceptance. People mentioned that he established a strong interpersonal connection and informal relations with people and had an understanding approach combined with an encouraging and supportive attitude. Authenticity as a person was displayed by being positive, genuine, along with being ethical, humane, honestly giving credit to team members where due and sharing information fairly and transparently. Above all, Dr Singh showed humility. In fact, humility has been found to contribute to developing supportive relationships with the employees (Richards, 1992) as has been evident in this case. When a reputed person in a powerful position displays this Level 5 attribute (Collins, 2007), it is viewed with admiration, and this is more so in hierarchical societies like India.

People experienced him as an impactful personality as indicated by the use of adjectives and phrases like impressive, passionate, reflective, emotionally sensitive, and good memory for names and events. Researchers have found that the leader's capacity to connect with followers results in the development of liking (Montoya & Horton, 2012), and feelings of trust and respect (Singh et al., 2016) among the team members. Warmth-related traits (highlighted by the sample) influence liking, whereas ability related traits predict respect (e.g., Hamilton & Fallot, 1974; Oden & Anderson, 1971; Singh et al., 1997; Singh & Teoh, 2000; Wojciszke et al., 2009). In fact, trust is the glue that creates a bond between the leader and the followers (Mineo, 2014). Examining the findings in the light of the above helps us to conclude that Dr Singh enjoyed both liking and respect from the subordinates.

In this section we analyse the perceived characteristics of Dr Singh as a person as evidenced in the research, using different theoretical lens—(a) the Jungian psychological types, (b) the five-factor model, (c) thinking style, (d) preference for heroes: ideal figures and (e) guiding values.

Theoretical Lenses to Understand the Person

An attempt has been made to understand the personality characteristics of Dr Singh using two prominent personality models. Personality refers to characteristic patterns of thinking, feeling, and behaving unique to an individual. The analysis is based on the data presented in various chapters as well as the authors' personal observation.

The Jungian Psychological Types

This is one of the most famous personality typologies. It is possible to frame the descriptions of Dr Singh's personality, using the MBTI model (1995), which is based on the Jungian types (2016). He was a self-declared ambivert (see the interview in Appendix A), which means he could be extraverted in one sphere of his life and introverted in the other sphere.

People's descriptions of Dr Singh in Chapters 2 and 3 tend to suggest that he was an extrovert in the professional sphere—for example behaviours like reaching out to people, building relationships, exuding self-confidence and positivity. At the same time, people also saw him as a good listener, who was both observant and sensitive to others' needs, which hints at a well-developed introverted side. Research brings out that individuals high in extraversion are described as friendly, gregarious and warm (Chernyshenko et al., 2011; McCrae & Costa, 1985). They enjoy social interaction and gain energy from it (McCrae & Costa, 1985). These statements match the descriptions of Dr Singh given in Chapter 2, Part 5 and in Chapter 3.

Those who worked closely with Dr Singh, found him to be creative and intuitive; besides, he was observed to be highly rational and logical while dealing with documents and data. This suggests that he used both sensing and intuition functions of the Jungian model for information processing. He was equally capable of perceiving things using a magnifying glass (metaphorically speaking), delving into details, as well as by scanning the horizon using binoculars. This gave him the powerful advantage of dealing with information through both kinds of cognitive capabilities—logical thinking as well as intuitive thinking, and this felicity with both types of cognitions, contributed to the speed of assessment, decision making and problem solving. Incidentally, the senior author also knows through the MBTI test scores of Dr Singh that he was an ENTJ (**E**xtroverted, **IN**tuitive, **T**hinking and **J**udgement focused) with balanced scores, indicating balanced development on all the eight attributes. Thus, his profile matches that of typical CEOs (eu.themyersbriggs.com).

The Five-Factor Model

The five-factor model (FFM) by McCrae and Costa (1985) is one of the most comprehensive models which conceptually brings together bulk of the personality attributes researched over the last many decades.

Findings presented show that it is also possible to view the descriptions of Dr Singh as a person using the Five-Factor model. This model consists of the following factors and their descriptors which we have then compared with the descriptions of Dr Singh given by the sample (Table 4.1).

Table 4.1. Comparison of FFM Descriptors with What People Said about Dr Singh

	Five-Factor Model (FFM) Descriptors*	Dr Singh: As a Person (Descriptions from the Study)
1	*Emotional stability:* self-confidence, self-esteem and stable moods	Good listener, patient, calm, accessible; smiled, laughed, and joked: these behaviours are indicative of emotional stability and self-confidence.
2	*Extraversion:* outgoing and energetic, assertive and enthusiastic	Positivity, warmth, reaching out to others, self-confidence and high energy
3	*Agreeableness:* compassionate, kind, tolerant and trustworthy and value getting along with other people	Warm hearted and friendly, nice person, helpful and concerned about others, humility
4	*Conscientious:* goal focused and organized, self-discipline, follow rules and planned	Highly goal focussed, very hard working, demonstrated a hands-on approach, highly organized and a stickler for time and not only was he planned, in fact, he believed in contingency planning**
5	*Openness to experience:* imaginative and creative, willing to try new things and open to ideas	Curious, listening, willing to consider different views, ability to find creative solutions to problems

Notes: * Erder and Pureur (2015); ** Contingency planning—personal observation.

As Table 4.1 indicates, the profile descriptions of Dr Singh given by the sample, fit the FFM model to a large extent. Research (Judge et al., 2002) has provided support for such a leader profile. For example, a meta-analysis has shown that people at the top of organizations tend to score low on neuroticism (the opposite of emotional stability) and high on extraversion, openness and Conscientiousness. Hogan and Judge (2013) report that one of the most important predictors of leadership success across various levels of the organization as well across industry sectors is personality. Characteristics like creativity—an element of openness to experience (Bass, 1990); conscientiousness (Judge et al., 2002) ; and agreeableness (Bass, 1990; Zaccaro et al., 1991) have been found related to leadership.

The two models—Jungian Temperament Model and the Five-Factor Model—thus significantly help in getting a deeper appreciation of the personality characteristics of Dr Singh.

Thinking Style

The world view or mindset of a top leader is crucial to how they handle complexity (Prahalad & Doz, 1987). Hambrick and Mason (1984) argue that the strategies and effectiveness of an organization are reflections of the values and cognitive capabilities of its powerful actors, among whom is the strategic leader (see also Schwenk, 1988). Thus, the thinking style of a leader and his senior team is key to how they perceive and interpret the organizational environment as well as the threats and opportunities. As was mentioned in Chapters 2 and 3, Dr Singh looked for opportunities even in tough situations rather than get fixated on problems. In addition, he shared his perceptions with the internal team and the collective thought process got imbued with a positive and 'can-do' spirit.

Holisticity of Thought

Dr Singh disliked Cartesian reductionism (Descartes, 1985), when applied to the human being, since it reduced the person to a set of sub-parts; and in the process, human complexities and the gestalt emerging from the integrated human entity are lost. He was a proponent of Gestalt Holisticity (Singh & Bhandarker, 2012, p. 453) which is also evident in his approach to organizational members, stakeholders and to organization building, that is, a holistic approach. For example, people were treated as people, not merely as human resources.

Intellectual Wanderer

It is apt to call Dr Singh an intellectual wanderer with a breadth of interests. He did a lot of reading in mythology, philosophy, psychology, Sanskrit, economics, finance and business management. He brought these to bear in teaching, advising and guiding in the core domain of leadership and individual potential identification, assessment and development. Being open minded and curious (openness to experience according to the FFM model) is an obvious characteristic of such a person, which is associated with having a wide range of interests and an exploratory thought process. This breadth of knowledge helped him to connect the synchronous dots across knowledge systems and disciplines. This also enabled him to anticipate the future, see patterns and develop strategy.

Another aspect of his breadth of interests is the restless exploration of ideas, curiously examining new and different concepts, creatively reframing them, never tiring of change and continuously internalizing new ideas into his core knowledge base. This is how his thoughts were fresh and new. Above all, he loved a good discussion, supported with logic and rationale.

Preference for Heroes: Ideal Figures

A hero is defined as a mythological or legendary figure often of divine descent endowed with great strength or ability; a person admired for achievements and noble qualities; and one who shows great courage (Merriam-Webster dictionary, n.d.). Kinsella et al. (2015) have identified 12 central traits of heroism, which consist of bravery, moral integrity, conviction, courage, self-sacrifice, being protective, honest, selfless, determined, saving others, inspiring and helpful. Allison and Goethals (2011) uncovered evidence for 'the great eight traits' of heroes consisting of wise, strong, resilient, reliable, charismatic, caring, selfless and inspiring.

From the psychological point of view, understanding one's heroes is important (Kinsella et al., 2016). Heroes function as 'a vehicle for the profoundest moral and metaphysical instruction' (Campbell, 1949, p. 257). On an individual level, heroes can be viewed as norms for social comparison which individuals can emulate (Klapp, 1954). Another important aspect consists of the role of mythological heroes in human life. According to Maddi (1980), mythological heroes and other phenomena can provide, among other things, culturally relevant inspiration and guidance for managing self. Thus, in order to develop deeper insight into a person and their aspirations and inspirations, it is helpful to know who their heroes are. Clearly, no one becomes, or fully actualizes their 'Hero'; they, however, help us understand the ideals that the person is striving towards. Understanding one's heroes thus provides insights into a person's inner world of aspiration and inspiration.

Dr Singh mentioned three kinds of heroes who influenced him (see Appendix A)—those figures from mythology like Krishna, Arjuna and Karna; well-known historical figures like Buddha and Chanakya; as well as more recent greats like Vivekananda and Gandhi. When we look at Dr Singh and his heroes from this prism, it provides deeper insights into his major sources of inspiration and striving. Each one of the heroes—whether mythological or actual—stood for a specific set of values. According to Dr Singh, Krishna stood for strategic thinking, leadership, friendship, and a capacity for joy, as well as detached observation and ego-lessness; Arjuna stood for bravery and single-minded focus. Karna was the epitome of the unconditional giver who could never say 'No' to anyone. Dr Singh admired the Buddha for his deep dive into managing the mind and Chanakya for his strategic thinking. Both Vivekananda and Gandhi were action heroes—Vivekananda for his pride in his country and culture and the fearlessness and command with which he represented India at the World Conference of Religions. Vivekananda's statement 'Arise, Awake and Stop not till the Goal is achieved' was etched on the Vivekananda statue at MDI Gurgaon. Gandhi was deeply admired for his multitude of leadership and personal qualities and his capacity to lead a movement and take the country towards Independence. Full-length portraits of these iconic figures adorned Dr Singh's office walls.

Given that heroes play an important role in human life by giving us wisdom; enhancing us; providing moral modelling; and by offering protection (Allison & Goethals, 2011), one can well imagine how Dr Singh inspired himself and shaped his character by studying these heroes and trying to emulate their qualities. In fact, many times he would advise the people he was mentoring 'when you are at a crossroads in your life and wondering which path to take, follow the path taken by great people.' This reflects how he viewed heroes. Quite possibly, all his personal heroes subconsciously coloured his perceptions as well as inspired him to action.

Dr Singh's Guiding Values

Dr Singh was known to quote extensively from the Upanishads, Bhagavad Gita and Mahabharata. In fact, he was steeped in these mythological works and strived to reinterpret the ancient wisdom contained therein, in the contemporary context of business and management. Many Indian writers and speakers have lately started using Indian wisdom to teach management and human behaviour. What made Dr Singh's usage different from others was the fact that he lived the words, believed and practiced them, thus imbuing his speeches and sessions with great power which emanates from conviction and personal experience. Above all, his genius lay in successfully linking them with modern management and human behaviour.

Some of the quotes which he mentioned in his conversation with the senior author (Appendix A), provide some insights. Incidentally, these were often quoted by him in numerous MDPs (Management Development Programs that were conducted jointly). As James Allen (2003) said, 'A man is literally what he thinks, his character being the complete sum of all his thoughts.' If we go by this logic, then repeatedly espousing something in public (which includes repetition of thoughts) leads to internalization, then becomes a habit and then becomes a part of a person's character.

We now examine Dr Singh's values through some of his favourite quotes mentioned in Chapter 4.

Lord Krishna talks to Arjuna in Bhagavad Gita:

'Yogah Karmasu Kaushalam'

Yoga is excellence at work.
Perform your duty with excellence,
without attachment to the fruits.

Bhagavad Gita, Chapter 2 Verse 50

This verse indicates the thrust on excellence in work without expectations. Clearly, Dr Singh placed high value on excellence and dedicated work. The focus was on producing high quality work and performance, without getting disappointed if the results were not commensurate with one's performance.

As indicated in Chapter 2, excellence and merit were the core values at the centre of organizational transformation. This further validates Dr Singh's belief in excellence. It is not that results were not valued; rather this approach helps to pre-empt disappointment in case the results fell short of expectations. This mindset makes one resilient, helps to maintain morale and continue to strive without getting into a negative emotional spiral. As Chapters 2 and 3 have indicated, Dr Singh did face some daunting challenging which he successfully overcame.

> *'Sukha dukhe same' kritva labha labhou jaya jayou'*
>
> In happiness and sorrow, profit and loss, victory,
> and defeat, keep equanimous.
>
> *Bhagavad Gita, Chapter 2 Verse 38*

This shloka highlights the need to be balanced and equipoised in the face of life's ups and downs. The emphasis here is on maintaining one's balance without getting affected by extreme destabilizing emotions. All human beings are both rational and emotional and traverse the range of emotions depending on life events. Dr Singh would be no exception to this law of nature. What differentiated him from others was his capacity to quickly bounce back He was so focussed on his vision and goals, that he did not allow anything to interfere and jeopardize the plans.

> *'Yatra yogeśhvaraḥ kṛiṣhṇo yatra pārtho dhanur-dharaḥ*
> *Tatra śhrīr vijayo bhūtir dhruvā nītir matir mama'*
>
> Wherever there is Shree Krishna, the Lord of all Yog, and wherever there is Arjun, the supreme archer, there will certainly be unending opulence, victory, prosperity, and righteousness. Of this, I am certain.
>
> *Bhagavad Gita, Chapter 18, Verse 78*

The shloka suggests that the person who has the outstanding capabilities of an Arjuna (the brave warrior and exceptional archer, who fought the war using fair means); as well as faith in the divine, is bound to be a winner. This shloka inspires one to do one's best, balance the mind and continuously sharpen one's capabilities while maintaining one's faith, because victory and well-being are certain.

A PERSPECTIVE ON HIS INCREDIBLE JOURNEY

By any stretch of imagination, Dr Singh's journey from a small Indian village to being part of India's elite (one of a miniscule number of 3242 Padma Shri awardees in India since 1954), based on sheer dint of merit and personal qualities, is nothing short of an Odyssey. Even today, traversing from 'Bharat' to 'India' and thereon to the globe is a Herculean task. Very few are able to bridge this yawning cultural chasm. Dr Singh successfully went (metaphorically speaking) from 'Bharat' to 'India', that is, from the mindset shaped by Indian traditions, to the mindset influenced by English education and Western thinking. What is striking is that unlike most western educated Indians, he neither lost himself nor forgot his roots, nor did he reject the best of Indian or Western values. He sought to integrate both Indian and Western knowledge and wisdom. As Sahasrabudhe put it, 'What I liked best was that while he was rooted in Indian knowledge, systems and traditions, he equally respected western knowledge without getting swayed to either extreme.' As Manoj Kohli said, 'He was a bridge between the East and the West.'

How he managed to straddle the two knowledge systems and effortlessly connect the two, moving back and forth between one and the other; and at the same time making this knowledge practical and useful to the corporate sector, is the uniqueness of his genius. He embraced and expounded both traditional wisdom of the Indian subcontinent—from the Upanishads, Bhagavad Gita, Mahabharata, Guru Granth Sahib, Buddhism and Sufism—and modern western knowledge in the domains of management and organizational psychology. He often illustrated modern Western principles of management with traditional Indian parables and tales from mythology. In fact, as a thinker and scholar, it appears that he was more on a quest to highlight similarities across various thought systems rather than look for differences and uniqueness.

Dr Singh's remarkable professional success is an outcome not only of strategic thinking, his mentoring and leadership as mentioned earlier but also based on his qualities as a person—the sheer positivity, drive, strong determination, high resilience, relentless efforts, clarity of personal beliefs and a creative and above all, an ever learning and agile mind. His level of aspiration was very high and he frequently used to inspire people by saying, 'shift the goal post further, when you reach the goal.' This was just as true for Dr Singh in his own life. In fact, his entire life he continuously worked to raise the bar of performance. After all, he became director of MDI-V2 at 62 and the Director of IMI at the age of 69—not only taking these positions but also living up to his own standards of performance and making significant contributions in the life of these institutions. When the research work on the book *In Search of Change Maestros* was completed (2011), the first author was taken aback to hear Dr Singh say at the age of 69, 'If we had done this work even 10 years ago, I would have been a different leader.' It reflects the learning orientation, open mindedness and the Olympian spirit to continuously soar beyond one's own level of performance.

APPENDICES

APPENDIX A: DR PRITAM SINGH IN CONVERSATION

This interview was conducted by the first author in April 2020. Emphasis has been given to understand the background, beliefs and values, aspirations and inspirations.

Dr Asha Bhandarker: Thank you for agreeing to talk about yourself. Dr Singh, I am curious to know about your early background. If you don't mind sharing?

Dr Pritam Singh: I grew up in a small town (Kachwwa) near Benares. I was the eldest son of six siblings. My father was a farmer and owned some land. I did my schooling from the village and then went to BHU, Banaras, for college education.

AB: Could you share some early memories from your life in the village?

PS: We lived in a joint family with my father's brothers and their families; at one time around 56 persons lived under the same roof. My father was the eldest and you know what that means in typical village societies in those days—he was the Karta or head of the joint family.

AB: Would you say that this early 'Kutumb' experience shaped your thinking? I remember the paper on Cultural Ethos in the organizational milieu which talked about these concepts.

PS: Maybe. When I look back...some powerful memories float up...my attitude towards conflict, my desire to bring people together, was probably influenced by those experiences.

AB: *It would be great if you can give us some glimpses of early memories...if that's not too intrusive....*

PS: My mother features in some of my earliest memories. I remember when I was little, she used to sing a song in Bhojpuri which roughly translated means, 'My son is so special, when he walks, the earth trembles.' I laugh thinking back—I was 6–7 years old at that time and I used to stomp my feet on the ground to check if it shook!

My father was a highly respected social leader—people from villages miles around used to visit him for help—either financial or to help resolve family disputes. When he lay ill in hospital there were large crowds that gathered and when he passed away, 5000 people from many nearby villages came to pay their respects. He helped so many people; I only came to know about this when many came up to me on his demise to say how he helped them. I wondered at that time; how many people will come when I pass away? And I ask myself the question: who was the bigger leader....

AB: *Any other memories of your childhood?*

PS: My father would take me regularly to the temple to listen to religious discourses. I remember asking him, 'Babuji, the Swami repeats the same thing every time, why go again?' He replied, 'Son, because good things need to be repeated again and again and heard again and again.'

Another memory is from my teenage years.... My mother used to worry about me. She would often say, 'once my son makes up his mind, no one can stop him.... I pray that my son takes up the right cause in life.' Maybe right from my younger days I was stubborn maybe determined, whatever you want to call it.

AB: *Who were your role models?*

PS: In high school, I was fascinated by Swami Vivekananda. In fact, for one week, I went around wearing the traditional headdress like he did. I was so impressed that I even contemplated giving up everything and becoming a Sanyasi.

I remember my high school teachers—they were so dedicated that before the Board exams they used to spend a month coaching us without any extra payment.

AB: *What about professors in BHU?*

PS: Well, we had some great professors—Professor A. K. Shah, Professor Bhandari, and others in the Department of Commerce at BHU. Some of them were trained in Stanford and Harvard. They maintained high standards of excellence and fostered a strong research temper in the department. BHU was a great place in those days, you know.

I hope you are aware about the great role Pandit Madan Mohan Malviya played in building BHU (Banaras Hindu University). Let me tell you an amusing story from his life. The man went from pillar to post looking for donations to set up the university. He approached the Nizam (the richest Indian in the world in those days) who refused to donate any money. The story goes that he threw his shoe at Malviya in exasperation. The latter picked it up and went out to execute a brilliant plan—he decided to auction the shoe. When the Nizam heard about this, he was dismayed and sent some of his men to buy back the shoe and that's how he donated a large sum of money to build BHU.

AB: *Growing up, what did you do in your spare time?*

PS: While in the village sometimes we would go for *Kushti*—wrestling; sometimes to swim in the river Ganges which flowed nearby. In college I developed a tremendous liking for ghazals, poetry and music. The annual festival on BHU campus brought some of the music greats to the college—Bhimsen Joshi being one of them. Our college group of friends used to regularly go for movies, especially soon after examinations. I have always had a great fascination for artists and poets—they are the ones who bring change in the world, by the power of the word. That is why, I believe that the 'Pen is mightier than the Sword'.

AB: *I am sure you must have been a studious person in school?*

PS: I enjoyed studies. I was a good student and in fact topped my boards in the district across arts, science and commerce. I am told that this record stands unbroken to this day.

AB: *What about friends from those days?*

PS: Kedarnathan and Ram Daur were my good friends while I was doing B. Com. We did a lot of group studies together. Of course, Dr B. R. Singh was also a close friend, but he was a year junior to me. We used to watch movies after our exams. Sometimes we used to go on picnics.

AB: *I heard from Dr B. R. Singh, Kedarnathan and Prabhu, that you were a quick learner in those days and would just listen to the lessons once in preparation for your exams.... I suppose it was because of your great memory.*

PS: Yes, very much so. I didn't need to read books more than once. As for faces, there was a time even when I was 52 years old, I could repeat the names of all 60 students in the class after hearing them once. I was quite good with numbers which is why I opted for Commerce.

AB: *Tell us something about your friends. Did you have many friends?*

PS: I don't know how to say this—I was friendly with many people in BHU; there were also a few close friends from my college days. I mentioned their names earlier. We are in touch even now.

AB: *Were you always gregarious and outgoing?*

PS: I don't think I am gregarious in that sense—you know, always extraverted, 'ho-ho ha-ha' type of personality. Both then and now, I see myself as more of an ambivert. I like to spend time by myself and I also meet people when needed—invariably that happens for professional reasons.

AB: *I have worked together with you for so long and have seen you interact with people, whether in a training program or while meeting corporates, or at the workplace; it is difficult to believe that you are not an extrovert.*

PS: (Chuckles) Connecting with people is an essential requirement, whether as a professor of management, or as a consultant and especially as a director. All along, I have been meeting professional demands of the role. And I have always been telling you that you should do more of this Dr Bhandarker!

AB: *You have a deep interest in the Mahabharata and the Gita and have mastery over the shlokas, from which you quote profusely. Where did it all start and who were your heroes?*

PS: It all started with listening to discourses in the village temple. I admired both Krishna and Arjuna. Krishna for his strategic thinking, extreme tolerance, sense of fun and enjoyment and above all his flexibility to do what needs to be done—imagine he became the charioteer to his protégé Arjuna so that the battle could be won! There was no ego at all! He is also known as the complete personality as he possessed all the 16 Kalas or qualities/competencies.

I admire Arjuna for his single minded focus—'what do you see?' asks the master—'I see the bird'; what next?; 'I see the eye of the bird'—and then he was told to shoot. His focus, bravery and courage were phenomenal.

AB: *Do you think your liking for Arjuna has anything to do with the fact that Arjuna is your birth name?*

PS: Maybe.... I don't know. You psychologists do such analyses. I leave it to you (chuckling).

AB: *Tell us briefly about your views on the Mahabharat.*

PS: The Mahabharata is as relevant today as when it was written thousands of years ago. I don't view it as a religious book. What attracts me to this treatise is the power of the story and its relevance to understand the complexities and dilemmas of the human condition even today as it was the case thousands of years ago. I am attracted to the premise of good over evil; of the triumph of truth; the strategy and tactics of war, the many shades of Good and the many shades of Evil presented through the characters. These are not black and white. I also wonder about another question—are we as humans more evolved or less evolved from those times?

On the other hand, if I have to talk about the Gita, the wisdom in this treatise is simply majestic and immortal.

AB: *What about the Gita and the Ramayana?*

PS: Well...the Ramayana belongs to a more innocent age in our history unlike the Mahabharata. The Gita is—civilizationally speaking—one of our greatest contributions to human heritage on many deep philosophical questions for which there are no easy answers. The discourse given by Krishna to Arjuna delves into many imponderables like Karma, Dharma, Immortality of the soul. As I have said before, read chapter 3 of the Gita to get insights into human psychology. The Gita provides a perspective on the human condition, and I believe it guides us on how to lead life. It helps cultivate detached attachment and attached detachment...helps us cope with failures, tragedies, misfortunes by strengthening the mind and keeps us ever hopeful.

AB: *I am not familiar with the Mahabharata beyond what I learnt from comic books and short stories. Could you share your favourite slokas?*

PS: There are many. Let me mention a few:

Lord Krishna talks to Arjuna in Bhagavad Gita:

'Yogah Karmasu Kaushalam'

Yoga is excellence at work.
Perform your duty with excellence,
without attachment to the fruits.

Bhagavad Gita, Chapter 2 Verse 50

*'Yatra yogeśhvaraḥ kṛiṣhṇo yatra pārtho dhanur-dharaḥ
Tatra śhrīr vijayo bhūtir dhruvā nītir matir mama'*

Wherever there is Shree Krishna, the Lord of all Yog, and wherever there is Arjun, the supreme archer, there will also certainly be unending opulence, victory, prosperity, and righteousness. Of this, I am certain.

Bhagavad Gita, Chapter 18, Verse 78

'Sukha dukhe same' kritva labha labhou jaya jayou'

In happiness and sorrow, profit and loss, victory, and defeat, keep equanimous.

Bhagavad Gita, Chapter 2 Verse 38

AB: *Why do these shlokas matter so much to you?*

PS: These shlokas succinctly capture how one can handle one's life and retain balance in the face of challenges.

AB: *Any other heroes from the Mahabharata?*

PS: Maybe Karna from the Mahabharata for his compelling urge to help everyone....

AB: *Would you describe yourself as religious?*

PS: No. I would call myself more spiritual than religious. I don't view the Mahabharata as a religious tome; I think it is a powerful text to understand human dynamics... what a range of topics it covers....

Let me add, I don't like rituals because they typify religion. Religion can be the biggest divider you know. When I say I am spiritual I mean that I am a believer of the Supreme Consciousness, and I also believe that we human beings are all connected. That is why I am a strong proponent of Humanism, the foundation stone for a good community and indeed a good society.

AB: *What about the women characters in the Mahabharata?*

PS: My grandson (Savita's son, Anvit) once told me that I am a chauvinist because I could not readily speak about Kunti as a character in the Mahabharata.

AB: *Considering that you are a strong proponent of gender balance at the workplace this is a bit surprising. Can you tell us more?*

PS: Well, I was visiting Savita once in Pennsylvania...Anvit was very young (10–12 years of age; now he is a doctor!). Like all daughters, she proudly praised her father as a wise scholar who was well versed in Mahabharata. Perhaps he was reading some stories/comics from the epic in those days. That's when he asked me, Nanuji, what do you think of Kunti? I could not immediately reply to his question and that's how he called me a chauvinist (laughs out loud). You know...it became a teachable moment for me.

AB: *Dr Singh, I admire your sense of humour. Many times, I have seen you laugh at yourself. Can you tell us more about this?*

PS: Look, Dr Bhandarker, it's about one's perspective in life. We can either choose to live life being happy or being sad.

Being sad helps no one and does not change the situation anyway. Why not be happy? There is so much in one's life to be grateful for. Being happy is contagious and a sense of humour helps a lot in spreading positivity and keeping up the morale.

AB: *In the Indian context somehow, humour seems to be equated with non-seriousness.*

PS: Well…isn't it about the type of humour and the timing of cracking a joke? One can be serious and humorous at the same time. I find that laughing at oneself is one of the best ways to lighten the mood. Laughing at a situation is also fine. Laughing at others is in poor taste.

AB: *Can you please share a humorous story from your life and how it helped you?*

PS: Well…this is a story from my Fulbright interview; it happened when I was in my late 20s. The interview started with various questions—you are familiar with the things they ask…well, after a few minutes there was an awkward silence. Then the American on the selection committee asked me a deceptive question, 'Dr Singh, what type of English do you speak?' I quickly realized what he was trying to say and was unfazed. Very coolly I replied, 'I speak Bhojpuri English!'

Everyone laughed (maybe at my guts or my composure) and I was awarded the fellowship. I could go to Indian Bloomington's Kelley School of Business where I successfully completed my MBA and started my PhD work. Although I am not a psychologist like you, I took the maximum number of courses possible in human behaviour; I was so fascinated to understand human behaviour.

AB: *I guess it was a great experience. Can you narrate any turning point in your life while in the US?*

PS: hmm…let me think…. In the 1970s and 1980s, the T-Group movement was very strong. I went for one such program; the facilitator was Professor Robert Chin of MIT. He conducted one exercise which really hit me hard. There was a feedback session in the program. Everyone wrote down whom they accepted as a leader, as a Colleague and as a Subordinate. When the data was collated, I came to know that no one had selected me as a Subordinate, or a Colleague and a couple of participants had selected me as a leader. I was very disturbed. It raised many questions in my mind. I used to be very arrogant in those days because of my intellectual capabilities. That's when I resolved to change my behaviour and now no one will call me arrogant. That was a major turning point in my life.

AB: *In those days Indians who went to the US rarely came back. What made you come back?*

PS: Well...many reasons. My father sent me a message, saying, *Jungle mein mor nacha, kisne dekha?* He was trying to convey that all my achievements were pointless unless my country and my own family could be a part of it. That's when I decided to come back home. I think that was the best decision I made in my life...no regrets.

AB: *You grew up in an era of Political Ideology. Can you share which one influenced you the most?*

PS: I have been and continue to be a voracious reader and was acquainted with the works of Karl Marx, the theories of Keynes and others. My experiences in the US demonstrated to me the qualities which I loved as a person— Freedom, Autonomy, Independence, Competitiveness, Quest for Innovation, etc. On the other hand, my experiences in East Europe—the erstwhile Yugoslavia, Romania and Hungary—as an ILO consultant, shook me. The professor, who was the Director of the institute which hosted my visit, was suddenly shifted. When I was leaving at the end of my stay there, the man who was driving the vehicle to the airport turned out to be the same person. On asking he replied that he was being punished for some decisions made by him as Director, which did not appeal to the political masters. It raised deep questions in my mind about human rights…my observation tells me that Communism seems to have built tremendous dependency of the individual on the state, with hardly any incentive for individual initiative.

On the other hand, Capitalism breeds its own set of excesses which only seem to widen the gap between the haves and the have-nots. The recent migrant crisis we witnessed in India during the lockdown was very painful. No system is perfect, whether it is Capitalism or Communism. I do wish however, that the underlying theme of Humanism is not forgotten by nations and leaders.

AB: *On many occasions I remember you mentioning (around 2005), that watching the movie Gandhi gave you immense inspiration. I am curious to know about this if you can kindly share?*

PS: You are right about my fascination with Gandhi. He personified among other things—Tolerance, Sacrifice, Patience and Determination, all the very qualities required by a leader. Above all was his aloneness (not loneliness)—*Ekla Cholo Re*. He did not have a personal life as such once he got into the national movement for Independence. I marvel at his moral strength, rooted in his faith in God. I learnt many things from Gandhi. In fact every time I watched the film, it gave me new insights. For example, I observed and learnt about the importance of sensitivity to one's constituency. When Gandhi arrived in India from South Africa, he quickly realized the importance of being accepted by the average Indian. As he told a reporter, 'this country never heard the language of kings and emperors, this country always heard the language of naked fakirs and saints. That's why I adopted the garb of a naked Fakir.' Gandhi followed Indians, Indians followed Gandhi. All these are the reasons why I used to watch this film many times over. It comforted me and gave me answers to some of my vexing questions.

Another figure that I admire is undoubtedly the Buddha and his teachings. His simple stories conveyed profound wisdom. I admire the lessons from Chanakya and his lessons for a good king. I have admired the intellectual ability of Acharya Rajneesh, his sheer mastery over philosophical teachings from around the world and the capacity to convey them to the masses in simple language.

AB: *You keep mentioning that there is a crisis of leadership in the contemporary world. Can you elaborate?*

PS: Well, at the individual level, D'Anta, the sense of duty has gone down. Hedonism is visible everywhere. People are more narcissistic, more self-focused. The ultrarich are focused more on their gains with no care or conscience about the very people from whom they gain. The ideals of Gandhi and his convictions on trusteeship are almost forgotten. Who thinks of duty to society today? That India had to mandate even CSR spends shows that given a choice, many businesses would not like to spend for social good. In a country like India, with its vast inequities, this is not only irresponsible, it is greedy and selfish. Such behaviour can only destabilize and create tensions in society. Those in leadership positions ought to think of doing business sustainably so that their businesses last and there is a win-win for all concerned.

AB: *I have observed you in the classroom setting over the years and have wondered about how you seamlessly adapted to change—there has been change in your thought processes* *over the years. It's almost like you keep reinventing yourself. What's your take on this statement?*

PS: Isn't that another way to say I am evolving and isn't that the way human beings are supposed to be? (laughs) To answer your question more directly, whatever I read impacts me, even the 'thought for the day' in the Times of India. I think and reflect and apply it afresh to the current situation, even if I have read it before. I believe in and practice intense listening. Whenever I am with a person, I am deeply immersed with what he or she is saying. I invariably find that there is something valuable in what each person says to me.

AB: *I am curious about one thing—you did face some challenging moments, whether it was dealing with villagers in IIM Lucknow, maintaining discipline on campus even if political figures are involved in some way, or buying land for the Noida campus. In MDI Gurgaon (V 1) you were faced with financial challenges—there was no money to even pay the salaries when you joined as Director. In IMI you were faced with the challenges of expanding activities on a physically small campus? What gave you the strength to handle all this?*

PS: That's a good question Dr Bhandarker. I was clear about my goal in each case—the goal was to transform and bring the institution to the top. Apart from this, when faced with any situation I clarify my priorities and likely consequences. Since my goal was clear the solution was pretty clear, I didn't bring any personal agenda into my decision making. I was prepared for the worst-case scenario. This made decision making much easier.

Many factors helped, especially the team. Once I am convinced that what I am doing is the right thing for the institutions, I do my very best to make it a reality. I back my team to the hilt so that they can give their best. Above all, I have an enduring faith in the power of doing good and believe that God helps those who help themselves. I was prepared to resign if necessary and this inner clarity helped me to take bold decisions.

AB: *You mentioned earlier that you dislike arguments. Management literature mentions that conflict has a positive side. How do you view this?*

PS: We need to learn the art of dialogue, not debate or argument. I don't care for arguments because when you win an argument, you lose a friend; when you lose an argument, in any case, you have lost. Conflicts have to be handled differently—we need to be Ok with the clash of ideas without the clash of individual egos. That's where many problems start.

AB: *Over the years, whenever you are faced with difficult times, I have heard you saying Good will always win over Evil. Where does this conviction come from?*

PS: All my life experiences have shown me this. Truth ultimately triumphs.

AB: *In various training programs there are discussions about the dilemma of job and career vs telling the truth. How do you view this human dilemma?*

PS: There is an ancient Sanskrit saying which is a good guide:

> 'Satyam bruyat priyam bruyat. Na bruyat satyam apriyam. Priyam cha nanrutham bruyat. Esha dharmah sanatanah.'
>
> Speak the palatable truth. If the other party cannot tolerate the blunt truth, what is the point in saying it? The goal should be very clear- if it is to help, if it is to bring change, then speak the palatable truth.

Secondly, you have to be true to your role. For example, as a Director it is my duty (dharma) to listen to all; take care of the interests of the institution and the people...after all we are all part of the same family and same community. I should be prepared for both the bouquets and the brickbats.

AB: *If you had to choose just one or two qualities you admire in a person, what would you say?*

PS: You mean a personal quality?

AB: *Yes*

PS: I think I admire many qualities. The one which I very much admire—perhaps because it is rare—is Gratitude. Most times people completely forget those who helped them. Another quality I like is that of helping others. I admire those who go out of their way to help others.

AB: *I was wondering if you can touch upon any qualities you possess, which you consider to be not very desirable for a leader?*

PS: As a human being I have my own share of such qualities—for example, I am a perfectionist to the T—not a bad quality but not very pleasant; sometimes I do get impatient and angry when people don't respect other people's time. I did mention earlier in this interview that I used to be very arrogant in my younger days.

AB: *As you rightly said, all of us have some undesirable qualities. How do you manage these qualities? I am asking because the qualities you mentioned are rarely visible to others.*

PS: It's not an easy task. Over the years I have been able to bring greater self-discipline. I think that meditation has really helped me to stabilize my thoughts and emotions.

AB: *Interesting. How long have you been meditating?*

PS: Let me see...many decades...maybe 35—40 years at least.

AB: *Nehru or Shastri whom do you admire more?*

PS: Nehru was born in such a distinguished family and was educated in the best of colleges; he was destined to be the PM (Prime Minister) of independent India. I admire Shastri much more because he did not let his humble beginnings daunt him. He became the PM of India based on sheer capability and drive. What a long and arduous journey!

AB: *Why did you give such a high focus on personal touch and Pygmalion approach when you dealt with people within the organization. After all, they would have followed you anyway as Head of the organization.*

PS: To answer your question—Leadership, especially academic leadership is not easy. Intellectuals are independent minded and may or may not follow the position holder. As Warren Bennis said, 'Leadership is like herding cats.' This applies so well in the academic context. In my experience, it is only the larger goal and personal touch that play an important role here, especially if your aim is organizational transformation. If anyone follows the leader, it is because they are convinced about the cause…. Many leaders make the mistake of thinking that people follow them…that's an illusion.

AB: *What is your major concern about the research conducted by management schools today?*

PS: The major focus is to find uniqueness and differences. Why not examine similarities also? Is it less exciting? Further, research (and knowledge) should contribute to society in some way, in bettering understanding and improving the quality of life, in increasing the efficiency of solving problems in organizing and managing things in a better way.

AB: *OK, I am getting you. Both contribute to building knowledge. What is your advice to the younger generations?*

PS: We all need to develop the art of joyful living. Life is both full of challenges and problems as well as opportunities and solutions. Therefore,

- People should clarify their life purpose. What do they want from life? That will give them meaning and focus and help channel their talent and energy.
- They must immerse completely in what they do and give it their best—joy comes from such immersion.
- Once a person does what s/he likes then they will enjoy what they do.
- Above all, don't forget to laugh.

Where is the joy in living if we don't feel fulfilled and satisfied at the end of the day?

AB: *Why is philosophy so important?*

PS: Because philosophy gives one a perspective in life which helps us make better life choices.

AB: *Tell us something about your take on the importance of the Art and Environment in life. I am asking because people that I interviewed said that you were very particular about the environment of the institutions you headed and brought some aspect of art/aesthetics onto the campus.*

PS: Number one—it creates an impact on anyone who visits the campus for the first time. As they say, the first impression is the last impression. Besides, I think living in a good environment, with gardens, fountains, statues and beautiful buildings with names, which remind us of the icons from history, has a great impact on inspiring and balancing the mind and provides a soothing touch. My intention was to create the best possible work environment.

AB: *You tend to use plenty of stories and quote either scriptures or some verses from poems while conveying management concepts in class. Can you explain the reason why?*

PS: It's difficult for people to absorb abstract concepts beyond a point. The point of teaching is lost if people either stop absorbing or they can't recall or remember what they learnt. Unless the message reaches the heart, it will neither be understood nor be remembered. Stories and poems have the capacity to involve both head and heart which is important for learning and retention.

AB: *People say that you have the knack of spotting talent. How do you do this?*

PS: Dr Bhandarker, everyone has some talent or the other. Few of them get enough backing and appreciation. I think everyone will flourish if they get some support and if someone believes in them. Somehow many of us are expert at seeing the flaws in people rather than in their capabilities. Having said that, it is also important to pay attention to academic pedigree and consistency of performance.

AB: *What do you think is your enduring contribution?*

PS: Building leaders for academia may be considered as a lasting contribution. Institutions rise and fall, go through trials and tribulations. As long as there are good leaders, institutions can be built again and again. I would like to think that the research that we have done and the books we have written may be considered important contributions especially since there is scarcity of documentation of India centric research on leadership.

AB: *What is your advice to future leaders?*

PS: As a leader you require a lot of goodwill and acceptance from all stakeholders. Wise leaders would never run down their predecessors regardless of the quality of their contribution to the institution. By doing that as a leader you will alienate a set of people. And let's face it, as a leader each one is building on something good which the predecessor has done. Why not focus on that?

AB: *Dr Singh, the interviews indicated that all of them had such positive feelings for you. Does it mean no one disliked you?*

PS: I have tried my level best to help in the professional development of everyone in organizations where I served as Director. I kept only one thing in mind—is the person aligned to the organization? Are they trying to contribute? I tried to give the signal to those who did not align. When someone was working against organizational interest which is rare, as you know, I have been tough. Of course, such a person would not have good feelings for me. That's why leadership is so tough, it's not a popularity contest, it's like piloting a plane for the long haul, carrying a huge load on one's shoulders, always alert and mindful.

AB: *Any regrets, Dr Singh?*

PS: Sometimes I think to myself, if I had put all my energy into research and scholarship, perhaps I could have tried for the Nobel Prize. I don't know (if it would have happened), but sometimes I wonder if I did the right thing by diverting my energy into institution building.

AB: *Many thanks for sharing your thoughts Dr.*

APPENDIX B: FESTSCHRIFT AUTHORS LIST

S. No.	Name	Current Designation
1	Dr Anil Khandelwal	Former Chairman, Bank of Baroda
2	Dr Sharad Sarin	Former Professor, Xavier School of Management (XLRI) Jamshedpur
3	Dr Rajan Saxena	Former Vice Chancellor, NMIMS (Narsee Monjee Institute of Management Studies); S. P. Jain Institute of Management and Research (SPJIMR) Mumbai; & IIM Indore
4	Dr Rajan George	Operations Consultant, Renaissance by the Creek
5	Dr Rattan Sharma	Professor Emeritus, Delhi School of Business; Vivekananda Institute of Professional Studies (VIPS-TC)
6	Dr Premila Verma	Former Faculty Member, Administrative Staff College of India (ASCI) Hyderabad
7	Dr M. P. Jaiswal	Director, IIM Sambalpur & Former Professor, Management Development Institute (MDI) Gurgaon
8	S. K. Bose	Executive Director-Human Resources (ED-HR), Indian Oil Corporation (IOCL) & Alumnus MDI Gurgaon
9	Dr Sunil Mithas	Professor, University of South Florida, Muma College of Business, School of Information Systems and Management; & Alumnus MDI Gurgaon
10	Dr G. N. Pandey	Advisor and Head of Department (HR-OB), Doon Business School-Group, Dehradun
11	Dr Ashok Banerjee	Professor, Indian Institute of Management Calcutta
12	Dr R. L. Raina	Vice Chancellor, JK Lakshmipat University, Jaipur & Former Professor IIM Lucknow

(Continued)

(Continued)

S. No.	Name	Current Designation
13	Dr Debashis Chatterjee	Director of IIM Kozhikode, Former D.G. International Management Institute (IMI) New Delhi & Former Professor IIM Lucknow
14	Dr Kala Seetharam and Dr V. Sridhar	Kala Seetharam Sridhar, Professor, Institute for Social and Economic Change, Bangalore; V. Sridhar, Professor, International Institute of Information Technology Bangalore; & Former Professors IIM Lucknow
15	Dr A. K. Rath	Professor IMI Bhubaneswar; former Professor, IMI New Delhi, MDI Gurgaon & Secretary Government of India (GOI)
16	Dr Nand Dhameja	Dean and Professor FMS, Manav Rachna International Institute of Research and Studies, Faridabad & Former Professor MDI Gurgaon
17	Dr Subir Verma	Director, Nirma Institute of Management, & Former Professor MDI Gurgaon and IMI New Delhi
18	Dr Reeta Raina	Associate Professor at FORE School of Management, New Delhi & Former Professor MDI Gurgaon
19	Dr Jyotsna Bhatnagar	Professor, Human Resource Management (HRM), MDI Gurgaon
20	Dr CN Narayana (CNN)	Sr. Professor & Director Pune Business School, Pune & Former Registrar IMI New Delhi
21	Mr Atul Sobti	Former Chairman & Managing Director (CMD), Bharat Heavy Electricals Limited (BHEL)
22	Dr Anu Singh Lather	Vice Chancellor, Dr B. R. Ambedkar University, Delhi
23	Dr D. P. Singh	Chairman, University Grants Commission (UGC)

(Continued)

(Continued)

S. No.	Name	Current Designation
24	Dr Sanjay Srivastava	Vice Chancellor, Manav Rachna International Institute of Research and Studies (MRIIRS)
25	Dr Anand Prakash	Professor & Head, Psychology Department, University of Delhi
26	Dr Yogesh Singh	Vice Chancellor, Delhi Technological University
27	Dr Nupur Prakash	Professor, University School of Information, Communication & Technology (ICT), GGS Indraprastha University, Delhi & Former Vice Chancellor, Indira Gandhi Delhi Technical University For Women
28	Dr Davide Sola	Professor of Strategy and Management, École Supérieure de Commerce de Paris (ESCP) Europe
29	Dr Jyoti Gupta	Professor Emeritus, ESCP Business School; Dean of Cotrugli Business School, Zagreb and Belgrade
30	Dr Alfredo Behrens	IME, University of Salamanca & FIA Business School, São Paulo
31	Dr Mamata Vegunta Singh	Director and Head Human Resources (HR), INVESCO INDIA

Note: Names in order of presentation of the essays.

APPENDIX C: LIST OF INTERVIEWEES

S. No.	Name (Dr/Mr)	Designation
1	Dr Anadi Pande	Professor, Strategic Management, IIM Lucknow and Former Head-Strategy, Hero Honda
2	Dr Anil Sahasrabudhe	Chairman, All India Council for Technical Education (AICTE)
3	Anurag Batra	Chairman and Editor-in-Chief, Business World & Alumnus MDI

(Continued)

(Continued)

S. No.	Name (Dr/Mr)	Designation
4	Arun Maira	Management consultant and former member of Planning Commission of India & Former India Head BCG
5	Arup Roy	Former Chairman, NTPC
6	Dr V. Chauhan	Ex-Chairman NAAC, Arturo Falaschi Emeritus Scientist—International Centre for Genetic Engineering and Biotechnology, New Delhi
7	Bhaskar Chatterjee	Former Secretary, Government of India, Department of Public Enterprises. Principal Adviser, Planning Commission
8	Dr Bhimaraya Metri	Director, Indian Institute of Management Nagpur; Former Professor MDI Gurgaon and IMI New Delhi
9	B. K. Chaturvedi	Former Cabinet Secretary, Government of India.
10	Dr B. R. Singh	Former Head HR, ISPAT Profiles & friend from college days
11	Deepak Hota	Chairman BEML Ltd.
12	Dhananjay Singh	Director General, National HRD Network
13	Dr Dilip Bandopadhyay	Former Vice Chancellor of Guru Gobind Singh Indraprastha University, and Former Professor IIM Lucknow
14	D. K. Bakshi	Chief Mentor & CEO, Global Talent Company Limited, & Former Head HR INDO-RAMA Thailand
15	Needamangalam Gopalaswami	Chairman PM's committee on IOE (Institutions of Eminence) and Former Chief Election Commissioner of India (CEC)
16	Dr Harivansh Chaturvedi	Director, BIMTECH and Alternate President, EPSI
17	Dr M. Jayadev	Professor, IIM Bangalore; Former faculty IIM Lucknow

(Continued)

(Continued)

S. No.	Name (Dr/Mr)	Designation
18	Jauhari Lal	Former Director Personnel, ONGC
19	Wing Commander Kedarnathan	Retired Indian Air Force and friend from college days
20	K. K. Sinha	Dean Executive Education, BIMTECH and Ex-Director HR, NTPC
21	Major Gen AVSM (Retd) D. N. Khurana	Former Director General, All India Management Association
22	M. Damodaran	Former Chairman, SEBI
23	Manoj Kohli	Country Head, India CEO SoftBank India
24	Dr Nagananda Kumar	Former Professor, MDI Gurgaon
25	P. Dwarkanath	Former Chairman, GSK
26	Dr M. P. Poonia	Vice Chairman, AICTE
27	Prabhu Singh	Friend from school days
28	Pradeep Dinodia	Non-Executive Director, Hero Moto Corp
29	Puneet Dalmia	Managing Director, Dalmia Bharat Group
30	Pushp Joshi	Director-HR, HPCL
31	Rajeev Dubey	Principal Advisor & Former Group President (HR and Corporate Services) Mahindra & Mahindra
32	Dr Ravi Kumar	Former Professor, IIM Bangalore
33	Dr R. A. Yadav	Former Chairman AICTE
34	R. B. Yadav	Former Officer MDI Gurgaon & Private Secretary to Dr Singh in MDI V1 and V2
35	R. K. Dubey	Former CMD, Canara bank
36	R. V. Shahi	Chairman, Energy Infratech Private Limited and Former Secretary to the Government of India, Ministry of Power

(Continued)

(Continued)

S. No.	Name (Dr/Mr)	Designation
37	Sanjiv Bikhchandani	Founder & Executive Chairman, Info Edge
38	Sarat Acharya	Director, Bhubaneswar Smart City Ltd. IEM, and Former CMD, NLC India Ltd
39	S. C. Tripathi	Former Secretary, Ministry of Petroleum and Natural Gas
40	Dr Sunil Maheshwari	Professor, IIM Ahmedabad and Former Faculty, IIM Lucknow
41	S. Y. Siddiqui	Chief Mentor, Maruti Suzuki India Ltd.
42	Udai Upendra	Founder CEO, The HR Company and Former President & Head, Global Human Resources, Ranbaxy
43	Vinod Rai	Former Comptroller and Auditor General (CAG) of India
44	Vivek Mehra	CEO and MD, SAGE Publications India
45	V. K. Nangia	Former Registrar, MDI Gurgaon
46	Yasho V. Verma	Business and Strategy Consultant; Former COO LG India

APPENDIX D: LIST OF COMMITTEE MEMBERSHIPS

S. No.	Chairmanship/ Committee Memberships
	Higher Education
1	Member IOE—The PM's Empowered Committee on Institutions of Excellence in Higher Education (only academician from India)
2	Chairman, Indira Gandhi Technical University
3	Visitor's Nominee, Delhi University
4	Visitor's Nominee, Banaras Hindu University
5	Member Executive Councils of Banaras Hindu University, University of Pondicherry, Central University of Himachal Pradesh and Central University, Tezpur
6	Executive Board, Punjab University, Chandigarh

(Continued)

(Continued)

S. No.	Chairmanship/ Committee Memberships
	Higher Education
7	Chairman, AICTE Committee for Accreditation of Management Institutes
8	Chairman, Sub-committee, 'Institutional Management and Leadership Development in Higher Education', instituted by the Planning Commission for 12th Five Year Plan (2012–2017)
9	Member, Search Committees for the Selection of Vice Chancellors and Directors
10	Member, 6th Pay commission for IITs, IIMs and NITs
11	Member, Tenth Five Year Plan for Higher Education
12	Member, NIT Reforms Committee
13	Chairman, Advisory Committee, Education Promotion Society for India (EPSI)
	Member, Board and Advisory Council of B-Schools
14	Narsee Monjee Institute of Management Studies (NMIMS), Fore School of Management, BIMTECH, Jaipuria group and Lal Bahadur Shastri Institute Of Management And Technology (LBSIMT)
	Other Government Committees
15	Chairman, Defence Acquisition and Procurement Committee, Ministry of Defence, Government of India (2016)
16	Member, Banking Selection Board for selecting CMDs and Executive Directors
17	Member, Search Committee for Selection of non-official Directors on the Boards of Central Public Sector Enterprises
18	Member, DOPT Committee on Leadership Building for IAS Officers
19	Member, Ministry of Home Affairs Committee for the Capacity Building of IPS Officers
	Member Corporate Boards
20	Member of prominent Boards like Hindustan Aeronautics Limited (HAL), Reserve Bank of India (RBI), Punjab National Bank, Unit Trust of India (UTI), Shipping Corporation of India, Hero Moto Corp and Godrej Properties Ltd

Note: This is not an exhaustive list.

APPENDIX E: LIST OF AWARDS RECEIVED

S. No	Dr Pritam Singh—List of Awards
1	Acharya Shrestha Award, MITWPU, Pune (2020)
2	Honorary Degree of D.Sc. (Honoris Causa) by National Institute of Technology (NIT) Kurukshetra (2015)
3	President's Award-National HRD Network (2014)
4	**Ranked 27 out of 50 Indian Thinkers by Thinkers 50 India (2013–2014)**
5	Sarvepalli Radhakrishnan Memorial Award: Teacher of Teachers—First Recipient (2009)
6	**AIMA Kewal Nohria Award for Academic Leadership in Management Education—First Recipient (2009)**
7	Lifetime Achievement Award—National HRD Network (2008)
8	**Global Thought Leader, Moscow International Higher Business School (MIRBIS), Moscow (2006–2007)**
9	Lifetime Achievement Award, Swami Vivekananda Foundation (2006)
10	Padma Shri—the first Padma Award given to a Professor and Director in the field of management education (2003)
11	Outstanding Entrepreneur Award, TIE-UP, California, USA—first recipient from the Indian academic community (2002)
12	Outstanding CEO Award, National HRD Network (2000)
13	Best Director Award of Indian Management Schools—First Recipient (1998)
14	Best Motivating Professor IIM Bangalore Award—First Recipient (1993)

APPENDIX F: NVIVO DATA ANALYSIS

Part 1 examines the data analysed from the two sources: Interview transcripts and Festschrift write-ups. There were 46 interviews and 31 Festschrift write-ups at this stage of the analysis. Both were considered separately, using NVivo.

Content analysis was conducted (Glaser and Strauss, 1967) with NVIVO software to analyse the data. Two layers of content analysis were conducted—a systematic analysis of the manifest content, followed by a more interpretive analysis of latent content. The transcripts were carefully read to come up with 'thought-units' and organized into emergent categories. These emergent thought-units were then categorized, and their frequencies calculated. Subsequently, latent analysis was carried out to put together the units with similar thematic contours. These latent themes were then segregated into two broad categories of personal attributes and leadership attributes.

NVivo as a tool for qualitative data analysis has been used by many researchers; The use of NVivo software was necessitated due to the multiple phases of coding conducted. NVivo facilitates a greater level of detail achievement in data analysis compared to manual analysis. NVivo helps to identify patterns and tabulate the data and can be used to organize open, axial and selective coding. NVivo facilitates both word frequency analysis and specific coding queries, which helps quantify the qualitative data. NVivo is also used to dissect, compare and categorize data to establish themes and theories. The transcribed data of interviews was uploaded in NVivo for assistance with coding. Subsequently, data were analysed and labels assigned.

APPENDIX G: MDI-GURGAON: KEY MILESTONES: 1996–1998 AND 2003–2006

1996
Training activities expanded; policy level programmes commenced
Advanced Management Programme (AMP) started
2004
Post Graduate Programme in Human Resource Management (PGP-HRM) launched
Executive Fellow Programme in Management (EFPM) launched

(Continued)

(Continued)

Key Financials* (2003–2004)	
Total revenue	1403.31 lakh
Revenue from PGP programs	801.14 lakh
Revenue from continuing education	520.77 lakh
Number of MDP programs	115 (31 open and 84 in-company)
Number of participants in MDP programs	2252 (431 open and 1820 in-company)
2005	
Post Graduate Programme in Energy Management (PGP-EM) established in association with the Ministry of Power and USAID	
MoU for School of Public Policy and Governance signed with Ministry of Personnel and Training, Government of India	
MDI accredited by South Asian Quality Assurance System (SAQS)	
Fellow Programme in Management (FPM) launched	
Post Graduate Programme in Management (PGPM-PT) launched	
Key Financials* (2004–2005)	
Total revenue	1822.15 lakh
Revenue from PGP programs	1034.61 lakh
Revenue from continuing education	747.07 lakh
Number of MDP programs	114 (29 open and 85 in-company)
Number of participants in MDP programs	2328 (483 open and 1865 in-company)
2006	
AMBA (Association of MBAs) UK accredited MDI's fulltime Post Graduate Programmes. MDI became the first and only B School in India to be internationally accredited.	
Post Graduate Programme in International Management (PGP-IM) launched in collaboration with European School of Management (ESCP-Europe), France	

(Continued)

(Continued)

Post-Graduate Programme in Public Policy and Management (PGP-PPM) launched	
Key Financials* (2005–2006)	
Total revenue	2883.90 lakh
Revenue from PGP programs	1480.20 lakh
Revenue from continuing education	1291.17 lakh
Number of MDP programs	127 (10 open and 117 in-company)
Number of participants in MDP programs	2652 (307 open and 2345 in-company)

Note: *From MDI internal sources.

APPENDIX H: IIM-LUCKNOW: KEY MILESTONES (1998–2003)

1998–1999	
Establishment of Agriculture Management Centre (AMC)	
Key Financials (1998–1999)	
Revenue from PGP	286.52 lakh
Revenue from CAT	136.16 lakh
Revenue from MDP	31.84 lakh
Revenue from research and consultancy	19.62 lakh
Revenue from other sources	40.25 lakh
Number of MDPs	22
Number of MDP participants	369
1999–2000	
Launched Fellow Program in Management (FPM)	
Launched Project Based MBA Program with the University of Hull, UK	
Key Financials (1999–2000)	
Revenue from PGP	346.48 lakh
Revenue from CAT	131.31 lakh
Revenue from MDP	102.97 lakh

(Continued)

(Continued)

Revenue from Agri Management Centre	72.62 lakh
Revenue from research and consultancy	58.74 lakh
Number of MDPs	56
Number of MDP participants	1152
Revenue from other sources	192.38 lakh

2000–2001

About 85 acres of IIM Land, which had remained unutilized and separated, due to various claims of farmers, spearheaded by the Bhartiya Kisan Union (Tikait Group), got released for development, and farmer's grievances settled through an MOU signed during October 2000.

Acquisition of 20 acres of land from the NOIDA authority for NOIDA (off Campus) centre, of the IIM Lucknow, exclusively devoted to executive education, the first of its kind in the country within the IIM system.

Key Financials (2000–2001)

Revenue from PGP	402.78 lakh
Revenue from CAT	132.49 lakh
Revenue from MDP	148.62 lakh
Revenue from Agri Management Centre	86.90 lakh
Revenue from research and consultancy	51.23 lakh
Revenue from other sources	196.18 lakh
Number of MDPs	79
Number of MDP participants	1745

2001–2002

Key Financials (2001–2002)

Revenue from PGP	524.36 lakh
Revenue from CAT	240.78 lakh
Revenue from MDP	251.49 lakh
Revenue from research and consultancy	182.43 lakh
Revenue from Fellow program	0.82 lakh
Revenue from other sources	54.94 lakh
Number of MDPs	95
Number of MDP participants	1927

(Continued)

(Continued)

2002–2003	
Key Financials (2002–03)	
Revenue from PGP	633.57 lakh
Revenue from CAT	258.36 lakh
Revenue from MDP	335.42 lakh
Revenue from Fellow program	0.80 lakh
Revenue from research and consultancy	275.05 lakh
Revenue from other sources	174.50 lakh
Number of MDPs	86
Number of MDP participants	1581

Source: G. N. Pandey, Former Registrar, IIM Lucknow.

APPENDIX I: IMI-DELHI: KEY MILESTONES (2011–2014)

Annual Revenue witnessed 2.5 times increase from 21 crore in 2011 to ₹50 crore in 3 years' time.
MDP revenue grew from 2 crore to more than ₹13 crore (2013–2014).
Number of ITEC programs and certificate courses increased manifold.
Fellowship Programme in Management (FPM) approved.
Banking and Insurance program launched.
National Board of Accreditation (NBA) approval and AIU approval for PGDM equivalent to MBA.
IMI New Delhi AMBA accreditation—the first institute in India to receive for straight 5 years approval.
South Asia Quality Assurance System (SAQS) reaccreditation was done during this period. IMI became a triple accredited institute (National, Asian and International).
Most of the statutory pending compliances like Completion Certificate, Fire Clearance Certificate, Occupation Certificate, NOC's from various agencies for expansion were obtained.

(Continued)

(Continued)

Chair Professorship was established with funding of ₹1 crore from Shri Budhi Raja.
Global Leadership Program was further strengthened with Advanced Management Program (AMP).

Source: CN Narayana, Former Registrar IMI New Delhi.

APPENDIX J: A SELECT LIST OF PUBLICATIONS

S. No.	Books
1	**P Singh**, A Bhandarker & S Verma (2021) *Role of Boards: Building Sustainable Competitive Edge.* SAGE Publications.
2	**P Singh**, A Bhandarker & S Rai (2015) *Leadership Odyssey-Darkness to Light.* SAGE Publications.
3	**P Singh**, A Bhandarker & S Rai (2012) *Millennials Meaning of Workplace: Challenges for Building the Organizations of the Future.* SAGE International.
4	**P Singh** & A Bhandarker (2011) *In Search of Change Maestros.* SAGE International.
5	**P Singh** & S Verma (Eds.) (2010) *Towards the Next Orbit, A Corporate Odyssey.* SAGE Response.
6	**P Sing**h and S Verma (Eds.) (2010) *Managing and Organizing in the Era of Globalization.* SAGE Publications.
7	**P Singh** & A Bhandarker (2002) *Winning the Corporate Olympiad: Renaissance Paradigm.* Vikas Publications.
8	**P Singh** & A Bhandarker (1993) *The IAS Profile: Myths and Realities* Pub. Wiley Eastern.
9	**P Singh** & A Bhandarker (1989) *Corporate Success and Transformational Leadership.* Wiley Eastern.
10	P Singh (1979) *Occupational Values and Styles of Indian Managers.* Wiley Eastern.
	Publications—Research Articles and Book Chapters
11	P Singh & A Bhandarker (2021) *Organizational transformation: New agenda for Indian Banks,* in Anil Khandelwal (Ed.), Transformational Leadership in Banking—Challenges of Governance, Leadership and HR in a Digital and Disruptive World. SAGE Publication.

(Continued)

(Continued)

S. No.	Books
12	P Singh & A Bhandarker (March 2002) 10 commandments for building corporate renaissance, IIM-B Review, 14(1), 9–26.
13	A. Bhandarker & P Singh (2002) 'Leading to win in 21st century', in *High Performing Organizations*. New Age.
14	P Singh & A Bhandarker (2002) *Contours of 21st century corporation*', S. G. Bhargava (Ed.). Excel Books.
15	P Singh & A Bhandarker (2001) Leading to win, *IIMB Management Review*, 13(1), 61–71.
16	P Singh & A Bhandarker (March 1999) Road map to transformational leadership, *IIMB Management Review*, 11(1), 39–50.
17	P Singh & A Bhandarker (1999) Parenting transformational leaders, *Vision, The Journal of Business Perspective*, 3(1), 1–13.
18	P Singh & A Bhandarker (Jul–Dec 1997) Five mantras to lead, *Vision: The Journal of Business Perspectives*, 1(2), 1–10.
19	P Singh, A Bhandarker & L Prasad (Jul 1996) Paradigm shifts in the Indian industry: The need for tolerance of ambiguity. *Vision: Journal of Business Perspective*, 9(2), 2–24.
20	P Singh & A Bhandarker (1993), Dilemma of change: Managing through leadership, in Rahim B. Talukdar (Ed.), *Management of Change in South Asia*. University Press Ltd.
21	P Singh & A Bhandarker (1992) Strategic thinking: New agenda for the Indian corporate sector, In B. L. Maheshwari (Ed.), *Innovations In Management for Development*, Tata McGraw Hill.
22	P Singh & A Bhandarker (Oct 1988) Cultural ethos in the organizational milieu: A framework for organization building. *Indian Management*, 27(10), 4–18.
23	A Bhandarker and P Singh, Managerial stress: A study in cyclical perspective, *Abhigyan*, 7–34.
24	P Singh & A Bhandarker (Sept. 1983) Managerial role: The need for clarity, *ASCI Journal of Management*, 13(1), 35–56.

REFERENCES

Aithal, P. S., & Kumar, P. M. (2016). Opportunities and challenges for private universities in India. *International Journal of Management, IT and Engineering*, 6(1), 88–113.

Aladwani, A. M. (2001). Change management strategies for successful ERP implementation. *Business Process Management Journal*, 7(3), 266–275.

Alam, P. A. (2017). Measuring organizational effectiveness through performance management system and McKinsey's 7S model. *Asian Journal of Management*, 8(4), 1280–1286.

Allen, J. (2003). *As a man thinketh*. Holmes Book Company.

Allison, S. T., & Goethals, G. R. (2011). *Heroes: What they do and why we need them*. Oxford University Press.

Amoroso, R. L., Albertini, G., Kauffman, L. H., & Rowlands, P. (Eds.). (2018). *Unified Field Mechanics II: Formulations and Empirical Tests* [Symposium]. Xth Symposium Honouring Noted French Mathematical Physicist Jean-Pierre Vigier. World Scientific.

Anderson, T. C. L. (2001). The leadership styles of effective beginning principals: Transformational or transactional? [Master's Thesis, Saint Louis University].

Astin, A. W., & Astin, H. S. (2000). *Leadership reconsidered: Engaging higher education in social change*. W. K. Kellogg Foundation.

Avolio, B. J., Gardner, W. L., Walumbwa, F. O., Luthans, F., & May, D. R. (2004a). Unlocking the mask: A look at the process by which authentic leaders impact follower attitudes and behaviors. *Leadership Quarterly*, 15(6), 801–823.

Avolio, B. J., Zhu W., Koh, W., & Bhatia, P. (2004b). Transformational leadership and organisational commitment: Mediating role of psychological empowerment and moderating role of structural distance. *Journal of Organisational Behavior*, 25(8), 951–968.

Avolio, B. J., & Gardner, W. L. (2005). Authentic leadership development: Getting to the root of positive forms of leadership. *The Leadership Quarterly, 16*(3), 315–338.

Avolio, B. J., Walumbwa, F. O., & Weber, T. J. (2009). Leadership: Current theories, research and future directions. *Annual Review of Psychology, 60*, 421–449.

Azanza, G., Mariano, J. A., Molero, F., & Mangin, J. P. L. (2015). The effects of authentic leadership on turnover intention. *Leadership and Organization Development Journal, 36*(8), 955–971.

Balwant, P. T. (2016). Transformational instructor-leadership in higher education teaching: A meta-analytic review and research agenda. *Journal of Leadership Studies, 9*(4), 20–42.

Barnard, C. (1938). *The functions of the executive*. Harvard University Press.

Bass, B. M. (1985). *Leadership and performance beyond expectations*. Collier Macmillan.

Bass, B. M. (1990). *Handbook of leadership: Theory, research, and managerial applications* (3rd ed.). The Free Press.

Bass, B. M. (1999). Two decades of research and development in transformational leadership. *European Journal of Work and Organizational Psychology, 8*(1), 9–32.

Bass, B. M. (2000). The future of leadership in learning organizations. *Journal of Leadership Studies, 7*(3), 18–40.

Bass, B. M., & Avolio, B. J. (1990). Developing transformational leadership: 1992 and beyond. *Journal of European Industrial Training, 14*(5), 21–7.

Bernard, M. B., & Riggio, R. E. (2006). *Transformational leadership*. Lawrence Erlbaum Associates.

Berson, Y., & Linton, J. D. (2005). An examination of the relationships between leadership style, quality, and employee satisfaction in R&D versus administrative environments. *R&D Management, 35*(1), 51–60.

Beyer, B. (2012). Blending constructs and concepts: Development of emerging theories of organizational leadership and their relationship to leadership practices for social justice. *International Journal of Educational Leadership Preparation*, 7(3), n3.

Bhagavad Gita, Ch 2, Verse 38. Sourced from https://www.holy-bhagavad-gita.org/chapter/2/verse/38, sourced on 30/05/2021.

Bhagavad Gita, Chapter 18, Verse 78. Sourced from https://www.holy-bhagavad- gita.org/chapter/18/verse/78, sourced on 30/05/2021.

Bhagavad Gita, Chapter 2, Verse 50. Sourced from https://www.holy-bhagavad-gita.org/chapter/2/verse/50, sourced on 30/05/2021.

Bhandari, H., & Yasunobu, K. (2009). What is social capital? A comprehensive review of the concept. *Asian Journal of Social Science*, 37(3), 480–510.

Blanchard, K. H., & Peale, N. V. (1996). *The power of ethical management*. Ballantine Books.

Blunkett, D. (2000). Modernizing higher education: facing the global challenge [Speech by the then Secretary of State at the University of Greenwich, UK]. http:cms1.ger.ac.uk/dfee#speech

Bollinger, A. S., & Smith, R. D. (2001). Managing organizational knowledge as a strategic asset. *Journal of Knowledge Management*, 5(1), 8–18.

Bourdieu, P. (1985). The forms of capital. In J. G. Richardson (Ed.), *Handbook of theory and research for the sociology of education* (pp. 241–250). Greenwood Press.

Boyatzis, E. R., Good, D., & Massa, R. (2012). Emotional, social, and cognitive intelligence and personality as predictors of sales leadership performance. *Journal of Leadership & Organizational Studies*, 19(2), 191–201.

Brown, M., Trevino, L., & Harrison, D. (2005). Ethical leadership: A social learning perspective for construct development and testing. *Organizational Behaviour & Human Decision Processes*, 97(2), 117–134.

Bryman, A. (1992). *Charisma and leadership in organizations*. SAGE Publication.

Burke, C. S., Stagl, K. C., Klein, C., Goodwin, G. F., Salas, E., & Halpin, S. M. (2006). What type of leadership behaviors are functional in teams? A meta-analysis. *The Leadership Quarterly*, 17(3), 288–307.

Burns, J. M. (1978). *Leadership*. Harper & Row.

Bushra, F., Usman, A. & Naveed, A. (2011). Effect of transformational leadership on employee job satisfaction and organisational commitment in the banking sector of Lahore (Pakistan). *International Journal of Business and Social Science*, 2(18), 261–267.

Calegari, M. F., Sibley, R. E., & Turner, M. E. (2015). A roadmap for using Kotter's organizational change model to build faculty engagement in accreditation. *Academy of Educational Leadership Journal*, 19(3), 31.

Campbell, J. (1949). *The hero with a thousand faces*. Princeton University Press.

Cavazotte, F. (2013). Transformational leaders and work performance: The mediating roles of identification and self-efficacy, *Brazilian Administration Review*, 10(4), 490–512. http//www.anpad.org.br/bar

Chappell, S., Pescud, M., Waterworth, P., Shilton, T., Roche, D., Ledger, M., Slevin, T. & Rosenberg, M. (2016). Exploring the process of implementing healthy workplace initiatives: Mapping to Kotter's leading change model. *Journal of Occupational and Environmental Medicine*, 58(10), e341–e348.

Chauhan, C. P. S. (2008). Higher education: current status and future possibilities in Afghanistan, Bangladesh, Bhutan, India, Maldives, Nepal, Pakistan, and Sri Lanka. *Analytical Reports in International Education*, 2(1), 29–48.

Cheng, B. S., Chou, L. F., Wu, T. Y., Huang, M. P., & Farh, J. L. (2004). Paternalistic leadership and subordinate responses: establishing a leadership model in Chinese organizations. *Asian Journal of Social Psychology*, 7(1), 89–117. doi: 10.1111/j.1467-839x.2004.00137.x

Chernyshenko, O. S., Stark, S., & Drasgow, F. (2011). Individual differences: Their measurement and validity. In S. Zedeck (Ed.), *Handbook of industrial and organizational psychology*, (Vol. 1, pp. 117–151). American Psychological Association.

Chi, N. W., Chung, Y. Y., & Tsai, W. C. (2011). How do happy leaders enhance team success? The mediating roles of transformational leadership, group affective tone, and team processes. *Journal of Applied Social Psychology*, 41(6), 1421–1454.

Childers, W. H. (2009). Transformational leadership and its relationship to trust and behavorial integrity. OSU Libraries, 1–7. http://hdl.handle.net/1957/21813.

Chrislip, D., & Larson, C. (1994). *Collaborative leadership*. Jossey-Bass.

Clapp-Smith, R., Vogelgesang, G. R., & Avey, J. B. (2009). Authentic leadership and positive psychological capital: The mediating role of trust at the group level of analysis. *Journal of Leadership and Organizational Studies*, 15(3), 227–240.

Cohen L., Manion L., & Morrison K. (2000). Research methods in education. *British Journal of Educational Studies*, 48, 446.

Coleman, J. S. (1990). *Foundations of social theory*. Harvard University Press.

Collins, J. (2007). Level 5 leadership. *The Jossey-Bass Reader on Educational Leadership*, 2, 27–50.

Conger, J. A. (1991). Inspiring others: The language of leadership. *Academy of Management Executive*, 5(1), 31–45.

Conger, J. A., & Kanungo, R. N. (1998). *Charismatic leadership in organizations*. SAGE Publication.

Dasborough, M. T. (2006). Cognitive asymmetry in employee emotional reactions to leadership behaviors. *The Leadership Quarterly*, 17(2), 163–178.

Denzin, N. K. (1978). *Sociological methods: A sourcebook*. McGraw-Hill.

Descartes, R. (1985). *The philosophical writings of Descartes* (R. Cottingham, Stoothoff, & D. Murdoch (Eds. & Trans), (vol 1, 1st ed.). Cambridge University Press.

Dinu, G. (2017). Romanian academic leadership: Representations of its dimensions. *Valahian Journal of Economic Studies*, 8(3), 21–29.

Doh, J., & Stumpf, S. (2005). Towards a framework of responsible leadership and governance. In J. Doh & S. Stumpf (Eds.), *Handbook on responsible leadership and governance in global business* (pp. 3–18). Edward Elgar.

Doh, J., & Stumpf, S. (2005). Towards a framework of responsible leadership and governance. In J. Doh & S. Stumpf (Eds.), *Handbook on responsible leadership and governance in global business* (pp. 3–18). Edward Elgar.

Downton, J. V. (1973). *Rebel leadership: Commitment and charisma in a revolutionary process.* Free Press.

Dubinsky, A. J., Yammarino, F. J., & Jolson, M. A. (1995). An examination of linkages between personal characteristics and dimensions of transformational leadership. *Journal of Business and Psychology*, 9(3), 315–335.

Dutton, J. E., Dukerich, J. M., & Harquail, C. V. (1994). Organizational images and member identification. *Administrative Science Quarterly*, 39(2), 57–88.

Dvir, T., Eden, D., Avolio, B. J., and Shamir, B. (2002). Impact of transformational leadership on followers' development and performance: A field experiment. *Academy of Management Journal*, 45(5), 735–744.

Eden, D. (1992). Leadership and expectations: Pygmalion effects and other self-fulfilling prophecies in organizations. *The Leadership Quarterly*, 3(4), 271–305.

Elwood, L. P., & Leyden, V. M. (2000). Strategic planning and cultural considerations in tertiary education systems: The Irish case. *Scandinavian Journal of Educational Research*, 44(3), 307–323.

Erder, M., & Pureur, P. (2015). *Continuous architecture: Sustainable architecture in an agile and cloud-centric world.* Morgan Kaufmann.

Erturk, A. (2014). Influences of HR practices, social exchange and trust on turnover intentions of public IT professionals. *Public Personnel Management*, 43(1), 140–175. doi: 10.1177/0091026013517875

ET Bureau. (February 2, 2021). Budget 2021: 6% cut in allocation for the education sector. The Economic Times.

Farh, J. L., & Cheng, B. S. (2000). A cultural analysis of paternalistic leadership in Chinese organizations. In *Management and organizations in the Chinese context* (pp. 84–127). Palgrave Macmillan.

Fiedler, F. E. (1967). *A theory of leadership effectiveness.* McGraw-Hill.

Fritz, S., & Sörgel, P. (2017). Recentering leadership around the human person: Introducing a framework for humanistic leadership. [Master's Thesis, Jönköping University].

Fukuyama, F. (1995). *Trust: The social virtues and the creation of prosperity.* Free Press.

Fukuyama, F. (1999). *The great disruption: Human nature and the reconstruction of social order.* Free Press.

Fullwood, R., Rowley, J. and Delbridge, R. (2013). Knowledge sharing amongst academics in UK universities. *Journal of Knowledge Management, 17*(1), 123–136.

Gansemer-Topf, A. M., Downey, J., Thompson, K., & Genschel, U. (2018). Did the recession impact student success? Relationships of finances, staffing and institutional type of retention. *Research in Higher Education, 59*(2), 174–197.

Geiger, R. (2010). Impact of the financial crisis on higher education in the United States. *International Higher Education, 59*(Spring), 9–11.

George, J. M. (2000). Emotions and leadership: The role of emotional intelligence. *Human Relations, 53*(8), 1027–1055.

Geyer, A. L. J., & Steyrer, J. M. (1998). Transformational leadership and objective performance in banks. *Applied Psychology: An International Review, 47*(3), 397–420.

Giallonardo, L. M., Wong, C. A., & Iwasiw, C. L. (2010). Authentic leadership of preceptors: Predictor of new graduate nurses' work engagement and job satisfaction. *Journal of Nursing Management, 18*(8), 993–1003.

Glaser, B. (1978). *Theoretical sensitivity. Advances in the methodology of grounded theory.* The Sociology Press.

Glaser, B., & Strauss, A. (1967). *The discovery of grounded theory: Strategies for qualitative research.* Aldine de Gruyter.

Glaser, B. (1992). *Emergence v forcing basics of grounded theory analysis.* Sociology Press.

Goel, R. K., & Göktepe-Hultén, D. (2018). Academic leadership and commercial activities at research institutes: German evidence. *Managerial and Decision Economics*, 39(5), 601–609.

Graen, G. B., & Uhl-Bien, M. (1995). Relationship-based approach to leadership: Development of leader-member exchange (LMX) theory of leadership over 25 years: Applying a multi-level multi-domain perspective. *The Leadership Quarterly*, 6(2), 219–247.

Greenleaf, R. (1970). *The servant as leader*. Robert K. Greenleaf Center.

GRLI. (2005). Globally responsible leadership: A call for engagement. http://www.grli.org/images/stories/grli/documents/globally_responsible_leadership_report.pdf

Gupta, A. (2008). International trends and private higher education in India. *International Journal of Educational Management*, 22(6), 565–594.

Gupta, D., & Gupta, N. (2012). Higher education in India: Structure, statistics and challenges. *Journal of Education and Practice*, 3(2), 17–24.

Gyanchandani, R. (2017). The effect of transformational leadership style on team performance in IT sector. *IUP Journal of Soft Skills*, 11(3), 29–44.

Hailey, V. H., & Balogun, J. (2002). Devising context sensitive approaches to change: The example of Glaxo Wellcome. *Long Range Planning*, 35(2), 153–178.

Hambrick, D. C., & Mason, P. A. (1984). Upper echelons: The organization as a reflection of its top managers. *Academy of Management Review*, 9(2), 193–206.

Hamel, G. (2000). *Leading the revolution*. Harvard Business School Press.

Hamel, G., & Prahalad, C. K. (1996). *Competing for the future*. Harvard Business School Press.

Hamilton, D. L., & Fallot, R. D. (1974). Information salience as a weighting factor in impression formation. *Journal of Personality and Social Psychology*, 30(4), 444.

Har-Evan, S. (1992). Four models of leadership persuade you. In *Seminar on Leadership*.

Hargreaves, A., & Fink, D. (2006). *Sustainable leadership*. Jossey-Bass.

Hassan, A., & Ahmed, F. (2011). Authentic leadership, trust and work engagement. *International Scholarly and Scientific Research & Innovation*, 5(8), 1036–1042.

Hitt, W. D. (1990). *Ethics and leadership: Putting theory into practice*. Battelle Press.

Hmieleski, K. M., Cole, M. S., & Baron, R. A. (2012). Shared authentic leadership and new venture performance. *Journal of Management*, 38, 1476–1499.

Holzman, Philip S. (2020). *Encyclopedia Britannica* (24 Feb. 2020). https://www.britannica.com/topic/personality.

Hoque, J. (2018). Quality concern in higher education in India. *EDULIGHT Journal*, 7(13), 662–668.

Howell, J. M., & Avolio, B. J. (1993). Transformational leadership, transactional leadership, locus of control and support for innovation: Key predictors of consolidated-business-unit performance. *Journal of Applied Psychology*, 78(6), 891–902.

Hogan, R., & Judge, T. (2013). Personality and leadership. In M. G. Rumsey (Ed.), *The oxford handbook of leadership* (pp. 37–46). Oxford University Press

Hsieh, C., & Wang, D. (2015). Does supervisor-perceived authentic leadership influence employee work engagement through employee-perceived authentic leadership and employee trust? *The International Journal of Human Resource Management*, 26(18), 1–20.

Hsu, C. F., & Peng, C. H. (2012). A case study of using 7S framework to improve business process for call centre reforming. *International Journal of Enterprise Network Management*, 5(1), 17–32.

Humphrey, A. (2012). Transformational leadership and organizational citizenship behaviors: The role of organizational identification. *The Psychologist-Manager Journal*, 15(4), 247–268.

Humphrey, R. H. (2002). The many faces of emotional leadership. *The Leadership Quarterly*, 13(5), 493–504.

Humphrey, R. H., Burch, G. F., & Adams, L. L. (2016). The benefits of merging leadership research and emotions research. *Frontiers in Psychology*, 7, 1022.

Hunt, J. G., Boal, K. B., & Sorenson, R. L. (1990). Top management leadership: Inside the black box. *The Leadership Quarterly*, 1(1), 41–65.

Indrawati, N. K. (2014). Management by inspiration: Implementation of transformational leadership on business at *Pondok Pesantren**) Sunan Drajat. *Procedia-Social and Behavioral Sciences*, 115, 79–90.

Ingram, D. (2018), Transformational leadership vs transactional leadership definition. https://smallbusiness.chron.com.

Jacobsen, C., & House, R. J. (2001). Dynamics of charismatic leadership: A process theory, simulation model, and tests. *The Leadership Quarterly*, 12(1), 75–112.

Jensen, S. M., & Luthans, F. (2006). Entrepreneurs as authentic leaders: Impact on employees' attitudes. *Leadership and Organization Development Journal*, 27(8), 646–666.

Judge, T. A., Bono, J. E., Ilies, R., & Gerhardt, M. W. (2002). Personality and leadership: A qualitative and quantitative review. *Journal of Applied Psychology*, 87(4), 765.

Jung, C. (2016). *Psychological types*. Routledge.

Jung, D. D., Wu, A., & Chow, C. W. (2008). Towards understanding the direct and indirect effects of CEOs' transformational leadership on firm innovation. *The Leadership Quarterly*, 19(5), 582–594.

Kahai, S. S., Sosik, J. J., & Avolio, B. J. (1997). Effects of leadership style and problem structure on work group process and outcomes in an electronic meeting system environment. *Personnel Psychology*, 50(1), 121–146.

Kan, M. M., & Parry, K. W. (2004). Identifying paradox: A grounded theory of leadership in overcoming resistance to change. *The Leadership Quarterly*, 15(4), 467–491.

Kang, S. P., Chen, Y., Svihla, V., Gallup, A., Ferris, K., & Datye, A. K. (2020). Guiding change in higher education: an emergent, iterative application of Kotter's change model. *Studies in Higher Education*, 1–20.

Kanter, R. M., Stein, B. A., & Jick, T. D. (1992). *The challenge of organisational change*. The Free Press.

Kanungo, R. N., & Mendonca, M. (1996). *Ethical dimensions of leadership*. SAGE Publication.

Kejriwal A., & Krishnan, V. R. (2004). Impact of vedic worldview and gunas on transformational leadership, *Vikalpa*, 29(1), 29–40.

Kelly, D. J. (1990). Ethics: The tone at the top. *Management Accounting*, 70(10), 18–19.

Kempster, S., & Parry, K. W. (2011). Grounded theory and leadership research: A critical realist perspective. *The Leadership Quarterly*, 22(1), 106–120.

Khazanchi, D., & Owens, D. (2018, January). *From strategic intent to implementation: How information technology initiatives take shape in organizations*. [Conference session] The 51st Hawaii International Conference on System Sciences, Hawaii, United States.

Khuse, H., & Singer, P. (2009). *What is bioethics: A historical introduction. A companion to bioethics* (pp. 1–10).Wiley-Blackwell.

Kinsella, E. L., Ritchie, T. D., & Igou, E. R. (2015). Zeroing in on heroes: a prototype analysis of hero features. *Journal of Personality and Social Psychology*, 108(1), 114.

Kinsella, E. L., Ritchie, T. D., & Igou, E. R. (2016). A brief history of lay and scademic perspectives. In *Handbook of heroism and heroic leadership* (pp. 18–19). Routledge.

Klapp, O. E. (1954). Heroes, villains and fools, as agents of social control. *American Sociological Review*, 19(1), 56–62.

Klein, K. J., & House, R. J. (1998). On fire: Charismatic leadership and levels of analysis. In F. Dansereau, & F. J. Yammarino (Eds.). *Leadership: The multiple level approach* (pp. 2–33). JAI Press.

Koh, W. L., Steers, R. M., & Terborg, J. R. (1995). The effects of transformational leadership on teacher attitudes and student performance in Singapore. *Journal of Organisational Behaviour*, 16(4), 319–333.

Koopman, P. L., & Wierdsma, A. F. M. (1998). Participative management. In P. J. D. Drenth, H. Thierry, & C. J. de Wolff (Eds.),

Personnel psychology. *Handbook of work and organizational psychology* (Vol. 3, pp. 297–324). Psychology Press.

Kotter, J. P. (1995). Leading change: Why transformational efforts fail. *Harvard Business Review*, 73(2), 59–67.

Kouzes, J. & Posner, B. (2002). *The leadership challenge* (3rd ed.). Jossey-Bass.

Kram, K. E. (1983). Phases of the mentor relationship, *Academy of Management Journal*, 26(4), 608–625.

Leithwood, K., Jantzi, D., & Steinbach, R. (1999). Do schools councils matter? *Educational Policy*. 13(4), 467–493.

Leroy, H., Palanski, M. E., & Simons, T. (2012). Authentic leadership and behavioral integrity as drivers of follower commitment and performance. *Journal of Business Ethics*, 107, 255–264.

Lewin, K. (1951). Force field analysis. In D. Francis, & M. Woodcock (1982). *Fifty activities for self-development*. GOWE.

Lewin, K., Lippitt, R., & White, R. K. (1939). Patterns of aggressive behavior in experimentally created "social climates". *The Journal of Social Psychology*, 10(2), 269–299.

Lian, L. K., & Tui, L. G. (2012). Leadership styles and OCB: The mediating effects of subordinates' competence and downward influence tactics. *Journal of Applied Business & Economics*, 13(2), 59–96.

Likert, R. (1967). *The human organization*. McGraw-Hill.

Lin, N. (2001). *Social capital: A theory of social structure and action*. Cambridge University Press.

Lowe, K. B., Kroeck, K. G., & Sivasubramaniam, N. (1996). Effectiveness correlates of transformational and transactional leadership: A meta-analytic review of the MLQ literature. *The Leadership Quarterly*, 7, 385–425.

Luthans, F., & Avolio, B. J. (2003). Authentic leadership development. In K. S. Cameron, J. E. Dutton, & R. E. Quinn (Eds.), *Positive organizational scholarship: Foundations of a new discipline* (pp. 241–261). Barrett-Koehler.

Maddi, S. R. (1980). Myth and personality. *The Journal of Mind and Behavior*, *1*(2), 145–153.

Makkar, S., & Waghmare, A. (2018, May 23). Why are Indian B-schools shutting down? Rediff. https://www.rediff.com/getahead/report/why-are-indian-b-schools-shutting-down/20180523.htm

Malivan, A., & Thanakunwutthirot, K. (2019, October). Modern office management: Mckinsey 7s framework. [Conference Session]. International Academic Multidisciplinary Research Conference, Berlin (pp. 92–95).

Maslow, A. H. (1954). *Motivation and personality*. Harper & Collins.

May, D. R., Chan, A., Hodges, T., & Avolio, B. J. (2003). Developing the moral component of authentic leadership. *Organizational Dynamics*, *32*(3), 247–260.

Mburu, R. M. (2013). Contribution of Mckinsey 7s model on employee productivity in the NGO sector: A case study of Maryland global initiatives corporation (Doctoral dissertation, United States International University-Africa).

McClelland, D. C. (1985). How motives, skills, and values determine what people do. *American Psychologist*, *40*(7), 812.

McColl-Kennedy, J. R., & Anderson, R. D. (2002). Impact of leadership style and emotions on subordinate performance. *The Leadership Quarterly*, *13*(5), 545–559.

McCrae, R. R., & Costa, P. T., Jr. (1985). Updating Norman's "adequate taxonomy": Intelligence and personality dimensions in natural language and in questionnaires. *Journal of Personality and Social Psychology*, *49*(3), 710–721.

McGregor, D. V. (1960). *The human side of enterprise*. McGraw-Hill.

Merriam Webster (n.d.). Merriam-Webster.com. Retrieved on July 6, 2021, from https://www.merriam-webster.com.

Mineo, D. L. (2014). The importance of trust in leadership. *Research Management Review*, *20*(1), n1.

Mishra, S. (July 24, 2019). Why IITs, NITs are facing faculty shortage in specialised streams. The Times of India. https://timesofindia.

indiatimes.com/home/education/news/why-iits-nits-are-facing-faculty-shortage-in-specialised-streams/articleshow/70359096.cms

Mohammad, S. I. S., Al-Zeaud, H. A., & Batayneh, A. M. E. (2011). The relationship between transformational leadership and employee's satisfaction at Jordanian private hospitals. *Business and Economic Horizons*, 5(2), 35–46.

Montoya, R. M., & Horton, R. S. (2012). The reciprocity of liking effect. In M. A. Paludi (Ed.), *The psychology of love* (pp. 39–57). Praeger.

Muna, F. A. (2011). Contextual leadership: A study of Lebanese executives working in Lebanon, the GCC countries, and the United States. *Journal of Management Development*, 30(9), 865–881.

Myers Briggs (n.d.). Myers-Briggs.com. Retrieved on May 30, 2021 from https://eu.themyersbriggs.com/en/tools/MBTI/MBTI-personality-Types/ENTJ

Nadler, D. A. (1997). *Champions of change: How CEOs and their companies are mastering the skills of radical change*. Jossey-Bass.

Nanus, B. (1992). *Visionary leadership: Creating a compelling sense of direction for your organisation*. Jossey-Bass.

Ndunge, W. E. (2014). Strategic leadership and change management practices at the Kenya wildlife service (Doctoral dissertation, University of Nairobi).

Njeru, K. N., & Kariuki, P. (2019). Influence of Mckinsey framework on competitive advantage of firms in the telecommunication industry in Kenya. *Journal of International Business, Innovation and Strategic Management*, 3(1), 68–81.

Oc, B. (2018). Contextual leadership: A systematic review of how contextual factors shape leadership and its outcomes. *The Leadership Quarterly*, 29(1), 218–235.

Oden, G. C., & Anderson, N. H. (1971). Differential weighting in integration theory. *Journal of Experimental Psychology*, 89(1), 152.

Oxford Bibliographies (n.d.). Oxfordbibliographies.com. Retrieved July 6, 2021 from https://www.oxfordbibliographies.com/view/document/obo-9780199766567/obo-9780199766567-0169.xml

Paquibut, R., & Al Naamany, A. (2019). Managing organizational change to meet the research–teaching nexus standard: The case of an HEI in the Sultanate of Oman. *International Journal of Educational Management*, 34(4), 782–793.

Patton, M.Q. (1999). Enhancing the quality and credibility of qualitative analysis. *Health Sciences Research*, 34, 1189–1208.

Paxton, P. (2002). Social capital and democracy: An interdependent relationship. *American Sociological Review*, 67(2), 254–277.

Pearce, C., & Conger, J. (2003). All those years ago: The historical underpinnings of shared leadership. In C. Pearce & J. Conger (Eds.), *Shared leadership*. SAGE Publications.

Pereira, C. M. M., & Gomes, J. F. S. (2012). The strength of human resource practices and transformational leadership: Impact on organisational performance, *The International Journal of Human Resource Management*, 23(20), 4301–4318.

Peters, T., & Waterman, R. (1982). *In search of excellence*. Harper & Row.

Peus, C., Wesche, J. S., Streicher, B., Braun, S., & Frey, D. (2012). Authentic leadership: An empirical test of its antecedents, consequences, and mediating mechanisms. *Journal of Business Ethics*, 107, 331–348.

Podsakoff, M. P., Mackenzie, S. B., Moorman, R. H., & Fetter, R. (1990). Transformational leader behaviours and their effects on followers' trust in leader, satisfaction and OCB. *Leadership Quarterly*, 1(2), 107–142. doi: 10.1016/1048-9843(90)90009-7.

Portes, A. (1995). Economic sociology and the sociology of immigration: A conceptual overview. In A. Portes (Ed.), *Economic sociology of immigration: Essays on networks, ethnicity, and entrepreneurship*. Russell Sage Foundation.

Prahalad, C. K., & Doz, Y. (1987). *The multinational mission, balancing local demands and global vision*. Free Press.

Putnam, R. (1993). *Making democracy work: Civic traditions in modern Italy*. Princeton University Press.

Putnam, R. D. (1996, Winter). The strange disappearance of civic America. *The American Prospect*, 7(24), 34–38.

Ramachandran, S., & Krishnan, V. R. (2009). Effect of transformational leadership on followers' affective and normative commitment: Culture as moderator. *Great Lakes Institute of Management*, 3(1), 23–38.

Ranjan, R. (2014). Private universities in India and quality of education. *International Journal of Humanities Social Sciences and Education (IJHSSE)*, 1(9), 140–144.

Rao, I. (2019). A brief note on the role of ethical leadership in higher education institutions for sustainability. *IUP Journal of Management Research*, 18(4), 70–79.

Rath, T., & Conchie, B. (2008). *Strengths based leadership: Great leaders, teams, and why people follow*. Simon and Schuster.

Reddy, D. P. V. (2018). Achieving academic excellence in private unaided engineering colleges in India. *Journal of Engineering Education Transformation*, 32(2), 100–104.

Richards, N. (1992). *Humility*. Temple University Press.

Rosenthal, R., & Babad, E. Y. (1985). Pygmalion in the gymnasium. *Educational Leadership*, 43(1), 36–39.

Rosenthal, R., & Jacobson, L. (1968). *Pygmalion in the classroom: Teacher expectation and pupils' intellectual development*. Holt, Rinehart, & Winston.

Rowland, P., & Parry, K. (2009). Consensual commitment: A grounded theory of the meso-level influence of organizational design on leadership and decision-making. *The Leadership Quarterly*, 20(4), 535–553.

Sarros, J. C., & Santora, J. C. (2001). The transformational-transactional leadership model in practice. *Leadership & Organization Development Journal*. 22(8), 383–393.

Sashkin, M. (1992), Strategic leadership competencies: what are they? How do they operate? What can be done to develop them?, in R. L. Phillips & J. G. Hunts (Eds.), *Strategic leadership: A multiorganizational-level perspective* (pp. 139–160). Quorum Books.

Schneider, I., Mädler, M., & Lang, J. (2019). Comparability of self-ratings and observer ratings in occupational psychosocial risk assessments: Is there agreement? *BioMed Research International*, 2019, 1–10.

Schraa-Liu, T., & Trompenaars, F. (2006). Towards responsible leadership through reconciling dilemmas. In T. Maak & N. Pless (Eds.), *Responsible leadership* (pp. 138–154). Routledge.

Schwenk, C. R. (1988). The cognitive perspective on strategic decision making. *Journal of Management Studies*, 25(1), 41–55.

Sharma, S., & Sharma, P. (2015). Indian higher education system: Challenges and suggestions. *Electronic Journal for Inclusive Education*, 3(4), 6.

Singh, P., & Bhandarker, A. (2011). *In search of change maestros* (p. 453). SAGE Publication.

Singh, P., Bhandarker, A., & Rai, S. (2012). *Millennials and the workplace: Challenges for architecting the organizations of tomorrow*. SAGE Publications.

Singh, R. (2016). The impact of intrinsic and extrinsic motivators on employee engagement in information organizations. *Journal of Education for Library and Information Science*, 57(2), 197–206.

Singh, R., & Teoh, J. B. P. (2000). Impression formation from intellectual and social traits: Evidence for behavioural adaptation and cognitive processing. *British Journal of Social Psychology*, 39(4), 537–554.

Singh, R., Onglatco, M. L. U., Sriram, N., & Tay, A. B. (1997). The warm–cold variable in impression formation: Evidence for the positive–negative asymmetry. *British Journal of Social Psychology*, 36(4), 457–477.

Skinner, B. F. (1938). *The behavior of organisms: An experimental analysis*. Appleton-Century.

Spreitzer, G. (2007). Participative organizational leadership, empowerment, and sustainable peace. *Journal of Organizational Behavior*, 28(8), 1077–1096.

Spreitzer, G. M., & Cameron, K. S. (2012). A path forward: Assessing progress and exploring core questions for the future of positive organizational scholarship. *The Oxford Handbook of Positive Organizational Scholarship*, 1034–1048.

Strauss, A. L. (1987). *Qualitative analysis for social scientists*. Cambridge University Press.

Strauss, A. L., & Corbin, J. (1990). *Basics of qualitative research. Grounded theory procedures and techniques*. SAGE Publication.

Strauss, A., & Corbin, J. M. (1997). *Grounded theory in practice*. SAGE Publication.

Strauss, A., Corbin, J. (1998). *Basics of qualitative research: Grounded theory procedures and technique* (2nd ed.). SAGE Publication.

Sukirno, D. S., & Siengthai, S. (2011). Does participative decision making affect lecturer performance in higher education? *International Journal of Educational Management*, 25(5), 494–508.

Taylor, C. M., Cornelius, C. J., & Colvin, K. (2014). Visionary leadership and its relationship to organizational effectiveness. *Leadership & Organization Development Journal*, 35(6), 566–583.

Teczke, M., Sansyzbayevna Bespayeva, R., & Olzhabayevna Bugubayeva, R. (2017). Approaches and models for change management. *Jagiellonian Journal of Management*, 3(3), 195–208.

Torlak, N. G., & Kuzey, C. (2019). Leadership, job satisfaction and performance links in private education institutes of Pakistan. *International Journal of Productivity and Performance Management*, 68(2), 276–295.

Tripathi, S. M., & Bajpai, A. (2017). Internationalization of higher education in India: Emerging trends, strategies and policies. *Productivity*, 58(3), 271–279.

Trivellas, P. T., & Dargenidou, D. (2009). Leadership and service quality in higher education: The case of the technological educational institute of Larissa. *International Journal of Quality and Service Sciences*, 1(3), 294–310.

Tse, H. M., Huang, Xu., & Lam, W. (2013). Why does transformational leadership matter for employee turnover? A multi foci exchange perspective. *The Leadership Quarterly*, 24(3), 763–776.

Unde, A. P., & Bhor, J. R. (2013). Emerging TQM issues in management education in India: Restructuring for global. *IBMRD's Journal of Management and Research*, 2(1), 167–180.

Varner, G. E. (2012). *Personhood, ethics, and animal cognition: Situating animals in Hare's two level utilitarianism*. Oxford University Press.

Voskuijl, O. F., & van Sliedregt, T. (2002). Determinants of interrater reliability of job analysis: A meta-analysis. *European Journal of Psychological Assessment*, *18*(1), 52.

Waldman, D. A., Siegel, D. S., & Javidan, M. (2004). CEO transformational leadership and corporate social responsibility. *Journal of Management Studies*, *43*(8), 1703–1725.

Walumbwa, F. O., & Hartnell, C. A. (2011). Understanding transformational leadership- employee performance links: The role of relational identification and self efficacy. *Journal of Occupational & Organisational Psychology*, *84*(1), 153–172. doi: 10.1348/096317910X485818.

Walumbwa, F. O., Avolio, B. J., Gardner, W. L., Wernsing, T. S., & Peterson, S. J. (2008). Authentic Leadership: Development and validation of a theory-based measure? *Journal of Management*, *34*(1), 89–126.

Waterman Jr, R. H., Peters, T. J., & Phillips, J. R. (1980). Structure is not organization. *Business Horizons*, *23*(3), 14–26.

Weber, M. (1947). The theory of economic and social organization. Oxford University Press.

Welzel, C., Inglehart, R., & Deutsch, F. (2005). Social capital, voluntary associations, and collective action: Which aspects of social capital have the greatest civic payoff? *Journal of Civil Society*, *1*(2), 1–26.

Wentworth, D. K., Behson, S. J., & Kelley, C. L. (2020). Implementing a new student evaluation of teaching system using the Kotter change model. *Studies in Higher Education*, *45*(3), 511–523.

Whicker, M. L. (1996). *Toxic leaders: When organizations go bad* (p. 189). Quorum VI.

Winkler, I. (2009). *Contemporary leadership theories: Enhancing the understanding of the complexity, subjectivity and dynamic of leadership*. Springer.

Winston, B. E. (2004). Servant leadership at Heritage Bible College: A single-case study. *Leadership & Organization Development Journal*, *25*(7), 600–617.

Wojciszke, B., Abele, A. E., & Baryla, W. (2009). Two dimensions of interpersonal attitudes: Liking depends on communion, respect depends on agency. *European Journal of Social Psychology*, *39*(6), 973–990.

Wong, C. A., & Cummings, G. G. (2009). The influence of authentic leadership behaviors on trust and work outcomes of health care staff. *Journal of Leadership Studies*, *3*(2), 6–23.

Wong, C. A., Spence Laschinger, H. K., & Cummings, G. G. (2010). Authentic leadership and nurses' voice behaviour and perceptions of care quality. *Journal of Nursing Management*, *18*(8), 889–900.

Woolcock, M., & Narayan, D. (2000). Social capital: Implications for development theory, research, and policy. *World Bank Research Observer*, *15*(2), 225–250.

Yammarino, F. J., & Bass, B. M. (1988). Long-term forecasting of transformational leadership and its effects among naval officers: Some preliminary findings. Center for Leadership Studies. http://www.dtic.mil/dtic/tr/fulltext/u2/a204110.pdf

Yang, F. H., Wu, M., Chang, C. C., & Chien, Y. (2011). Elucidating the relationship among transformational leadership, job satisfaction, commitment foci and commitment bases in the public sector. *Public Personnel Management*, *40*(3), 265–278.

Yıldız, I. G., & Şimşek, Ö. F. (2016). Different pathways from transformational leadership to job satisfaction: The competing mediator roles of trust and self-efficacy. *Nonprofit Management and Leadership*, *27*(1), 59–77.

Yin, R. (1994). *Case study research: Design and methods* (2nd ed.). SAGE Publication.

Yukl, G. A., & Becker, W. S. (2006). Effective empowerment in organizations. *Organization Management Journal*, *3*(3), 210–231.

Zaccaro, S. J., Gilbert, J. A., Thor, K. K., & Mumford, M. D. (1991). Leadership and social intelligence: Linking social perceptiveness and behavioral flexibility to leader effectiveness. *The Leadership Quarterly*, *2*(4), 317–342.

ABOUT THE AUTHORS

Asha Bhandarker, a distinguished Professor of Organizational Behaviour at International Management Institute (IMI) New Delhi, India, is well known for her contributions to research, teaching, training and consulting in the field of organizational behaviour. She has published over 40 research papers as well as articles in peer-reviewed journals, both nationally and internationally. She has published eight books with reputed publishers like SAGE. Dr Bhandarker has received many awards for her work, including the Senior Fulbright fellowship, Best Paper Award, Best Case Award and Best Teacher Award. She is the Director on the Board of Punjab National Bank and IMT Ghaziabad, India. As a trainer and consultant, she has worked with numerous organizations in the public and private sectors. She has been a visiting professor at the School of Public Policy, George Mason University, Fairfax, USA, and at the Darden School of Business, University of Virginia, Charlottesville, USA, and visiting fellow at the London Business School, London, England. She recently co-authored the book, *Role of Boards: Building Sustainable Competitive Edge* along with Late Dr Pritam Singh and Dr Subir Verma.

Subrat Kumar is the CEO of People Labs, now a leading name in Experiential Learning interventions for corporate and higher educational institutes alike. An MBA from Management Development Institute (MDI) Gurgaon and a FPM fellow from IMI New Delhi (thesis submitted), Subrat started People Labs Pvt Ltd in 2010 (then known as Cinque

Education). Before that, Subrat worked as Brand and Sales Manager at Asian Paints. In his 11 years of entrepreneurial journey, Subrat has trained more than 25,000 students and corporate professionals. He has delivered learning interventions for companies across private and public sectors including Airtel, ADP, Axis Bank, GSK, Maruti, Trident, Asian Paints, IOCL, NTPC, Canara Bank, Union Bank, PNB, Powergrid to name a few. His academic clients include MDI, XLRI, NMIMS, IIM Kashipur, IIM Trichy, IMT, IMI, BIMTECH, FLAME University, NIRMA University, IIFM to name a few, wherein his interventions range across student capability building, faculty capability building and helping institutions prepare for accreditation and rankings. Subrat has also presented and published internationally. He was the only Indian at the ABSEL 2017 conference (largest conference in the world for experiential learning practice), wherein he presented two papers. His case study titled *New Holland Tractors India: Community Management and Employee Relations* has been published at Richard Ivey Case Centre. He has also published in SCOPUS indexed journals and contributed a book chapter titled 'Humanistic Leadership and its impact on Organizational Effectiveness' in edited book.

STAY ENCOURAGED • STAY CREATIVE • STAY MOTIVATED

What do influential leaders do differently? Get inspired and change the way you think, act and lead.

For special offers on these books and more visit **stealadeal.sagepub.in**

www.sagepub.in